"Antonio Nieto-Rodriguez's *Powered by Projects* marks a shift from the mechanistic philosophy of the industrial age to the organic paradigm of the digital era—and from hierarchical bureaucracy to self-organization."

—**ZHANG RUIMIN,** founder and former CEO, Haier;
Chairman Emeritus of the Board of Directors, Haier Group

"It's hard to disagree with this great new book's provocative claim that we live in a project economy. More and more of today's work is project work calling for simultaneous execution and perpetual rethinking while challenging traditional management approaches. Antonio Nieto-Rodriguez brings valuable insight and advice for navigating our world of projects more effectively."

—**AMY C. EDMONDSON,** Novartis Professor of Leadership and
Management, Harvard Business School; author,
Right Kind of Wrong and *The Fearless Organization*

"Powerful transformations and the spirit of constant reinvention have become defining traits of L'Oréal's culture. *Powered by Projects* embodies this forward-thinking mindset perfectly: shifting from perfecting the present to imagining the future while keeping people at the center."

—**MATTHIEU SERRES,** Chief Transformation Officer, L'Oréal

"Today transformation is a top priority, demanding focus on what truly creates value for people, business, and society. *Powered by Projects* captures this shift with insight and precision. It's a timely guide for executives ready to lead their organizations into the future."

—**BÉATRICE GUILLAUME-GRABISCH,** President,
Group HR and Business Services, Nestlé

"Project professionals are the force multipliers of this era, anticipating customer needs, aligning people, and delivering value end to end. *Powered by Projects* is essential reading for practitioners committed to lifelong mastery and for leaders determined to build enterprises that stay resilient, relevant, and ahead."

—**PIERRE LE MANH,** President and CEO, Project Management Institute

"*Powered by Projects* brilliantly illuminates the often-overlooked truth that while project-driven structures are undeniably critical for modern success, transformative projects ultimately succeed or fail based on culture and leadership. Nieto-Rodriguez reminds us that amid all our technological and corporate evolution, it's still the human element of motivation, guidance, and authentic change management that makes the difference."

—**ABIGAIL POSNER,** former Director, Creative Works, Google; founder and CEO, Human Code Company

"Antonio Nieto-Rodriguez is the world's premier champion of the project-driven organization. In a transformative age, the only way leaders and their teams are going to successfully achieve change is through knowledge of the skills and thinking required to make projects work. *Powered by Projects* deserves to be—needs to be—read by leaders of organizations large and small."

—**STUART CRAINER,** cofounder, Thinkers50

"Antonio Nieto-Rodriguez reframes how we think about work in the modern era. *Powered by Projects* makes the compelling case that the future belongs to organizations that master the art of project execution, not as a tactical skill but as a core strategic discipline. This book is a road map for getting the most important initiatives done and leading with impact."

—**DORIE CLARK,** Instructor, Executive Education Program, Columbia Business School; *Wall Street Journal* bestselling author, *The Long Game*

"At APM we're committed to positioning project management at the heart of strategic decision-making and societal impact, and *Powered by Projects* does exactly that—it offers leaders a clear road map for moving beyond operational thinking and unlocking the transformational power of projects."

—**ADAM BODDISON,** OBE, CEO, Association for Project Management

"*Powered by Projects* offers a timely and actionable framework for mastering complexity, leading change, and working through projects—reframing project work not as a technical function but as a core leadership discipline and critical enabler of transformation and future readiness in any organization."

—**SELINA NERI,** CEO, Dean, and cofounder, Institute for Future Readiness (UAE)

POWERED BY PROJECTS

POWERED BY PROJECTS

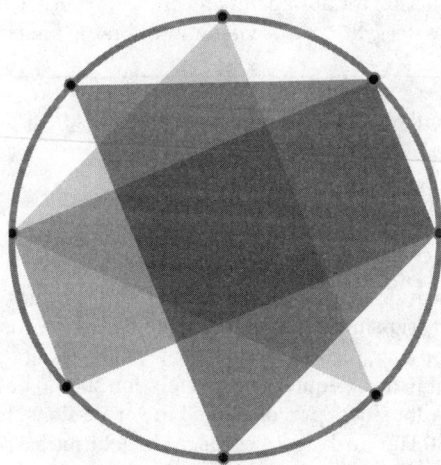

LEADING YOUR
ORGANIZATION
IN THE
TRANSFORMATION AGE

ANTONIO
NIETO-RODRIGUEZ

HARVARD BUSINESS REVIEW PRESS
BOSTON, MASSACHUSETTS

The web addresses referenced in this book were live and correct at the time of the book's publication but may be subject to change.

Library of Congress Cataloging-in-Publication Data

Names: Nieto-Rodriguez, Antonio author
Title: Powered by projects : leading your organization in the transformation age / Antonio Nieto-Rodriguez.
Description: Boston, Massachusetts : Harvard Business Review Press, [2026] | Includes bibliographical references and index.
Identifiers: LCCN 2025023232 (print) | LCCN 2025023233 (ebook) | ISBN 9798892790604 hardcover | ISBN 9798892790611 epub
Subjects: LCSH: Project management | Organizational change
Classification: LCC HD69.P75 N543 2026 (print) | LCC HD69.P75 (ebook) | DDC 658.4/04—dc23/eng/20250523
LC record available at https://lccn.loc.gov/2025023232
LC ebook record available at https://lccn.loc.gov/2025023233

ISBN: 979-8-89279-060-4
eISBN: 979-8-89279-061-1

The paper used in this publication meets the requirements of the American National Standard for Permanence of Paper for Publications and Documents in Libraries and Archives Z39.48-1992.

To those, in every corner of the world, who believe that meaningful change begins with a project—and have the courage to lead it forward. The future is built by you.

CONTENTS

PART THREE

VALUE GENERATION IN THE TRANSFORMATION AGE

PREFACE

If you're reading this book, you already know that modern project management matters. You've seen it drive strategy, innovation, and growth—and you've likely seen poor project management tank even the most promising initiatives.

But what if I told you that many project failures aren't really about project management at all? In fact, some of the biggest reasons projects fail can't be traced to missed deadlines or flawed Gantt charts. They stem from something more profound—from leadership blind spots and organizational structures that were never designed to support a world powered by projects.

That's what drove me, in 2019, to introduce a more disruptive shift—the concept of the *project economy*. It wasn't just about doing projects better. It was about recognizing that projects had become the primary engine of value creation. Operations keep the lights on—but projects move organizations forward.

The basics of the project economy were clear:

- Today, value, growth, ROI, and so forth comes from projects, not just from operations.

- Everyone—regardless of role or title—is a project manager.

- Senior leaders spend more time sponsoring projects and overseeing operations.

- Companies and governments must get far more return on their project investments—and address the trillions lost each year to failed or underperforming projects.

The idea resonated with many leaders and gained traction across industries. And then the pandemic hit. Suddenly, the project economy wasn't a future trend; it was a reality. Everything became a project: standing up digital infrastructures overnight, reconfiguring supply chains, and launching new services at record speed. Transformation wasn't optional—it was urgent. Projects became the center and the front line. Everyone, all the way up to CEO, became a project manager.

And yet despite this awakening, project failure remains exceptionally high. Organizations and leaders are not adapting fast enough. The understandable instinct has been to focus on running projects better—tighten timelines, upgrade tools, train more project managers. That's where my previous book, *HBR Project Management Handbook*, thrived.

But that's only half the battle. The truth is, the problem is deeper. At many organizations, 50 percent of the value is lost before a project even begins, not because of poor project management, but because of outdated organizational models and old-fashioned leadership.

Most organizations are still operating with nineteenth-century structures built for stability and efficiency—not for speed and transformation. Their people have twentieth-century skills: functional expertise, process thinking, and problem-solving. But in the twenty-first century, that's no longer enough. Adaptability, creativity, and bold decision-making are the new baseline.

Worse still, their approach to projects remains rigid and linear. They commit to too many initiatives. They mistake output for value. They are unable to pull fully dedicated cross-functional teams together. They rely on lengthy, costly, all-or-nothing transformation initiatives to deliver returns. They don't have executives who act as true project sponsors. They rely heavily on consultants to drive their strategic projects. And they're unable to adapt or stop projects that are no longer viable.

These aren't just project problems—they're leadership problems and organizational design problems. We can't do what needs to be done by managing projects better. The project economy calls for a new kind of leadership—one that goes beyond the day-to-day comfort zone—and a new organizational model that places projects at the core: the *project-driven organization*. It represents the next evolution of the agile organization—a twenty-year-old concept that, while valuable in its time, is no longer sufficient for the scale and complexity of transformation required today.

But there's a twist: just as everyone has become a project manager (whether they know it or not), every organization is now a project-driven organization—they just don't behave like one. And that's what this book is about.

This mission is personal. After two decades leading large-scale transformations at companies like GlaxoSmithKline, BNP Paribas, and PwC, I saw firsthand how traditional structures and leadership models were falling short. Projects, not operations, were driving the real value, yet they were too often treated as secondary. That disconnect inspired me to write five books on the issue, and now this book. My work since—advising leaders, training thousands, pioneering concepts like the project economy and the project canvas, and speaking around the world—has focused on one question: How can leaders significantly increase and accelerate project success and transform their organizations through projects?

Along the way, I've worked to elevate modern project management into the core of management thinking. I've helped persuade top business schools to incorporate it into their MBA curricula and collaborated with executives to reframe project capabilities as essential to strategy execution. As the first project management expert recognized by Thinkers50 and one of the most published authors on project management in *Harvard Business Review*, I've had the privilege of helping reshape how the world sees this discipline. I've served as chairman of the Project Management Institute (PMI), currently serve as vice president of the UK's Association for Project Management (APM), and founded Projects & Company as well as cofounded the Strategy Implementation Institute and the Brightline Initiative. All of that work has led to a deeper realization: what's needed isn't just better project execution, but a fundamental shift in how we lead and structure our organizations.

This book is my answer.

It's not a guide to running projects more efficiently. It's a blueprint for how leaders can remake their organizations—and themselves—for a world powered by projects. Only leaders can create the conditions where projects and the people behind them can truly thrive. Only leaders can stop treating projects as exceptions and start building organizations where projects are the norm, the strategy, the culture. If you're a CEO, an executive, a manager, a transformation leader, a project sponsor, or a project leader—this book is for you.

The transformation age is here. The question is: Are you and your organization ready?

POWERED BY
PROJECTS

All Organizations Are Now Project-Driven Organizations

Nobody now doubts that we are living in the transformation age—a time when organizations must move from viewing transformation as a one-time initiative to seeing it as a permanent state. This is a time of relentless upheaval, rapid technological progress, and profound socioeconomic shifts. AI and new technologies are reshaping industries at an unprecedented pace, market shifts are challenging long-held assumptions, and global challenges such as climate change and geopolitical instability demand constant adaptation.

According to Accenture's Global Disruption Index, disruption increased by an astounding 200 percent between 2017 and 2022, compared to just 4 percent from 2011 to 2016.[1] The pandemic and political and trade instability have largely driven this shift, along with emerging technologies such as quantum computing, gen AI, Web3, robotics, 5G, and the metaverse. These advancements are not only transforming industries but also enabling entirely new business models and reshaping how we work and live.

Where companies face a constant state of flux, speed and adaptability are paramount. Organizations today face a simple but critical question: Can they evolve fast enough to not only survive but thrive? Those that succeed will recognize that projects are no longer occasional initiatives but the engine driving transformation, growth, and competitive advantage. In my previous book, I explored this new paradigm, called the *project economy*.[2]

Change is no longer optional or occasional—it is the defining condition of our time. In this new reality, projects rather than operations become the focus of the organization. This is the foundation of the project economy: a world where projects are how organizations evolve, innovate, and deliver value in a state of continuous change.

The project economy didn't emerge overnight. It is the result of a century-long shift in how organizations allocate their time, budgets, and leadership attention. The importance of operational work—once the dominant focus—steadily declined as businesses pursued efficiency through mass production, reengineering, continuous improvement, ERP systems, outsourcing, and process automation. These improvements freed up capacity and pushed organizations to redirect resources toward change-driven efforts. The trend is accelerating as disruptive technologies such as AI and robotics are rapidly reshaping or eliminating traditional operational roles. The core focus of organizations is shifting from running the business—traditionally their comfort zone—to changing the business, which often lies outside of it. (See figure I-1.) Organizations that once relied on stable, repeatable processes must now become adept at continuous transformation through initiatives that are complex, fast-moving, and high-stakes.

Many organizations have responded to this new environment by investing in improving how they run projects. They have started to adopt hybrid methodologies and upskill some of their employees and managers. There are signs that execution has progressed—projects are better defined and managed than they were a decade ago. And yet the value isn't showing up where it counts. Far too many projects still underdeliver or fail altogether. The outcomes don't match the intent. The impact doesn't justify the investment. Transformation programs stall and strategic initiatives get bogged down in complexity and bureaucracy.

Better project management alone isn't enough. Often, the missing piece isn't in the execution—it's in the ecosystem. Value is lost not in the delivery phase, but in how organizations prioritize, sponsor, adapt, and embed projects into their strategic core. These are not project management problems: they are leadership and organizational design problems.

FIGURE I-1

From operations to transformations

Organizations are reallocating time, resources, and leadership focus from operations to projects in response to constant disruption in the project economy.

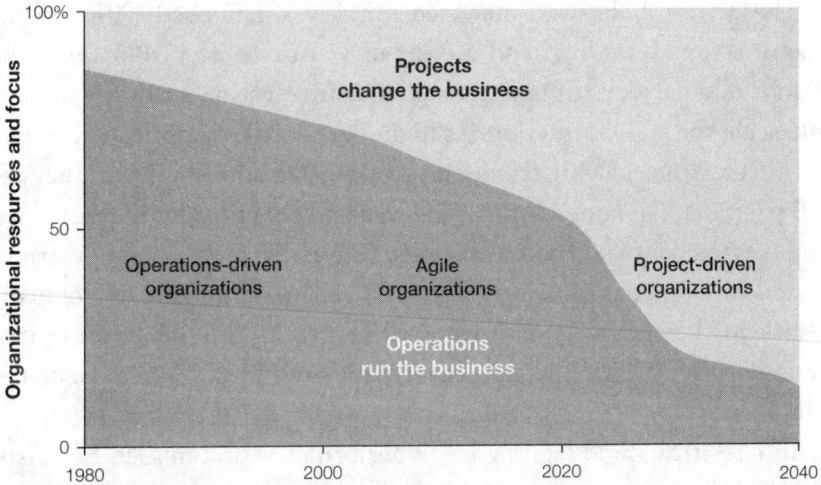

I'd like to share two stories of organizations that executed key projects perfectly but failed to create value.

In 2022, global professional services giant Ernst & Young set out to execute a sweeping corporate transformation: splitting its consulting and audit divisions into two separate firms. The rationale was strong—resolving long-standing conflicts of interest and unlocking growth on both sides of the business. The planning was rigorous. Executional elements were put in place: project teams mobilized, financing secured, and timelines set.

But Project Everest, as it was called, ultimately collapsed.[3] Why? Because despite sound project-related execution, leadership wasn't aligned. Senior leaders disagreed on core elements—financial arrangements, brand implications, and strategic priorities. With no unified voice at the top, the project lost momentum and credibility. Eventually, it was scrapped, leaving behind cost overruns, internal confusion, and reputational damage. This wasn't a failure of project management—*it was a failure of project-driven leadership.*

Now consider Nike's digital transformation between 2020 and 2024.[4] In the four years following the start of the pandemic, the company accelerated its shift to a direct-to-consumer model, investing heavily in e-commerce, digital platforms, and consumer data analytics. Nike executed a series of projects with precision—revamping its SNKRS app, expanding the Nike Training Club app, and pushing into virtual retail experiments, including NFTs and the metaverse.

These were bold, well-managed initiatives, launched with capable teams, strong branding, and a clear digital-first vision. But the value didn't follow. Nike's organizational structure wasn't ready to support and scale the transformation. As digital grew, Nike significantly pulled back from wholesale distribution—straining relationships with key retail partners like Foot Locker. This weakened its broader market reach and created confusion across regions. Internally, innovation efforts operated in silos, disconnected from core business units. The company also leaned too heavily into trend-driven tech like Web3 and virtual goods without building structural pathways to sustained customer value.

In late 2023, amid lagging stock performance and missed forecasts, Nike announced that CEO John Donahoe would step down in 2024. Again, it wasn't the project that failed—it was the structure around it.

These examples make one thing clear: in the transformation age, it takes more than just modern project management to succeed. Without project-driven structures and leadership, even the most well-executed initiatives will fail to deliver value. You must bring together modern project methods with project-first leadership and organizational structures that are designed for projects to flourish. I call this new organizational model the *project-driven organization* (PDO).

The Project-Driven Organization: The Next Evolution beyond Agile Organizations

A project-driven organization places projects at the heart of its strategy, growth, value creation, operations, and culture. In this model, leaders sponsor and align strategic initiatives, empower teams to make decisions closer to the action, and ensure that resources, skills, and support are aligned with project priorities. The structure becomes agile not just at the team level, but across the entire enterprise.

Becoming project-driven is more than adopting tools, frameworks, or agile methods—it's a deep cultural and structural shift. It requires seeing projects as the vital connection between vision and execution, strategy and results, ideas and impact.

For the past two decades, agile organizations have served as the gold standard for thriving in a fast-paced, technology-driven world. Agile introduced critical innovations: smaller teams, shorter feedback loops, customer-centric design, and iterative development. These tools helped companies break free from rigid planning models and adapt more quickly. But as we move deeper into the transformation age, the magnitude and velocity of change now demand something more integrated—an enterprise-wide capacity for continuous transformation, not just localized speed or flexibility.

Organizations today face challenges that agile frameworks were never designed to address. Entire industries are being redefined overnight. AI and advanced analytics are collapsing decision cycles. Customers and employees expect personalized, real-time experiences. In this new context, PDOs represent the next logical evolution—re-architecting the business itself around dynamic, empowered, cross-functional project teams.

The shift—from operations-driven to agile to project-driven—reflects a broader transformation in how organizations create value, drive ROI, and reallocate resources to compete. See table I-1 for an illustration of this evolution across key dimensions of strategy, structure, and culture.

This evolution makes clear that PDOs don't replace agile—they build on its foundation and expand it across the enterprise. They embed the spirit of agility—empowerment, adaptability, speed, focus on value—into every layer of the organization, from strategic planning to frontline execution. Projects become the operating system of the business.

This shift isn't just conceptual—it's urgent. In a world defined by disruption, traditional operating models leave organizations vulnerable to irrelevance. Legacy hierarchies are too slow, and isolated innovation labs lack impact. The project-driven model brings together structure, leadership, and culture to enable speed, clarity, and sustained value creation. It also elevates modern project management from a delivery discipline to a strategic capability. Projects are no longer just how work gets done—they are how strategy comes to life. Organizations that embrace

TABLE I-1

The path to project-driven organizations

	Operations-driven organizations	Agile organizations	Project-driven organizations
Inception period	Late nineteenth to early twentieth century	Early 2000s	2025 onward
Primary focus	Efficiency, stability, and control	Speed and flexibility within teams	Enterprise-wide transformation driven through projects
Value creation	Cost optimization, productivity gains, and operational leverage	Faster time-to-market, iterative customer-value delivery, and improved responsiveness	Strategic execution, innovation, and dynamic resource reallocation toward high-impact initiatives
Scope of application	Business units and functional departments (e.g., manufacturing, finance)	Mostly software, product development, and innovation	Across all business areas—strategy, operations, customer experience, technology
Organizational structure	Hierarchical, siloed departments	Agile teams within existing hierarchies	Flat, decentralized structures where projects are the primary units
Leadership model	Command-and-control	Leaders enable and unblock teams	Leaders sponsor, prioritize, and align multiple strategic projects
Culture	Standardization and risk aversion, focus on compliance and process control	Iterative learning, adaptability, and small-team empowerment, experimentation within defined limits	Continuous transformation, outcome orientation, and entrepreneurial accountability across teams
Skills	Process execution, compliance, domain expertise	Collaboration, iteration, product thinking	Project leadership, cross-functional execution, value creation

this model consistently outperform, particularly in transformation contexts. And McKinsey research shows that firms adopting project-based approaches during digital transformations experienced a 30 percent increase in market share.[5]

The drivers are clear: the need to integrate digital strategy with execution, adapt to volatile environments, and meet rising stakeholder expectations. A project-first mindset enables leaders to prioritize, mobilize talent, and make decisions in real time. It's how modern organizations navigate uncertainty—and thrive.

How Project-Driven Organizations Work

Transformation and project successes and failures are multifaceted, rooted in three key dimensions: project-promoting organizational aspects, project-first leadership, and project-centric value generation.

Reimagining Organizations

The daunting—or exciting—reality is that transitioning to a PDO profoundly impacts every level of business strategy and operations. Organizations that have realigned their culture, structure, and governance to be more project-driven have observed significant improvements in project success rates.

Transitioning to a project-based model involves creating an organizational structure that promotes cross-functional collaboration and enhances communication and decision-making within project teams. Transformation leaders and project managers feel empowered by direct control over resources and project execution, facilitating a more coordinated approach to project management. Nike's story serves as a reminder: even well-executed projects can falter when organizational structures aren't built to support integration at scale.

An organizational culture that supports innovation, risk-taking, and collaborative problem-solving is crucial to success. When such a culture is absent and organizational structures are hierarchical or rigid, silos emerge, information flow is hindered, decision-making becomes slow, and resistance to change is heightened. In this environment, project teams cannot respond swiftly to changing circumstances or emerging challenges.

Furthermore, as we saw with EY and Nike, ambitious initiatives can be undermined by a lack of internal alignment. Where the structure, culture, and governance aren't designed to support transformative projects, the success rate of such initiatives will inevitably suffer. Project success without organizational readiness will fall short of delivering strategic impact.

Project-Driven Leadership

In project-driven organizations, leadership transcends traditional management practices by emphasizing adaptability, swift decision-making, and a holistic approach to team dynamics. Unlike conventional leaders who often operate within the comfort zone of functional expertise and routine operations, project-driven leaders thrive in ambiguity. They embrace the discomfort of unfamiliar contexts—navigating complex, rapidly evolving project landscapes—and are adept at cross-cultural communication to unify diverse teams toward common goals.

To thrive in the transformation age, leaders must foster a culture where project success is a shared responsibility, encouraging autonomy and trust among team members. This involves delegating tasks and empowering teams to make decisions that align with strategic goals, enhancing engagement and accountability.

Many leadership-related challenges in this environment revolve around a need for proper prioritization and strategic alignment. Senior leaders frequently initiate too many projects and transformations simultaneously, straining resources and causing critical initiatives to compete for limited attention, funding, and personnel. When every project is a priority, none truly is, resulting in diluted focus and fragmented efforts. These not only impact the success rate but also place a substantial burden on middle managers and employees. Project-driven leadership is required to prioritize resource allocation and manage tensions between multiple projects.[6]

Another significant leadership gap lies in the disconnect between the strategic vision of senior leadership and execution. This gap can manifest as unclear or conflicting objectives, insufficient sponsorship, inadequate support from executive leaders, or a lack of timely decision-making or guidance when project teams encounter obstacles. Without strong executive sponsorship, transformational projects lack the necessary visibility, resources, and authority to navigate challenges, significantly reducing their likelihood of success. Strategic ambition without unified leadership not only derails execution but can undermine credibility across the organization.

Leaders may also fail to cultivate an organizational culture that embraces agility and adaptability in transformations. Resistance to change and risk aversion can stifle innovation, preventing organizations from learning from past mistakes. Consequently, projects often continue beyond their financial viability, resulting in wasted investment, poor capital efficiency, and opportunity costs, which emerge after project launch. Without a transformation-ready culture—reinforced and modeled by leadership—organizations lack the resilience to pivot or pause, even when it becomes clear that a project's value trajectory is off course.

Another core aspect of project-driven leadership is helping your people understand their new roles in the organization. Have you ever heard your employees saying, "Can we go back to normal?" or "I can't wait to get back to normal"?

But in today's business environment, the idea of returning to a "normal" state of operations is no longer viable. Stability is no longer the default—it's the exception. As a leader, you must inspire them to embrace transformation as a constant, rather let them "set and forget."

One of the significant triggers of the Great Resignation that followed the onset of the Covid-19 pandemic was the substantial increase in project-based work. This shift led to heightened stress, uncertainty, and increased workload for many employees. According to organizational strategist Michael Mankins, the phenomenon was not solely a result of the pandemic but rather a continuation of a trend driven by factors such as reconsideration and reshuffling, exacerbated by the pandemic's impact on work dynamics.[7] The increase in project work often required employees to juggle multiple projects simultaneously, which many found overwhelming and unsustainable.

A McKinsey report on Covid's implications for business further observes that many companies had to adapt their business models rapidly to survive. Unfortunately, the accelerated shift to project-based work, while necessary, also contributed to employee burnout and dissatisfaction.[8] The increased prominence of project work has highlighted organizations' need for greater adaptability and resilience and emphasizes the importance of a raft of skills that are rarely identified in many workplaces and even more rarely part of an active development program.

Value Generation in the Transformation Age

In successful PDOs, projects are the primary vehicles through which strategy comes to life. These organizations treat projects as dynamic capital investments aimed at generating future returns and growth, not as pure incremental improvement changes. High-performing PDOs excel at selecting the right mix of initiatives, aligning them with strategic priorities and executing them with empowered, multidisciplinary teams. They build strong project ecosystems equipped with modern tools, hybrid methods, real-time data, embedded learning loops, and continuous up-skilling of teams with modern project management capabilities, allowing them to deliver benefits faster and with more significant impact.

Yet it is increasingly clear that many organizations and individuals don't have the right tools and skills to execute. Too many organizations continue to rely on outdated methods, either too rigid or too undisciplined, that lack the customization and flexibility required in today's dynamic environment. When confronted with unforeseen challenges—such as sudden market shifts, technological disruptions, or changes in regulatory landscapes—they often fail to adapt, leading to a breakdown in execution and, ultimately, the derailment of transformation efforts.

The Emergence of the Project-Driven Organization

The definitive end of business as usual is reshaping industries from manufacturing and services to technology as organizations shift their focus from optimizing stable, long-term processes to an ambidexterity that involves executing discrete, variable projects with precision and agility alongside a progressively leaner and more automated operational core.

This shift is already happening at the highest levels of global business. Take the recent transformation launched by Bill Anderson, CEO of Bayer, the 160-year-old German pharmaceutical and life sciences giant.[9] Confronted with declining share prices, investor pressure, and operational inefficiencies, Anderson is leading a radical corporate restructuring. His approach replaces layers of traditional management with self-directed, project-based teams that dissolve and reassemble every ninety days to tackle new initiatives.

This concept, which Anderson calls "dynamic shared ownership," is designed to break through bureaucracy and accelerate decision-making. It aims to boost innovation, reduce costs by €2 billion, and revitalize employee engagement. While many organizations have attempted similar transformations with mixed results, Anderson believes that Bayer's experiment will serve as a blueprint for others.

While many contemporary leaders are starting to embrace PDOs, W.L. Gore & Associates has embodied these principles since its inception. Bill Gore, a former DuPont engineer, founded the company in 1958. His vision was to foster innovation through a nonhierarchical, lattice organizational structure.[10] In this system, traditional chains of command are absent. Instead, associates engage directly with one another, promoting open communication and collaboration. Leadership emerges naturally based on expertise and the ability to inspire followership rather than through formal appointments. This approach has enabled Gore to cultivate self-managed teams that form organically around projects, allowing the company to respond swiftly to market opportunities and technological advancements.

Gore's cultural principles—freedom, fairness, commitment, and lowering the risk waterline—further reinforce its project-driven ethos. Associates are encouraged to pursue initiatives they are passionate about (freedom), ensure equitable treatment (fairness), uphold personal and collective responsibilities (commitment), and consult with peers before making significant decisions that could impact the company (waterline). This enduring model has facilitated continuous innovation at Gore. By maintaining a structure that prioritizes agility and empowers employees, Gore is a testament to the effectiveness of PDOs.

PDOs Are Powering Digital Transformations Worldwide

Digital tools are critical to support the development of a project economy by providing the infrastructure needed for rapid adaptation and collaboration. The EU's Digital Economy and Society Index highlights how European countries are advancing digital transformation to support project-based work. The EU has committed significant resources to digital-related reforms and investments, with countries like Austria, Germany, and Lithuania dedicating over 30 percent of their Recovery and Resilience Facility allocations to digital transformation efforts.[11]

In Africa, the World Bank's Digital Economy for Africa initiative has delivered numerous digitalization projects since 2019, aiming to build the foundation for a project-based economy. Over 160 million Africans gained broadband internet access between 2019 and 2022, enabling more flexible and innovative work environments.[12] In Asia, the Asian Development Bank reports that regional growth is supported by robust domestic demand and digital transformation efforts.[13] Countries like India and China are investing heavily in digital infrastructure to support project-based work, recognizing the need for flexibility and rapid decision-making in a competitive global market.

These investments are essential for fostering a project-driven economy that can adapt to new challenges and opportunities. PDOs will be well positioned to leverage the power of AI and automation, significantly improving project success rates and overall productivity. Companies like Haier and Google offer examples of what PDOs can achieve by integrating agile, project-centric structures with cutting-edge technology. Haier's flat organizational model empowers teams to make decisions rapidly, fostering a culture of constant innovation. Google's matrix structure similarly combines hierarchical oversight with substantial project autonomy, enabling rapid product development and adaptation to market shifts.

As organizations start to realize the full transformative potential of AI, they will use it to simulate possible project outcomes as well as guide them in designing the organizational structures and systems that will enable these outcomes. PDOs will no longer simply design their project delivery around their current capabilities and resources; instead they will adapt their capabilities, resources, and leadership to enable the projects that they can deliver. Companies that pivot successfully will lead the way with technological advancements, fostering a resilient and adaptable culture capable of navigating the complexities of a project-driven world.

Reading This Book

At the heart of this book is the *project-driven organization blueprint* designed to guide leaders in understanding and implementing a project-driven approach to steer their organizations through the transformation age. (See figure I-2.) This comprehensive framework illustrates how eight critical elements must align around projects as the primary drivers

FIGURE I-2

The project-driven organization blueprint

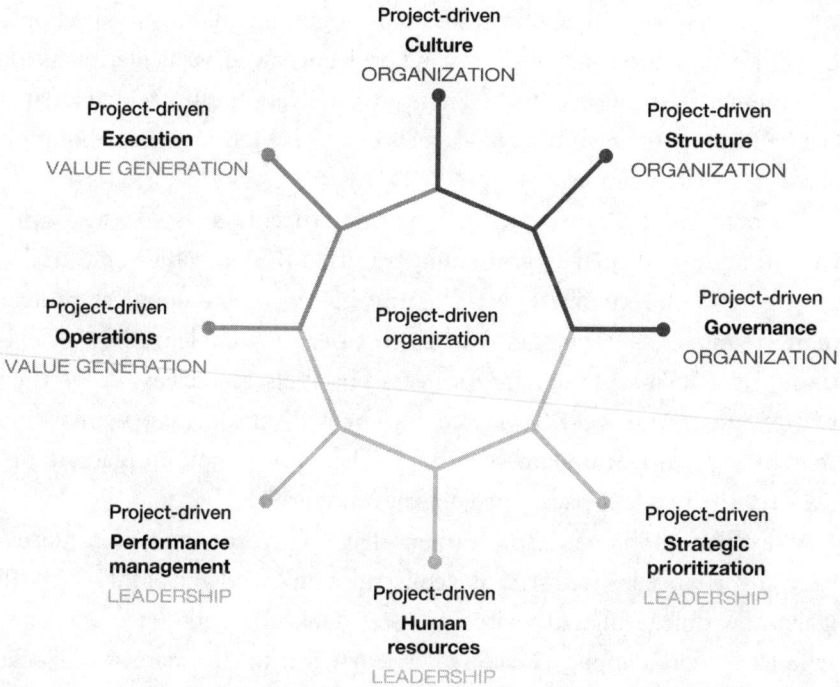

Project-driven
Culture
ORGANIZATION

Project-driven
Execution
VALUE GENERATION

Project-driven
Structure
ORGANIZATION

Project-driven
Operations
VALUE GENERATION

Project-driven
organization

Project-driven
Governance
ORGANIZATION

Project-driven
**Performance
management**
LEADERSHIP

Project-driven
**Human
resources**
LEADERSHIP

Project-driven
**Strategic
prioritization**
LEADERSHIP

of value. Throughout the book, we return to this chart as a blueprint for building, scaling, and sustaining a high-performing PDO.

The book is structured in three parts, each reflecting a critical dimension of what it takes to build and lead PDOs. Part 1 reimagines how organizations must evolve to enable project success. It explores the structural, cultural, and governance shifts required to promote project work at scale. Part 2 shifts the focus to project-driven leadership, defining the mindset and behaviors leaders must adopt to fuel transformation: prioritizing strategically, staffing projects for peak performance, sponsoring actively, and implementing project-based performance systems that incentivize return on investment, strategic value creation, and collective ownership of results. Finally, part 3 examines how value is delivered in a PDO. It examines how to structure operations around projects, embed execution excellence, and integrate technologies like AI to thrive in the project economy.

Chapter 1 explores project-driven culture—a mindset that empowers organizations to prioritize the right work, execute with purpose, and stay aligned. We begin by examining the habit of stopping projects—a critical yet often overlooked discipline that helps organizations stay focused on a few initiatives. We'll also explore how projects can serve as platforms for an exponential mindset culture. Finally, we look at the culture that creates the conditions for fast, informed decisions and high-trust collaboration across the organization.

Chapter 2 focuses on project-driven structure. In a world where agility and adaptability are paramount, traditional hierarchies can hinder progress. We'll explore how flattening hierarchies empowers project teams to move faster and take ownership. Leaders will learn how prioritizing transformation-driving projects channels resources where they matter most. And we'll cover staffing for peak performance, ensuring that your organization can swiftly put the right people in place to deliver results in a fast-paced, project-driven world.

The third chapter is about project-driven governance. While necessary, governance is often seen as a constraint on speed and agility. We will learn how delegating authority for faster decisions puts power closer to where the work happens. Leaders will learn how to eliminate bottlenecks to reduce friction and accelerate execution—and how to design lean, effective governance bodies to ensure oversight without sacrificing agility while supporting rapid decision-making across the project portfolio.

With the organizational foundations in place, part 2 turns to the essential role of leadership in enabling project-driven transformation. Chapter 4 takes a deep dive into project-driven strategic prioritization. We will explore how defining purpose and measurable benefits from the start sets a clear direction and builds momentum. Leaders will learn to ruthlessly prioritize a few high-value initiatives, ensuring focus and impact. We will also show how to activate sponsors to champion execution, turning strategic intent into sustained delivery through visible, committed leadership.

Chapter 5 covers project-driven human resources. We will examine how adopting dynamic resource allocation models enables organizations to respond quickly to shifting priorities. Leaders will learn how to build high-performing, collaborative project teams that thrive in cross-functional environments and demonstrate a strong sense of ownership and entrepreneurial drive. We will also explore strategies for upskilling for the future of work and leadership, ensuring that talent is ready to meet the evolving demands of the project economy.

In chapter 6, we examine project-driven performance management. Traditional performance metrics and reward systems often fail to capture the collaborative, dynamic nature of project work. Here, we'll discuss innovative approaches to developing performance measurements and incentives, tailored specifically to a PDO, where success and rewards are team-based, linked to measurable value creation, and aligned with long-term financial and strategic outcomes, supported by frameworks to track benefits.

With leadership and organization aligned, part 3 shifts focus to the operations and execution that deliver real value. In chapter 7, we enter the realm of project-driven operations. We will look at what it means to lead in an era of automation and robotization, where operational excellence is redefined by speed, flexibility, and intelligent systems. Leaders will learn how to shift the center of value creation from operations to projects, aligning core activities with strategic execution. We'll also examine how to orchestrate operations through project-aligned service models that reduce friction, increase responsiveness, and support high-impact delivery.

Chapter 8 explores project-driven execution, examining the frameworks, methodologies, and technologies that enable organizations to execute projects with agility and impact. We will introduce the project canvas, a structured yet flexible tool that ensures clarity of purpose, bolsters stakeholder buy-in, and drives measurable outcomes. We also move beyond the waterfall-versus-agile debate, embracing hybrid methods that tailor approaches to project needs. Finally, we explore how integrating AI and emerging technologies elevates execution by enhancing decision-making, automating workflows, and enabling smarter, faster collaboration.

In the concluding chapter, we turn our attention to shaping the future through PDOs, where we explore how the most resilient and influential enterprises leave a lasting legacy by embedding adaptability, innovation, and purpose into their core. This chapter highlights the evolution of PDOs, focusing on their ability to foster resilience in uncertain times, cultivate leaders who can balance complexity with purpose, and embrace a mindset of continuous transformation.

Every organization begins this journey—from the foundational shifts driving the rise of the project economy to the practical realities of building and leading a PDO—from a different starting point, with varying levels of maturity and urgency. The ideas and examples in this book are meant to support your ongoing evolution—not toward a fixed end-state but toward building lasting capability. Start where you are, engage your stakeholders to join you on this journey, and learn and adapt as you go.

Haier: A Project-Driven Exemplar

Haier is an exemplar of project-driven success. The world's largest appliance manufacturer has been at the forefront of redefining organizational structure and leadership, evolving from traditional hierarchies to agile networks, and now to a fully project-driven model under the visionary leadership of Zhang Ruimin, first as CEO over many years and now as chairman emeritus. Ruimin's leadership philosophy is deeply rooted in the concept of entrepreneurial self-organization, which he believes is essential for companies to become truly people centric.[14]

Haier's transformation is anchored in its micro-enterprise (ME) model, where thousands of small, autonomous teams function like independent startups within the larger organization. These teams are empowered to make decisions, own their profit and loss accountability, and pursue customer-focused opportunities. This model is part of a broader philosophy known as RenDanHeYi, which translates roughly to "combining the value of employees with the value created for users." It's a system built to dissolve bureaucracy, unleash initiative, and directly link individual contributions to market outcomes.

The core elements of Haier's micro-enterprise model neatly showcase the essence—and the promise—of the PDO:

- *Extend accountability beyond project delivery.* By requiring and enabling leaders to think *beyond* project completion, organizations can focus on the long-term impact and investment returns.

- *Provide autonomy in decision-making.* Establishing clear boundaries and guidelines—and trusting leaders to navigate within these parameters—provides strategic direction and intent but allows local innovation and enables decisions to be taken close to where the work happens.

- *Align incentives with value creation.* The reward and incentive structures are designed to align personal success with project success; consequently, they act as powerful forces for behavior change.

- *Foster an entrepreneurial mindset.* Transformation leaders need to be trained and mentored to encourage a calculated attitude toward risk, an appetite for innovation, and a continual focus on value creation—not just in ideas, but in measurable business outcomes such as ROI, strategic impact, and long-term growth.

- *Create cross-functional teams.* Silos limit both speed and value realization. By going beyond agile team models and embedding project teams across business functions, organizations can unlock broader capabilities, improve capital utilization, and ensure alignment with enterprise-level goals.

- *Implement an autonomous lean governance model.* Project governance is often a source of greater friction rather than being enabling. An autonomous lean governance model should provide guidance and support without stifling innovation. This could involve regular check-ins, peer reviews, or advisory boards that offer guidance rather than top-down control.

- *Invest in capability development.* Organizations require fundamental reskilling to transition from delivering projects to becoming project-driven. This may include training in business strategy, leadership, finance, and modern project management—skills typically associated with CEOs and business owners.

- *Cultivate a culture of continuous learning.* Complex change requires experimentation, which will depend on a culture where mistakes are seen as part of learning, experimentation is encouraged, and lessons learned are shared openly across the organization.

- *Provide access to resources.* The PDO recognizes that resource allocation extends beyond the financial and has routes and techniques to enable project teams to access technology, talent, and senior leadership support.

- *Celebrate and showcase success.* Regularly highlighting the achievements of your empowered project leaders will both recognize their efforts and signal the value of their approach to the wider organization.

Throughout this book, I will begin each chapter with examples from Haier, demonstrating what's possible when organization, leadership, and project-related factors are all aligned around transformation.

A Final Word

We're ready to get started. This is the last time we'll speak about project-driven organizations in the abstract. From here on, we're in the real world, where every organization is already a PDO—whether it knows it or not. And that includes yours.

For the rest of this book, I'll speak directly to you: a leader, or future leader, of a PDO. Your company may not yet behave like one—but it is one by default simply because projects have become how work gets done and value gets created. The only question is whether you're leading it that way.

Understanding and acting like a PDO will help you build the organization of the future—one that adapts continuously, engages its people deeply, and earns their pride as it thrives in the decades to come. Staying stuck to leadership models and organizational structures from another era will almost certainly ensure the opposite.

Let's kick off this transformation project.

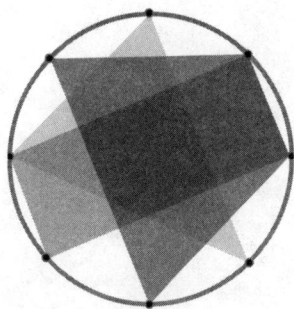

REIMAGINING ORGANIZATIONS

n the first part of this book, we explore the foundational elements that enable organizations to thrive in the transformation age. This section unpacks how culture, structure, and governance must evolve to support a world where projects are not just strategy components—they *are* the strategy.

Consider Honeywell's transformation under the leadership of then-CEO Darius Adamczyk. Beginning in 2017 and accelerating through the early 2020s, Honeywell undertook a sweeping digital reinvention.[1] It modernized its IT infrastructure, centralized its data environment, and embedded digital capabilities across its business units. It also launched new business models, including software platforms and connected services, that opened up fresh revenue streams. This transformation was delivered through a series of coordinated, high-impact initiatives—all characteristics of a project-driven organization.

By 2023, Honeywell achieved 4 percent organic sales growth, with total sales reaching $36.7 billion.[2] Operating income grew by 10 percent, and the company reported adjusted earnings per share of $9.16. Its backlog rose to a record $31.8 billion, up 8 percent year-over-year, reflecting strong demand for its newly integrated, technology-driven offerings.

Organizations that succeed in this era don't simply add more projects—they reimagine themselves to be powered by projects. That means cultivating a culture of empowerment and exponential growth, designing adaptive structures that support execution, and implementing governance models that promote speed, alignment, and accountability. Unlike operations, projects thrive with minimal hierarchy and require governance frameworks that enable cocreation, not control.

Before we explore how leaders drive these changes (part 2) and how execution turns strategy into reality (part 3), we must first understand the organizational architecture that makes project-based transformation scalable and sustainable.

CHAPTER 1

Project-Driven Culture

Haier's transformation under Zhang Ruimin provides a master class in cultivating a project-driven culture. Central to this revolution is the company's RenDanHeYi philosophy, which emphasizes decentralization, self-organization, and user-centric innovation.

At Haier, the *ability to decisively stop underperforming or misaligned projects* is embedded in the organizational DNA. The company is organized into *micro-enterprises* (MEs): decentralized, entrepreneurial teams that drive the company's growth and innovation. MEs operate autonomously but are held accountable for creating measurable user value. If a project fails to meet predefined value-creation goals within three months, it is either restructured or terminated. This rigorous system prevents the misallocation of resources and ensures that time and capital are channeled into high-potential initiatives. This culture is evident in the continuous evolution of Haier's ecosystem microcommunities (EMCs), which dynamically reassemble, split, and evolve based on users' changing needs. For example, Haier's Smart Medical sub-EMC evolved from a failing business unit by identifying critical inefficiencies in hospital pharmacy management and pivoting to develop personalized automated solutions. This move allowed Haier to reallocate resources and maintain momentum in innovation.

Haier's project-driven approach *fosters an exponential mindset culture*. Employees are encouraged to think like entrepreneurs, embracing risk and learning from failure. In fact, failure is reframed as an essential part of the iterative process. Zhang often cites the adage, "If you're not embarrassed by the first version of your product, you've launched too late."

For instance, Haier's Incaier comprehensive health ecosystem brand—which specializes in life sciences, clinical medicine, and biotechnology—boasts three listed companies: Haier Biomedical, Incaier Life Sciences, and Shanghai RAAS.

Enabling an open and transparent execution culture is another cornerstone of Haier's project-driven culture. Haier's decentralized structure demands open information flow and real-time strategic visibility. To support this, Haier has developed digital platforms that democratize access to operational data, empowering MEs and EMCs to make informed decisions, respond to change, and align more closely with end-user expectations.

Chery Automobile used Haier's COSMOPlat intelligent interaction model to engage directly with users throughout the development of a new off-road vehicle. This engagement surfaced over fifty thousand specific demands, which led to thirty-five customization scenarios. By transforming customer input into real-time design insights, Chery launched a vehicle tailored to a previously underserved segment, demonstrating how open collaboration can unlock new market opportunities.

On the execution side, COSMOPlat's digital infrastructure enabled flexible manufacturing and supply chain coordination, helping Chery reach a production rate of sixty vehicles per hour. This wasn't just an operational win; it was the outcome of transparent, cross-functional execution powered by shared data and user engagement.

By embedding openness into both strategy and execution, Haier and Chery have shown how transparency and feedback loops can elevate project outcomes. They reinforce a core truth of the transformation age: in fast-moving, project-driven environments, clarity and collaboration are cultural imperatives.

———————————

One of the most important lessons I share with my clients is that changing an organization's culture is a long journey, but transformation projects can't wait. When launching major initiatives, you have the opportunity (and the obligation) to deliberately establish its own culture from scratch.

Projects inevitably bring together people from different business units, functions, and backgrounds, each with its own cultures, ways of working, and assumptions. If you don't consciously define the cultural principles for the transformation at the start, teams will default to old habits, often pulling in conflicting directions.

Taking time at the beginning of every transformation to establish the appropriate cultural values and principles—how to collaborate, decide, learn, and adapt—is one of the most strategic leadership actions you can take. It creates the micro-culture a project needs to succeed even before the broader organization fully evolves.

Albert Bandura's research on social learning emphasizes the importance of organizational culture: "Perceived collective efficacy [the shared beliefs that group and community members hold about their capability to achieve desired goal] will influence what people choose to do as a group, how much effort they put into it, and the staying power when group effort fails to produce results."[1] The concept, which encompasses the values, beliefs, and behaviors that shape how work gets done within an organization, introduces perspectives into the way project organizations are managed that are anything but common language. Yet they reflect ideas such as those championed by Stephen Covey, who advocated "sharpening the saw" by increasing motivation, energy, and vitality by making time for renewal activities."[2]

In a PDO, the focus must shift to the strategies and practices necessary to cultivate a culture that supports project-driven initiatives and transformative growth. (See the sidebar, "What Are Projects—and Why Do They Hold the Key to Your Future?")

In this chapter, we explore how companies across various industries cultivate a project-centric culture by focusing on three main areas—the habit of stopping projects, projects as platforms for an exponential mindset culture, and enabling an open and transparent execution culture—all of which were visible in the examples from Haier seen earlier.

These practices can help project-driven leaders redefine their organizations and govern their projects to foster innovation, agility, and alignment with strategic objectives (see figure 1-1 for a summary).

What Are Projects—and Why Do They Hold the Key to Your Future?

Projects are much more than temporary endeavors with a defined start and end date—they are the building blocks that determine the future of your organization.

A project is a focused effort to create something new, solve a problem, or seize an opportunity. Whether delivering a digital transformation, implementing a sustainability initiative, or redesigning a business model, projects are how organizations adapt, grow, innovate, and transform.

In today's business landscape, projects are the lifeblood of strategy. They translate ambition into action, bridging the gap between what an organization aspires to achieve and what it delivers. Projects are not just tools—they are how progress happens. By mastering the art and science of projects, leaders can position their organizations to thrive in a world defined by constant transformation.

The Habit of Stopping Projects

One of the most critical principles of success in a PDO is that less is more—focusing on fewer, high-impact transformations and projects leads to stronger performance and higher value, while pursuing too many initiatives often results in inefficiencies and value losses.

In a survey we carried out in June 2024, we found that most organizations struggle with stopping projects that no longer align with strategic goals. Only 8 percent reported having a formal, monthly review process, while 16 percent cancel projects quarterly but in an ad hoc manner. The majority (44 percent) stop projects only occasionally, a few times a year, when significant misalignment is identified. Only 26 percent rarely stop projects—and 7 percent never do, continuing all initiatives regardless of their relevance. These findings underscore the need for systematic practices to evaluate and stop projects.

Many organizations remain reluctant to terminate projects, even when they are no longer viable, creating a culture in which resources are wasted,

FIGURE 1-1

Project-driven culture

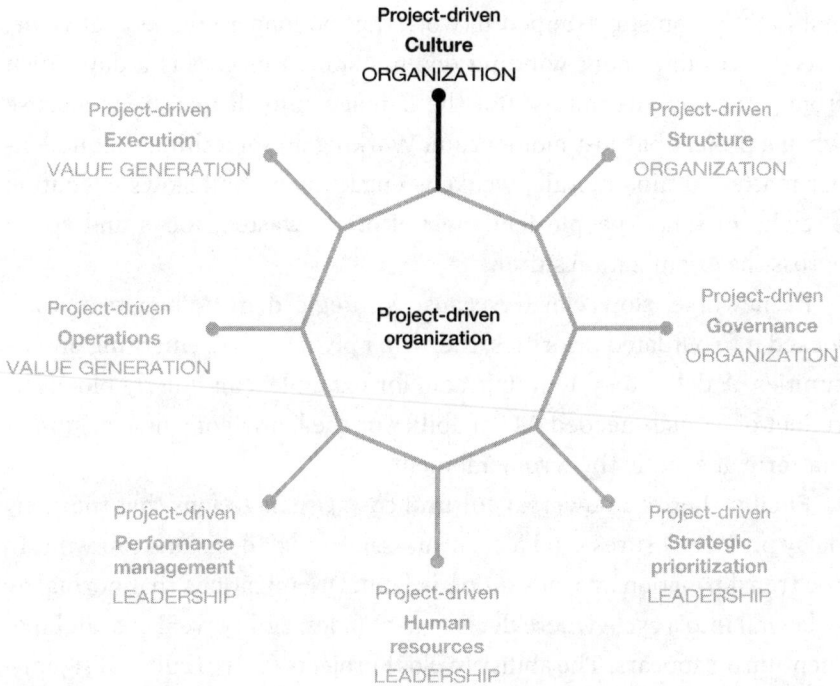

Project-driven
Culture
ORGANIZATION

Project-driven
Execution
VALUE GENERATION

Project-driven
Structure
ORGANIZATION

Project-driven
Operations
VALUE GENERATION

**Project-driven
organization**

Project-driven
Governance
ORGANIZATION

Project-driven
Performance
management
LEADERSHIP

Project-driven
Human
resources
LEADERSHIP

Project-driven
Strategic
prioritization
LEADERSHIP

opportunities are missed, and strategic focus is undermined. Cultivating the habit of stopping nonviable projects is crucial for maintaining agility and ensuring that resources are directed toward the most promising opportunities. By embracing failure, organizations can view project termination not as a loss, but as a strategic decision.

The Hidden Costs of Letting Projects Linger

In transformation environments where speed is everything, few mistakes are more damaging than letting projects drag on once their usefulness has ended. When closure decisions are slow or when shuttering projects takes weeks or months after the decision, the costs pile up quickly. At first, they might seem invisible. Over time, they quietly drain energy, stretch budgets, and blur strategic focus.

The most obvious cost is wasted resources. People, budgets, and leadership attention stay trapped in work that no longer creates real value. Every extra day spent winding down a stalled project is a day stolen from future opportunities. But the damage runs deeper. Teams sense when a project has lost momentum. Working on something that no longer matters drains morale, weakens engagement, and slows execution elsewhere. When people feel their effort is wasted, focus and speed across the organization suffer.

Even worse, slow closures cause strategic drift. When teams are locked into outdated priorities, they can't pivot to seize emerging opportunities. A delayed system upgrade, for example, can quietly block the rollout of a much-needed AI capability or the launch of a new customer platform at exactly the wrong moment.

Finally, there's a powerful cultural cost. Organizations that routinely delay project closures send a clear message: tough decisions can wait. In the transformation age, hesitation is fatal. Organizations that normalize delay fall into a cycle where decisiveness fades, agility weakens, and momentum disappears. The ability to close projects fast is a cultural signal—and a leadership capability—that separates companies that keep moving forward from those that fall behind. As Cicero reportedly said, "More is lost by indecision than wrong decision."

Understanding When to Kill a Project

Understanding when to terminate a project is not a matter of simple calculations or rigid thresholds. It requires a combination of hard data, gut instinct, context awareness, and leadership judgment. Timelines shift, assumptions evolve, and priorities change. But what remains constant is this: the cost of indecision is almost always higher than the cost of stopping.

In 2023, Wales's government scrapped a raft of road building and improvement projects, following a yearlong review of their impact. Over fifty schemes were reassessed, with only fifteen set to go ahead in their original form and others amended, postponed, or scrapped. The government's net-zero commitments drove the decision: at the same time, they signaled that "all future roads must now pass strict criteria which mean they must not increase carbon emissions or the number of cars on the road, lead to higher speeds or negatively impact the environment."[3]

Although it was a painful decision, the care that the government took in the review and involvement of key stakeholders provides useful insight into how to approach project closure: "What we've just been through has created uncertainty, but we can start to get clarity on investments in infrastructure, whether that's maintaining what we've got or new investment in energy, for instance, then that will go a long way to ensure that jobs, business, and communities are safeguarded," said Ed Evans, director of the Civil Engineering Contractors Association.

Nestlé, the global food and beverage leader, has a history of making tough decisions to terminate projects that do not align with its strategic goals. Under the leadership of CEO Mark Schneider, the company has demonstrated a strategic approach to project and business termination as part of its broader portfolio optimization strategy. For example, it announced in February 2023 that it would terminate its frozen food project in Canada. Schneider explained that the challenges of importing products from the United States to Canada, including the lack of local manufacturing and the impact of currency fluctuations, made the project unfeasible.

This is not an isolated incident but part of a larger strategy to optimize Nestlé's portfolio. The company is conducting a "very targeted review SKU by SKU, brand by brand," to determine where it has the best chance to succeed and what the potential rewards are. Further terminations of specific projects may occur as Nestlé refines its portfolio.[4]

Cultivating Decisive Project-Termination Practices

Even with clear strategic goals, many organizations struggle to stop projects at the right time. Recognizing danger signals is only the first step. To truly protect focus and accelerate learning, organizations must build the habit of decisive project termination.

Drawing lessons from the pharmaceutical industry, where disciplined project closure is critical to success, organizations can adopt a structured, high-trust model to stop nonviable projects quickly and confidently. This isn't about being ruthless; it's about ensuring that re-sources and attention are continually redirected toward initiatives with the greatest potential for impact.

Here's a refined approach for embedding fast and strategic project closure as a cultural habit:

- *Set clear evaluation criteria.* Establish clear and holistic evaluation criteria that combine measurable project performance with strategic relevance. Go beyond abstract goals—focus on whether tangible benefits have already been realized and whether the project aligns with your organization's current strategy. The project termination matrix (figure 1-2) helps categorize projects based on three key dimensions: project fundamentals, strategic alignment, and intuitive signals. This tool provides a clear visual framework for deciding whether to continue, adjust, or stop a project. The project canvas, discussed in chapter 8, can further support your analysis by mapping a project's core logic—why it exists, what it delivers, and how it's executed. Combined, these tools promote faster, more confident decisions when it's time to close, pivot, or double down.

- *Limit project time frames to three to six months.* Even in multiyear transformation programs, breaking initiatives into tightly scoped three- or six-month project cycles creates natural decision points that support timely and objective termination decisions. At the end of each cycle, it becomes significantly easier to assess whether the project should be continued, adjusted, or stopped altogether. This time-boxed structure reduces the psychological and political barriers to ending underperforming initiatives, while helping teams maintain focus, momentum, and a clear connection to strategic priorities.

- *Accelerate closure once the decision is clear.* Limiting projects to three- to six-month cycles helps surface tough decisions—but once a project has been flagged for termination, speed becomes critical. Aim to move from decision to execution within a week. That means communicating clearly, initiating offboarding steps, and

FIGURE 1-2

Decision matrix for project continuation or termination: A holistic approach

Project fundamentals

	Poor	Sound
High	**Stabilize or terminate** Objective criteria • Partial benefit realization, but delivery challenges persist • Strategic fit remains valid Intangibles • Team fatigue or delivery strain • Sponsor support weakening Gut feeling • Confidence in success is mixed • Uncertainty about continued momentum	**Continue or double down** Objective criteria • Tangible benefits already realized • Strong fit with current strategy and priorities Intangibles • High team energy and ownership • Active and visible executive sponsorship Gut feeling • Strong conviction and momentum to scale • Broad organizational confidence
Low	**Terminate immediately** Objective criteria • Minimal or no benefit realization • Misaligned with current strategic direction Intangibles • Stakeholder disengagement • Lack of team motivation or relevance Gut feeling • Repeated doubts • No sense of urgency or direction	**Reassess for repositioning** Objective criteria • Some delivery capacity or progress • Strategic intent unclear or outdated Intangibles • Passive sponsor support • Teams showing mixed signals Gut feeling • Feels salvageable with adjustments • Worth validating through realignment discussion

Left axis: Strategic alignment and benefits (High to Low)

reallocating resources without delay. Fast follow-through not only preserves momentum and minimizes waste—it reinforces a culture where responsiveness, accountability, and strategic clarity take precedence over defending past investments.

• *Reinforce ownership and transparency.* Teams must feel responsible not just for launching projects, but also for speaking up when they see misalignment or drift. Leaders must create a culture where surfacing concerns about a project's viability is considered strategic maturity, not career risk. Maintaining transparency—through open project reviews, visible risk reporting, and inclusive decision-making—helps remove the stigma around project closure and strengthens overall strategic discipline.

- *Celebrate tough calls, not just delivery.* Organizations that celebrate not only completed projects but also courageous decisions to stop projects early send a powerful signal: smart choices matter more than simply pushing projects to the finish line. Recognizing teams for making tough calls reinforces a culture of learning, resilience, and speed. It encourages employees to focus on delivering outcomes, not just outputs.

By embedding fast, decisive project termination into organizational habits, companies sharpen their focus, accelerate execution, and strengthen their ability to adapt to changing realities. In chapter 4, we will build on this foundation.

Projects as Platforms for an Exponential Mindset Culture

The next frontier is executing projects effectively and using them as engines to unlock exponential growth. That transformation starts with an exponential mindset. Many organizations still operate with a fixed or linear mindset focused on predictability, perfection, and incremental gains. In such environments, mistakes are penalized, risk-taking is discouraged, and change is approached cautiously. But this mindset severely limits innovation and resilience. Running a PDO successfully requires something fundamentally different: an exponential mindset culture. Projects are nonlinear engines of continuous improvement, capable of unlocking disproportionate impact—*if* the surrounding culture is designed to support that potential.

An exponential mindset culture is built on three core principles:

- *Timely decision-making,* enabling teams to pivot, adjust scope, or redefine benefits without fear, reducing wasted effort and accelerating value creation

- *A culture of continuous learning,* where experimentation is encouraged, and failures are treated as essential steps toward breakthrough outcomes

- *Dual-speed ambition,* locking in early value while continuously pursuing larger, exponential opportunities that can shift the project's trajectory

Cultivating this mindset doesn't just improve project outcomes—it fundamentally reshapes how an organization thinks, learns, and grows. It turns projects into platforms not just for execution, but for evolution.

IKEA's exponential mindset culture under the leadership of CEO Jesper Brodin transformed not only its operations but also its entire business trajectory. While many companies treat sustainability as a parallel or isolated function, IKEA made it central to its strategy, despite being in a business where the environmental stakes are especially high.

As one of the world's largest wood users, IKEA faced a fundamental challenge: reconciling high-volume furniture production with environmental responsibility. An incremental mindset might have led to modest changes—swapping out a few materials, reducing packaging, or launching a small eco-friendly product line. Yet IKEA chose a far bolder path. Under Brodin's leadership, the company committed to becoming fully circular and climate-positive by 2030.[5] This includes using only renewable or recycled materials, eliminating all plastic packaging by 2028, and rethinking the entire product life cycle—from design to reuse.

This kind of innovation emerges only when exponential thinking is part of the cultural fabric. IKEA has built a deeply collaborative and decentralized environment where employees at all levels are encouraged to experiment, challenge conventions, and contribute to major initiatives. One example is the launch of the company's Preowned platform—a marketplace for secondhand IKEA products that blends sustainability goals with customer engagement and new business models.

By turning its biggest environmental liabilities into platforms for innovation and growth, IKEA shows what's possible when projects are aligned with long-term vision and empowered by a culture of experimentation and adaptability. It's a powerful example of how an exponential mindset culture can scale across an entire organization—not just in ambition, but in measurable, transformative impact.

From Fixed to Exponential: Rethinking the Mindset behind Projects

An exponential mindset builds on the belief that capabilities—whether human, technological, or organizational—can grow dramatically through bold experimentation, learning, and scaled ambition. The exponential mindset is about designing and executing projects that radically accelerate value creation and redefine what the organization believes is achievable. Cultivating this mindset is essential for transforming projects from tools of gradual improvement into engines of strategic reinvention. It fuels innovation, accelerates execution, and empowers teams to reimagine impact—not in 5 percent gains, but in tenfold shifts.

The Ocean Cleanup is a Dutch nonprofit founded in 2013 by Boyan Slat. On vacation in Greece, then sixteen-year-old Slat went scuba diving and was struck by what he saw: more plastic bags than fish in the sea. That moment sparked a simple but radical question in his mind: *Why can't we just clean this up?*[6] What started as a high school science project soon evolved into one of the most ambitious environmental initiatives of the twenty-first century. Just two years later, Slat took the stage at a TEDx event and publicly declared his goal—not to clean a beach, a bay, or even a coastline, but the world's oceans.

Rather than rely on traditional, slow, and resource-intensive cleanup methods, The Ocean Cleanup developed scalable technologies that tackle the problem at both ends. Its System 03, now deployed in the Great Pacific Garbage Patch, uses passive ocean currents to collect massive amounts of plastic debris efficiently. Meanwhile, Interceptor systems installed in some of the world's most polluted rivers are preventing plastic from reaching the oceans in the first place.

Slat's vision—to remove 90 percent of floating ocean plastic by 2040— would seem unrealistic through an incremental lens. But it's precisely this kind of exponential thinking that has ignited global interest, attracted engineering talent, and mobilized millions in funding. The Ocean Cleanup stands as a vivid example of what happens when bold ideas are pursued with focused execution, learning loops, and scalable project design.

TABLE 1-1

From an incremental to an exponential mindset

Type of project	Incremental mindset	Exponential mindset
Launching a new mobile app	Add two new features to existing functionality	Build a platform supporting 100+ third-party integrations
Redesigning the online customer journey	Improve customer satisfaction score by 5%	Increase digital engagement tenfold across all channels
Transitioning to sustainable packaging	Replace 10% of current packaging with recycled material	Eliminate 100% of single-use plastic packaging by 2028
Modernizing distribution operations	Reduce delivery time by two days	Enable 90% of orders to ship same-day through automation
Migrating legacy systems to the cloud	Move one business unit's system to the cloud	Achieve 100% cloud-native infrastructure across all functions in two years
Launching a digital skills academy	Train 200 employees in one new tool	Provide real-time, AI-driven learning paths for 100% of employees
Restructuring the sales organization	Merge two regional sales teams for cost efficiency	Reorganize into 50+ agile sales squads aligned by customer segment
Running a multi-channel marketing campaign	Grow email list by 10%	Build a digital community of 10 million brand followers
Automating a finance process	Automate one routine finance report	Automate 70% of financial reporting across all departments
Implementing a cybersecurity initiative	Update 2024 security compliance checklist	Deploy real-time threat detection system with 95% predictive accuracy

Exponential thinking can, and should, apply across every type of project and function. Table 1-1 contrasts how different projects might look when approached with an incremental versus an exponential mindset.

The Importance of Embracing Experimentation and Project Failure

The ability to experiment and learn from failures is crucial for organizations to stay competitive. Organizations that foster a culture of experimentation in their project teams are better equipped to adapt to changing market conditions, identify new opportunities, and continuously improve their products and services.

In our survey, we found that 53 percent of organizations rely on leadership-led discussions on lessons learned to promote an exponential mindset around projects, while 31 percent use regular debriefings on failed projects. However, only 16 percent reward innovative attempts regardless of outcome, and only 20 percent integrate failure analysis into performance assessments. Notably, 35 percent admitted they lack a specific approach to learning from project failures, highlighting the need for cultural shifts to fully embrace learning and innovation.

Using an approach called "real options logic," Ilias Krystallis and Michel-Alexandre Cardin of University College London's Bartlett Centre explain how even large infrastructure projects can design-in for the risk of project failure. They describe the Health Care Services Corporation building in Chicago, which was constructed in two distinct phases of thirty-three and twenty-four floors each. This was completely different from designing either a thirty-three-story or a fifty-seven-story building. The project team had to plan for the additional load, but they didn't know if they were going to use it. Ten years after the first phase was completed, the company exercised its option and added an additional twenty-four floors. Interestingly, the same team was responsible for the new phase in the project, which is unusual in the world of infrastructure, where a new operations team takes over from the delivery team, and continuity and knowledge is lost.[7]

Not all experiments are successful, so a culture of embracing failure must be seen as fundamentally entrepreneurial. Entrepreneurs often have numerous ideas before one gains traction. They do not regard this as a failure but rather as a learning process that leads to eventual success. For example, at Business Forum Group, Europe's leading business events company, learning from failure is not just a mantra—it's an organizational discipline. Its CEO, Hans-Peter Siefen, shared with me that his team evaluates projects daily, critically assessing whether to continue, pivot, or stop based on real data and outcomes. "We don't wait for the end of a project to decide if it's working," he explained. "We constantly challenge ourselves during execution." This proactive and evidence-driven approach fosters a true culture of growth, ensures that resources are continually reallocated toward the most promising opportunities, and prevents stagnation. (See the sidebar, "A Framework for Assessing Maturity in Cultivating a Culture of Experimentation.")

Siefen's leadership illustrates the kind of disciplined, agile thinking that PDOs must adopt if they are serious about scaling impact. It's not about avoiding failure—it's about making failure safe, visible, and useful at every stage of the journey.

A Framework for Assessing Maturity in Cultivating a Culture of Experimentation

CEOs must first understand their organization's current maturity level to cultivate a culture of experimentation and acceptance of failure. By assessing their company's strengths and weaknesses, they can identify areas for improvement and develop targeted strategies to foster an impact-driven mindset.

For the banking group DBS, business transformation involved learning a whole new discipline from those with which they were familiar. According to chief information officer David Gledhill, "Perhaps the thing that was most difficult was that we had to learn how to learn. What I mean by that is we understand banking, and we understand credit and market risk and how to build great mortgage systems. But when you get into this new digital space of experimenting with ecosystems, with start-ups, with launching a brand-new product that nobody's ever tried in a new market, you get lots of things wrong."[a]

Here is a simple framework that CEOs can use to evaluate their organization's maturity in cultivating a culture of experimentation and acceptance of failure:

- **Leading with a growth mandate.** Assess the leadership team's mindset, including the CEO and senior executives. Do they actively promote an impact-driven mindset and encourage experimentation? Are they willing to take calculated risks and learn from failures? A growth-oriented leadership team is essential for driving cultural change throughout the organization.

(continued)

- **Turning employees into "owners."** Evaluate the autonomy and decision-making authority level given to employees. Are they encouraged to take ownership of projects and experiment with new ideas? Do they feel safe to voice their opinions and challenge the status quo? Empowered employees are more likely to embrace a culture of experimentation.

- **Learning as a strategic advantage.** Examine the organization's approach to learning and development. Are there opportunities for leaders and employees to continuously upskill and acquire new knowledge? Are failures viewed as learning opportunities, or are they met with punishment and blame? A strong focus on continuous learning and development is crucial for fostering an exponential mindset.

- **Engineering for experimentation.** Assess the processes and systems that support experimentation. Are there dedicated resources and budgets for testing new ideas? Are there clear guidelines and metrics for evaluating the success or failure of experiments? Well-defined experimentation processes can help organizations learn and iterate more effectively.

- **Normalizing smart failure.** Evaluate the organization's tolerance for failure. Are failures celebrated as learning opportunities or met with negative consequences? Do leaders and employees feel comfortable sharing their failures and lessons learned? A high tolerance for failure is essential for cultivating a culture of experimentation.

- **Making learning contagious.** Examine the organization's level of collaboration and knowledge sharing. Are there platforms and channels for employees to share their experiences, successes, and failures? Effective collaboration and knowledge sharing can accelerate learning and foster an exponential mindset across the organization.

NOTE

a. "Transforming a Bank by Becoming Digital to the Core," DBS, April 2018, https://www .dbs.com/media/digital-transformation/dbs-cio-david-gledhill-on-transforming-a-bank-by -becoming-digital-to-the-core.page.

Encouraging an All-One-Organization Project Culture

An *all-one-organization* culture, where every employee is aligned with the organization's goals and collaborates across functions, is essential for reaching your potential as a project-driven organization. This holistic approach breaks down silos, fosters cross-functional collaboration, and ensures that every team member, regardless of their role, contributes to the success of the organization's projects.

Under the leadership of CEO Kenichiro Yoshida, Sony has emphasized the importance of cross-functional collaboration through the "One Sony" initiative.[8] This initiative encourages different business units to work together toward common goals, leveraging the strengths of Sony's various divisions, such as electronics, entertainment, and gaming. By fostering a culture of unity and collaboration, Sony has been able to innovate and maintain its competitive edge in multiple industries, exemplifying the benefits of a PDO.

This effort embeds project thinking into the DNA of every business unit. Cross-functional project teams now routinely form around strategic priorities like AI integration or immersive user experiences, bringing together engineers, creatives, marketers, and data analysts. With this project-first, cross-enterprise alignment, a large, complex organization can move with the speed and focus of a startup when built on shared purpose and connected execution.

In India, the Tata Group, led by chairman Natarajan Chandrasekaran, has implemented an integrated corporate social responsibility (CSR) approach involving all its subsidiaries and employees.[9] Tata Group's commitment to CSR is reflected in projects that address issues such as education, health care, and rural development. By inviting employees across all levels and subsidiaries to cocreate CSR initiatives, Tata Group exemplifies an all-one-organization project culture— one where purpose and performance are intertwined. These cross-company projects harness local expertise while reinforcing shared values, creating a sense of unity across Tata's diverse portfolio. The result is not just stronger cohesion, but a culture where every project, whether commercial or societal, advances the organization's collective mission.

Implementing an all-one-organization culture depends on several key actions:

- *Unite around a shared purpose.* Ensure all employees understand the organization's purpose and strategic goals. Communicate these elements regularly and clearly so everyone knows how their work contributes to the organization's success. A shared purpose is crucial for a PDO, ensuring that every project aligns with the strategic direction.

- *Build cross-functional teams.* Encourage the formation of fully dedicated cross-functional teams for projects. This approach leverages diverse skills and perspectives, leading to more innovative solutions and better project outcomes. Cross-functional collaboration is critical to achieving comprehensive and innovative solutions in a PDO.

- *Celebrate collective wins.* Acknowledge and reward teams and individuals who exemplify collaborative efforts and contribute to the organization's projects. Recognition can motivate others to adopt similar behaviors and strengthen the all-one-organization culture. Celebrating collaborative success is essential in a PDO to maintain high morale and continuous engagement.

- *Equip everyone to contribute.* Offer training programs that enhance collaborative skills such as teamwork, communication, and conflict resolution. Developing these skills ensures that leaders and employees can work effectively in cross-functional teams. Continuous development is crucial to ensure that teams have the skills needed to tackle complex projects.

An exponential mindset culture redefines how organizations think, learn, and execute. It's about empowering teams to take bold action, learn continuously, and scale impact through projects. Rather than aiming for incremental improvements, PDOs foster a culture where experimentation is safe, failure is informative, and every project becomes a platform for transformative growth.

Building an Open and Transparent Execution Culture

And at the heart of it all that we've discussed so far is an open and transparent culture of execution—ensuring that information flows in real time, decisions are shared, and everyone moves forward with clarity and confidence. In many companies, information about transformation projects is siloed, fragmented, and often contradictory. This lack of transparency leads to misalignment, inefficiencies, and a breakdown of trust within organizations. As projects become the primary drivers of value, these breakdowns become operational risks and strategic liabilities.

The Pitfalls in Building a Project-Driven Culture

As organizations strive to become project-driven, they often encounter significant roadblocks. While the promise of agility, innovation, and execution is enticing, the reality is that many organizations fall into predictable traps. These pitfalls often stem from legacy mindsets and cultures ill-suited to the project economy. Below are three of the most common pitfalls that can derail transformations.

Reluctance to Terminate Misaligned Projects

In many organizations, projects are launched with great fanfare but are rarely ended with equal decisiveness. Leaders and teams become emotionally invested, clinging to initiatives even when evidence suggests they no longer align with strategic priorities. The sunk cost fallacy, internal politics, and fear of reputational damage often prevent timely decisions to shut down underperforming projects.

A striking example is Meta's multibillion-dollar push into the metaverse.[a] Starting in 2020, the company invested more than $60 billion into its Reality Labs division to drive virtual reality and augmented reality innovation. Yet, despite the scale of investment, returns remained

(continued)

elusive—Reality Labs posted a $4.2 billion loss in Q1 2025 alone. While AI rapidly gained traction across the tech industry, Meta was slow to pivot, continuing to back the metaverse long after its strategic relevance waned. Analysts widely criticized this delay, arguing that it diverted capital and attention from more promising innovation frontiers. This underscores a key principle in project-driven leadership: the ability to recognize misalignment and act decisively is not weakness—it's strategic maturity.

Becoming Trapped in an Incremental Mindset

Despite the potential of projects to drive exponential outcomes, most organizations still approach them through an incremental lens. In my own experience, roughly 95 percent of projects across industries focus on doing the same things slightly better—streamlining processes and systems, shaving costs, meeting regulations, or marginally improving performance. These "improvement projects" amount to operational optimization, not transformational change. This mindset limits the role of projects to maintenance rather than innovation, missing the opportunity to leverage them as strategic platforms for exponential thinking—where bold ideas are paired with disciplined execution and clear value creation.

Take the widespread approach to ERP (enterprise resource planning) consolidation. Large organizations routinely invest hundreds of millions of dollars and engage extensive consulting support to migrate from multiple ERP systems—such as SAP or Oracle—to a single, standardized version. While these projects are framed around harmonization, compliance, and cost control, they seldom unlock significant business value. Moving from one ERP version to another—or consolidating systems across business units—often becomes a painful exercise in internal alignment rather than strategic transformation. The outcome is typically improved reporting or reduced IT complexity but rarely any exponential change in customer experience, innovation capacity, or competitive agility.

Transparency Is Too Little, Too Late

Transparency is often treated as a formality—an end-of-quarter report or a static dashboard rather than a real-time flow of information. But in project-driven environments, delayed or fragmented communication creates dangerous blind spots. Risks go unflagged, early signals are ignored, and teams operate on outdated assumptions. The result? Slower decisions, diminished trust, and a higher chance of failure.

Birmingham City Council's 2023 ERP rollout was intended to modernize core HR and finance functions. But despite early signs of technical issues and delays, flaws were allowed to fester beneath surface-level reporting. When the system finally went live, it caused widespread disruption—payroll errors, halted supplier payments, and costly manual work-arounds. The lack of dynamic transparency and timely escalation ultimately contributed to a financial collapse so severe that the council was forced to declare effective bankruptcy.

NOTE

a. Tim Bajarin, "Meta's Strategic Pivot, Again," *Forbes*, February 25, 2025, https://www.forbes.com/sites/timbajarin/2025/02/25/metas-strategic-pivot-again/.

In a PDO, cultivating an open and transparent execution culture means ensuring that everyone from project teams to senior leadership has a shared, real-time understanding of priorities, progress, and performance. This doesn't require overwhelming detail or micromanagement; it involves high-trust systems and rhythms that make key information visible, timely, and actionable. This approach fosters a culture of open collaboration, real-time insight sharing, and collective problem-solving while discouraging information hoarding and internal politics.

Netflix, under the leadership of founder and CEO Reed Hastings, has fostered a culture that emphasizes freedom and responsibility coupled with radical transparency. Employees are granted access to a wide range of company information, including strategic plans and performance metrics, creating an environment where informed decision-making is encouraged at all levels. Hastings has articulated this philosophy by contrasting Netflix's openness with other companies' compartmentalization, stating, "We're like the anti-Apple. They compartmentalize: we do the opposite. Everyone gets all the information."[10] This transparency is designed to build trust, promote accountability, and empower employees to act in the company's best interests.

By embedding transparency into its operational fabric, Netflix has created a workplace where information flows freely, enabling swift decision-making and cohesive execution. This culture not only enhances alignment and efficiency but also cultivates a sense of ownership and engagement among employees, contributing to the company's agility and sustained success.

Under the leadership of CEO Emma Walmsley, GSK has undergone a significant cultural transformation, emphasizing transparency to maintain its competitive edge in the pharmaceutical industry. I had the opportunity to work under her leadership until the end of 2024. I witnessed firsthand how she championed a shift toward open communication and continuous learning, fostering an environment where information flows freely across all levels of the organization.

A cornerstone of this transformation is GSK's commitment to clinical trial transparency.[11] The company has published over eight thousand protocol summaries and more than seven thousand results summaries on its public register. It has listed thousands of clinical trials for data sharing via platforms like Vivli, enabling researchers worldwide to access anonymized patient-level data. This openness not only enhances scientific collaboration but also builds trust with stakeholders, including patients, health-care professionals, and regulators.

The transparent approach also extends to operations and decision-making processes. The company regularly publishes comprehensive reports detailing its progress on various fronts, such as environmental sustainability, access to medicines, and ethical business practices. By openly sharing both achievements and challenges, GSK fosters a culture of accountability and continuous improvement.

Internally, the company encourages open dialogue among employees, with mechanisms in place for feedback and knowledge sharing across departments. These practices have been instrumental in breaking down silos, enhancing collaboration, and ensuring that all team members are aligned with the company's strategic goals. Through these concerted efforts, GSK exemplifies how embracing an open and transparent execution culture can drive innovation, build stakeholder trust, and position a company for long-term success in a dynamic industry.

Policies for Openness and Transparency in Projects Start at the Top

Transparency starts with deliberate choices made at the top. When CEOs and senior leaders model openness, demand visibility over vanity metrics, and ensure strategic intent is clearly communicated, they lay the foundation for an open and transparent execution culture.

The participatory democracy movement advocates for greater public participation in government-funded projects. A 2020 Grattan Institute report revealed that "of 32 projects larger than $500 million committed to by the Australian government since 2016, only eight had a business case either published or assessed by a relevant infrastructure body at the time of commitment. This means politicians are committing to projects without knowing whether they are in the community's interest to build, let alone whether they are the best choice for the money."[12] This lack of transparency at the very top of project decision-making undermines stakeholder trust and discourages public engagement (and consequently reduces the project's resilience). Since the whole purpose of public infrastructure investment is to drive changes in the habits of citizens, it may even threaten the ultimate success of the projects concerned.

The same principle applies in corporate environments. When major projects are launched without clear communication of goals, expected outcomes, or rationale, teams are left navigating ambiguity, making alignment nearly impossible. Even well-funded initiatives can falter when the broader organization lacks clarity about the "why" and "what for." On the other hand, when project selection, prioritization, and progress tracking are shared openly—through regular town halls, cross-functional forums, or transparent objectives and key results (OKR) systems—people engage more deeply, contribute more meaningfully, and align their work with the organization's strategic North Star.

Salesforce has become a model for dynamic transparency by embedding openness directly into its operating model. CEO Marc Benioff communicates regularly and publicly through stakeholder letters that include updates on major projects, strategic pivots, social impact initiatives, and company performance. For instance, in his 2023 letter to stakeholders, Benioff emphasized the company's commitment to environmental, social, and governance (ESG) transparency, highlighting initiatives such as achieving net-zero residual emissions and investing in racial equality and justice programs.[13]

Internally, Salesforce employees have access to shared dashboards and internal briefings that keep everyone from engineering to sales aligned on progress and priorities. These dashboards provide real-time insights into KPIs, project statuses, and benefits and strategic goals, enabling teams to track execution status using the same Salesforce platforms the company offers to its customers. This approach ensures that everyone involved is aligned and informed, fostering a collaborative environment crucial for sustained growth.

Leadership transparency in project governance doesn't mean handing over every decision to consensus. It means being explicit about how decisions are made, what data is used, and how progress will be measured. It means sharing what's working and what isn't, early and often. And most importantly, it means modeling the behaviors—such as admitting uncertainty, correcting course, and celebrating learning—that make transparency sustainable. By institutionalizing transparency in how projects are chosen, launched, and led, executives not only improve project execution—they elevate the credibility and resilience of their entire transformation strategy.

Making Strategic Decisions Visible and Actionable

In a project-driven organization, transparency shouldn't be limited to task-level progress or project dashboards—it should extend to strategic decision-making at the highest levels. Employees don't just need to know what they're doing—they need to understand *why*. When the purpose is clear and compelling and the decisions are visible, it creates alignment, motivation, and accountability across the entire enterprise.

CEOs and senior leaders play a pivotal role in this shift. They must move beyond one-way communication and embrace consistent, participatory dialogue around strategy. This means sharing not only decisions but the context, trade-offs, and anticipated impact and doing so in a way that employees across all levels can connect to their daily work. By making decisions visible, leaders can ensure that everyone understands the organization's direction and how their work contributes to overall success.

Here are three powerful ways to bring strategic decisions into the open and make them meaningful:

- *From town halls to trusted rituals.* Regular updates from leadership—whether through town halls, internal podcasts, or video briefs—should evolve into predictable, trusted communication rhythms. These are opportunities not just to inform, but to inspire and align. When done consistently, they reinforce transparency as a cultural norm, not a sporadic gesture.

- *Put the strategy on the (digital) walls.* Make your strategic priorities and performance metrics accessible, visual, and alive. Share annual objectives, transformation road maps, and OKRs in digital workspaces that teams can actually use—not just tucked away in quarterly presentations. Visibility leads to accountability and helps employees connect their projects to enterprise-wide outcomes.

- *Close the loop with two-way strategy.* Transparency doesn't stop at visibility—it requires voice. Embed structured feedback mechanisms like pulse surveys, open Q&As, and cross-functional review forums. These not only help leaders adjust course with real-time insight—they also foster deeper trust by showing that employee perspectives matter in shaping the path forward.

The UK government's Transforming Infrastructure Performance (TIP) program adopted a platform called Meeting Quality to enable near-real-time capture and (anonymized) sharing of the perceptions, beliefs, and emotions of the delivery team at every weekly progress meeting. The initiative involved providing ratings around key questions such as the team's perception of the program's chances of success, the clarity of its vision, and the sustainability of their working practices. Sharing the data from the platform with everyone in the team within twenty-four hours of each meeting quickly established trust and transparency and provided a platform for the team to agree on and cocreate a series of activities and interventions to address their needs and concerns.[14]

Unilever, under former CEO Paul Polman, embedded openness and accountability into its transformation strategy, especially around sustainability. Rather than keeping environmental goals internal or vague, the company made its sustainability targets, project progress, and even setbacks publicly available through detailed annual reports and external communications. This bold visibility wasn't just for PR; it was strategic. It created stakeholder trust, invited public scrutiny, and made internal teams feel accountable and motivated. Employees at all levels could clearly see how their work contributed to the company's broader vision, turning corporate strategy into a shared commitment. Polman's approach demonstrated that when transparency is modeled from the top and embedded into how performance is tracked and shared, it becomes a force multiplier for cultural and strategic alignment.

An open and transparent execution culture is about accelerating alignment, trust, and action. When leaders model transparency, when strategic intent is visible and accessible, and when teams are empowered to contribute and respond in real time, organizations move faster and more effectively toward their goals. In a project-driven world, transparency isn't a soft value—it's a strategic capability. It transforms visibility into velocity.

Conclusion

To foster a dynamic and resilient project-driven organization, developing the habit of stopping projects is the first step. Understanding when to terminate nonviable projects, cultivating decisive project termination practices, and ensuring timely closure and resource reallocation for new initiatives will free time and resources to focus on the projects that really matter. Promoting an exponential mindset, encouraging an all-one-organization culture, fostering experimentation and innovation, and embracing failure as a learning opportunity form the foundation. Lastly, enabling an open and transparent execution culture and making strategic decisions visible creates an environment of trust and collaboration. By integrating these strategies, your organization can thrive as a dynamic and resilient project-driven entity capable of achieving sustained success and growth in an ever-evolving business landscape.

In the next chapter, we will look at how a project-driven structure can further empower project teams and enhance overall agility.

CHAPTER 2

Project-Driven Structure

Haier's transformation offers one of the clearest examples of how organizations evolve beyond traditional agile models. As companies seek greater speed, innovation, and resilience, many have embraced agile working methods. However, leading organizations are moving a step further—becoming project-driven organizations, where empowered project teams, not rigid hierarchies, are the true engines of value creation.

To unlock the full potential of its workforce, Haier *radically flattened its structure,* eliminating over twelve thousand middle-management positions. In this way, it was able to reposition talent where it could create greater value. Many former managers moved into roles within MEs or EMCs, decentralized, entrepreneurial, and hierarchy-less teams that now drive the company's growth and innovation.

Each ME operates like an independent startup, empowered to make strategic and operational project decisions, set its direction, recruit talent, and allocate resources based on market needs in real time. By pushing decision-making closer to customers and emerging opportunities, Haier dismantled bureaucratic bottlenecks and dramatically accelerated its ability to respond to change. This structure fosters an environment where innovation thrives. For example, Haier Biomedical's transformation from a hardware supplier to a life sciences ecosystem was driven by autonomous MEs identifying market opportunities and acting decisively without needing top-down approvals.

Haier's structural evolution *prioritizes transformational initiatives over traditional operations*. This shift is evident in its focus on high-value, user-centric projects that drive long-term growth. The RenDan-HeYi model emphasizes continuous evolution, pushing MEs and EMCs to pursue opportunities that redefine user experiences rather than simply maintaining the status quo.

To support this prioritization, Haier allocated resources strategically, introducing flexible, rolling budgets tailored to the needs of specific projects. This approach allows resources to be reallocated dynamically based on project performance and emerging market demands. The result is a structure that supports bold innovation while maintaining operational sustainability. This flexibility was particularly critical in initiatives like the Smart Medical EMC, which required iterative funding to develop automated solutions for hospital pharmacy management.

At Haier, strategic resource allocation transcends mere financial considerations. The company prioritizes *dedicated staffing to enhance project outcomes* and minimize inefficiencies. Each ME and EMC comprises fully committed team members, ensuring that projects receive the focused expertise necessary to deliver high-quality results, eliminating the multitasking inefficiencies often associated with traditional organizational models, where employees juggle multiple roles and priorities.

Central to Haier's HR strategy is its full-staff entrepreneurship system. Employees are granted rights to labor income, capital gains, and value-added sharing, transforming them from mere executors into entrepreneurial partners. This system fosters a culture of ownership and accountability, aligning individual success with the company's performance.

Haier's staffing practices also prioritize adaptability. EMCs can dynamically reconfigure their teams based on evolving project needs, bringing in additional expertise or redistributing talent as necessary. This fluid approach ensures that projects remain aligned with organizational goals and user expectations, even as conditions change.

By integrating dedicated staffing, global resource networks, entrepreneurial empowerment, and adaptive team structures, Haier exemplifies a strategic resource allocation model that supports an open and transparent execution culture.

––––––––––––

This chapter examines how forward-thinking companies are reengineering their internal structures to thrive in the transformation age. One of the most persistent—and personal—lessons I've learned in working with organizations around the world is this: structure often stands in the way of transformation.

I've seen ambitious projects stall not because of a flawed strategy or lack of talent, but because leaders were forced to navigate outdated hierarchies, rigid approval layers, and slow decision paths. These organizations are still operating in structures built for stability and efficiency, not for the speed and adaptability that today's challenges demand.

Unlike operations, where hierarchy is necessary to drive consistency and efficiency, projects thrive on flatter, more flexible structures—often no more than two levels of decision-making. Many companies have tried to fix this by going agile—introducing squads, tribes, or flatter team models. But as we explored in the introduction, that surface-level change isn't enough. Without rethinking how authority, resources, and collaboration actually flow through the organization, agility becomes cosmetic—a set of new labels on the same old system.

Structure often emerges not through deliberate strategy but as an organic response to growth. As businesses expand, their frameworks often evolve haphazardly, shaped more by historical circumstances than intentional design. The larger and older the organization, the more entrenched and complicated this structure becomes and the less open it is to meaningful change.

Consider Taylor & Francis, a publishing business that grew from a modest £10 million in 1990 to a substantial £500 million enterprise by 2015. This exponential growth might seem like a remarkable success story. But beneath the surface, there was a persistent tension: the structure of the business had never been purposefully designed to accommodate its expanding scale. Instead, it simply "got bigger," with layers and processes added as needed, but without any overarching strategy to guide its development.

Many of the managers who had grown up with the company during this period of rapid expansion were never taught how to adapt their leadership styles to reflect the organization's changing needs. The result was a business where synergy was noticeably absent. There was little collaboration—strategy and programs operated in silos, uncoordinated and disconnected. The digital publishing arm, for instance, burgeoned in response to the rise of e-books, riding the wave of a rapidly changing industry. Yet when the transition from paper to digital was largely complete, the division hit a brick wall. Without an intentional strategy or innovative vision, it struggled to imagine or create the next generation of publishing products. Ultimately, this led to layoffs and a decision to outsource development and coding to India.

This story illustrates a common challenge in organizations that grow without deliberate attention to their structure. While the business expands outwardly, internal cohesion and adaptability falter. Without a clear strategy, the organization risks stagnation, inefficiency, and missed opportunities for innovation.

For PDOs, structure needs to integrate with both the requirements of project execution and of value realization associated with operations. This requires an understanding of the current organizational structure and the capability to adapt it intentionally to create the perfect "ambidexterity"—the ability to balance the needs of transformational change and asset delivery associated with projects with the needs of value realization associated with operations.

As organizations seek to move beyond agile, the next evolution is clear: the rise of project-driven structures—where empowered project teams, not departments or titles, become the engines of execution, innovation, and growth. (See figure 2-1.) This chapter explores three structural shifts that high-performing, project-powered organizations are embracing—Shimizu Corporation, which flattens hierarchies to empower project teams; General Motors, which prioritizes projects that drive transformation; and SpaceX, which staffs projects for peak performance.

FIGURE 2-1

Project-driven structure

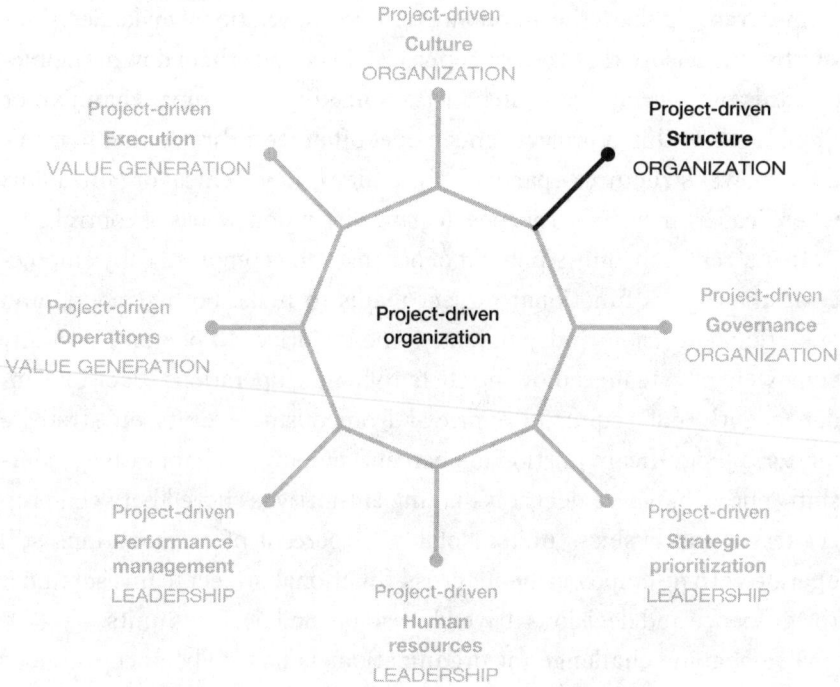

Structures built around projects—not rigid hierarchies—are what enable organizations to seize opportunities faster, innovate at scale, and deliver meaningful outcomes in real time. Let's explore how to design, scale, and lead a truly project-driven structure built for the realities of the transformation age.

Flattening Hierarchies for Empowered Project Teams

In the transformation age, traditional hierarchical structures often hinder agility and responsiveness. In project-driven organizations, by contrast, everyone working within a project needs to be a reflective practitioner, committed to delivering the required outputs and outcomes while continually questioning the purpose and progress of their work and their approach to it.

By flattening hierarchies, organizations can empower their project teams, granting them the autonomy to cocreate solutions, make decisions swiftly, and ensure that layers of approval do not bog them down. In practice, this often means reducing decision-making to no more than two or three levels within a project. This model often feels threatening to traditional power structures—particularly in highly hierarchical organizations where leaders may resist the idea, fearing disruption or loss of control.

In our research, only 9 percent of organizations reported fully empowering their cross-functional project teams to make both strategic and operational decisions independently. The majority (40 percent) partially empower these teams, allowing them to handle operational decisions independently but requiring approval from business units on strategic matters. A significant portion (33 percent) employ a collaborative leadership approach, where decision-making authority is shared between project teams and business units. Notably, 17 percent of organizations still operate with no empowerment—cross-functional project teams act under the guidance and decisions driven by established business units.

The ongoing challenge for organizations is how to balance the need for agility, local autonomy, and changes driven from the bottom up, while maintaining strategic alignment and control.

Shimizu Corporation, a 220-plus-year-old Japanese architectural, engineering, and construction firm, has developed a new mindset—*choukensetsu*—which it is using to transform innovation across the company, shaping the future together with its customers and society.[1] Using this mindset, Shimizu is experimenting with a fluid organizational structure in some of its innovation activities. Rather than relying on rigid, top-down hierarchies typical in the industry, Shimizu seamlessly integrates full-time staff, part-time contributors, and volunteer champions into project teams, which form dynamically across departments and functions, based on the needs of each project. This allows diverse skills and perspectives to converge quickly. Volunteer champions, often employees with deep expertise or strong community ties, step forward to lead initiatives without formal reassignment or bureaucratic approval, creating an innovation-oriented culture where an initiative is recognized, not resisted.

During a recent collaboration with communities on remote islands in Japan, Shimizu applied this approach to develop and deliver a highly customized infrastructure project for connecting the community there. Rather than establishing a large organizational structure, they assembled a cross-functional team of visionaries, engineers, designers, and volunteer champions, and, together with people from the island, they considered the local challenges and opportunities to cocreate solutions. Shimizu's team started with shared discovery to truly understand what the island community really needed and wanted. They then defined a platform as a candidate solution and finally refined it before scaling it further. This ability to use the *choukensetsu* mindset to integrate exploration (discovery) and exploitation (delivery) across the project, with direct support from the CEO, has become a hallmark of the company's innovative approach.

By removing silos and repositioning talents dynamically, Shimizu embodies the attributes of a startup within a large established organization, where empowerment, flexibility, and shared ownership drive project success. Its experience shows that in the transformation age, it's not just about the speed of execution—it's about the ability to mobilize the right people, at the right time, around the right opportunities.

Yet flattening hierarchies is not easy. See table 2-1 for some of the obstacles senior leaders face when transitioning to a less hierarchical structure—and the opposing forces they must balance and reconcile.

Let's explore practical strategies for removing hierarchies in PDOs, building on the challenges discussed here.

Radical Removal of Middle Management

Flattening hierarchies and radically removing layers of middle management is often seen as a bold and risky move. Yet in project-driven organizations, it's increasingly clear that the traditional middle layer, built to coordinate static functions, often becomes a bottleneck when speed, innovation, and decentralized execution are critical.

Removing layers is often about cost-cutting, but in a PDO, it's more. Done right, it's about releasing entrepreneurial energy, accelerating decision-making, and pushing ownership closer to those creating value. By reducing approval chains and directly empowering project teams,

TABLE 2-1

Competing forces in flattening hierarchies

Driving force	Area	Counterforce
Fear of loss of influence and relevance by middle managers leads to resistance to (and even in some cases sabotage of) change.	Middle management	The actual loss of middle managers can lead to a loss of experience and the means of providing oversight, coordination, and assurance of work.
Change often brings confusion and ambiguity to decision-making processes and authority.	Roles and responsibilities	The absence of clearly defined roles in the new structure can lead to overlaps, gaps, and accountability issues.
Hierarchical authorities are often out of touch with the reality of the project; their decision-making processes introduce delay and the decisions themselves are suboptimal.	Cocreation and collective agreement	Collaboration, cocreation, and collective agreement can themselves paralyze decision-making and introduce inconsistencies within and between projects.
The absence of opportunities for advancement due to organizational hierarchy encourages employees to move elsewhere for career progression.	Career paths	Developing overly broad, generalist career paths can dilute deep expertise, create role ambiguity, and weaken accountability across functions.
The formal management and decision-making structures within organizations are becoming increasingly unreflective of how things really get done.	Shadow organizations	Informal hierarchies and cliques can emerge, which can make it hard to build a sense of all-one-organization working toward a set of common goals.
As the number and complexity of projects increase, the loss of centralized functions can lead to unintended competition for resources or local initiatives that effectively run counter to each other.	Scalability	Fragmentation across smaller, semiautonomous teams can lead to duplication of efforts, misaligned priorities, and inefficiencies at scale.

organizations can become faster, more adaptive, and more customer focused.

However, the radical removal of middle management is not without challenges. Many organizations rely heavily on these managers for institutional memory, relationship management, and operational continuity. Ripping them out without a plan can create chaos, confusion, and cultural backlash. But there are several ways to mitigate this effect.

Different Paths to Address This Tension. Some companies, like Haier, have redesigned their operating model completely around empowered project teams, repositioning many former managers into new entrepreneurial roles rather than eliminating them. Others, like Sonic Healthcare, a global leader in laboratory medicine, pathology, and radiology services, offer a different kind of response.[2] Instead of stripping away middle management entirely, it moved to a federated structure that preserved local leadership autonomy while embedding strategic alignment at the corporate level.

Rather than erasing middle management, Sonic transformed its role: from control and coordination to entrepreneurship and localized decision-making. Local management teams were retained—trusted to manage branding, service delivery, and customer relationships specific to their communities—while being supported by global resources and unified by a shared culture and strategic vision.

Sonic's Federated Model balances empowerment with cohesion. Knowledge sharing, best practice development, and innovation now flow horizontally across the group, not just vertically through headquarters.

Both paths—radical flattening or smart federation—show that rethinking the role of middle management is critical for building PDOs. The choice isn't simply whether to remove layers, but how to rewire accountability, decision-making, and ownership across the enterprise.

Incremental Hierarchy Removal in Strategic Projects. For many organizations, the alternative approach to radical flattening involves gradually reducing layers of management, starting with specific projects, business units, or departments. This method allows organizations to move forward stepwise, minimizing the risks associated with large, untested, "big bang" changes.

Incremental flattening enables organizations to learn and adjust as they go, minimizing disruption while building internal confidence and capabilities for more decentralized ways of working. It also provides opportunities to engage employees directly in designing and refining the new operating model, creating greater ownership and smoother adoption.

But incremental change also carries risks. There's always a gravitational pull back to the old hierarchy. Without discipline and imagination, early momentum can stall. But when done thoughtfully, this approach allows organizations to adapt flattening strategies to the realities of different teams, divisions, and changing external environments—making the evolution more sustainable.

Buurtzorg, the Dutch health-care organization, chose to introduce self-managed teams gradually across its care network rather than dismantling its structure overnight:[3]

- *Starting small.* When it was founded in 2006, Buurtzorg began with a small project team of ten nurses who were given full autonomy to manage all aspects of patient care and business operations. This initial team served as a pilot project to test the feasibility of the self-managing model in home-care delivery.

- *Gradual expansion.* Over time, Buurtzorg expanded its model through multiple projects. By 2016, the organization had grown to over fourteen thousand nurses in 950 self-managing project teams. Each team comprises ten to twelve nurses handling everything from patient care projects to administrative tasks.

- *Minimal central management.* Buurtzorg maintains a lean central management structure with only about forty staff members at headquarters. This minimal oversight allows project teams to operate independently and quickly decide on their care delivery projects.

- *Custom IT system.* The organization's custom IT system, BuurtzorgWeb, facilitates communication and allows teams to share best practices. This system supports the decentralized structure by providing the necessary tools for project coordination and information sharing.

- *Solution-driven decision-making.* Buurtzorg uses a framework for project decisions called "Solution-Driven Methods of Interaction." This approach ensures that project teams can make decisions efficiently and autonomously.

- *Integrated care approach.* Buurtzorg's project teams aim to engage patients and families in the care process, teaching them essential practicalities of care provision. This integrated approach is a key project focus for each team.

Jos de Blok, Buurtzorg's founder, explained:

> My idea was to create small teams with nurses who organize everything themselves. We would let them focus on outcomes; let them work with patients in a way they think is the best, based on professional standards; and create a support system around them, including a back office and IT system that helps them in their daily work. It would grow by itself and improve quality. I started with one team at the end of 2006 and started working again as a nurse myself. Based on these principles, we started to grow from one to almost 1,000 teams in around 10 years.[4]

Buurtzorg's project-driven approach has led to remarkable outcomes. The organization has become the largest home care provider in the Netherlands while achieving a 40 percent reduction in costs compared to its competitors. Additionally, it consistently scores higher in patient and employee satisfaction than any other health-care organization in the country.

Prioritizing Transformational Projects

In a project-driven structure, not all projects are created equal. Organizations that succeed in the transformation age prioritize projects that drive meaningful, strategic change—not just incremental improvements. This demands disciplined, focused leadership and new approaches to budgeting and resource allocation that reflect the organization's highest priorities. Prioritization is no longer a periodic exercise; it must become an ongoing capability ensuring that resources, executive attention, and organizational energy flow to the projects that will define the future.

Moving from Traditional Operations to Transformational Projects

In a 2021 McKinsey Global Survey, 93 percent of executives reported that their organizations were undergoing some form of digital transformation.[5] However, only 30 percent of these initiatives fully succeeded in improving performance and equipping their organizations to sustain changes in the long term. This gap underscores the challenges and opportunities in prioritizing transformational projects.

GM demonstrates how prioritizing transformational projects can reshape an entire industry position. Under the leadership of CEO Mary Barra, GM made a structural pivot: shifting organizational focus and resources toward electric and autonomous driving technologies—sectors critical to the future of mobility.

This prioritization wasn't incremental—it was bold and decisive. In 2021, GM announced it would invest $35 billion in electric and autonomous vehicle development through 2025, a 75 percent increase from its pre-pandemic plans.[6] By making transformational projects the strategic core of its investment and operational planning, GM accelerated its transition and positioned itself at the forefront of automotive innovation. The results are already tangible: GM's EV sales grew by 38 percent year-over-year in 2022, reinforcing how disciplined prioritization, backed by structural resource reallocation, can drive not just future ambitions but immediate performance gain.

In traditional organizations, operations have long been structured to optimize performance around existing products, processes, and markets. These models favor efficiency, predictability, and scale—attributes that served well in more stable, slower-moving environments. Core work was centered around maintaining the status quo and continuously improving it through incremental refinements. Project work, by contrast, was often treated as exceptional—an initiative occurring outside the day-to-day flow of operations, typically managed as a temporary deviation from business-as-usual.

In PDOs, however, the paradigm shifts completely. Instead of treating projects as occasional or peripheral, these organizations place transformational initiatives at the very heart of how they operate. Project work becomes the default mode through which value is created, strategy is executed, and innovation is realized. To support this, the organizational structure must evolve to continuously deliver transformation—not as a bolt-on to daily work, but as the backbone of how work gets done.

This shift requires bold and deliberate leadership actions. It's not enough to launch projects on the edges of the enterprise. Instead, leaders must:

- *Make transformational projects structurally central.* These are not side programs or special initiatives—they are the main vehicle for driving growth, entering new markets, digitizing processes, or building future capabilities. Their centrality must be reflected in how the organization allocates its best talent, budgets, executive attention, and strategic oversight. This also means linking project success directly to business outcomes, with clear accountability for impact rather than activity.

- *Integrate project prioritization into operational rhythms.* Many organizations treat project governance and prioritization as an annual budgeting or planning exercise. In project-driven enterprises, it must become a continuous discipline embedded into regular operational reviews. Strategic projects should be actively monitored, reprioritized, and adapted in response to changes in market conditions, technology, or performance. This creates a culture of agility, where focus and investment follow value—not legacy assumptions.

Reorienting the organization in this way sends a powerful message: transformation is the new normal. And because of this, transformation must be systematized and scaled—not left to chance or individual heroics.

Of course, making transformation central to operations requires a fundamental rethinking of how organizations fund and manage projects. Traditional annual budget cycles—fixed, siloed, and often outdated by the time execution begins—are not fit for purpose in a world where the speed of change is lightning fast. Instead, dynamic funding models must be introduced. These allow high-priority projects to receive rapid approvals, stage-gated investments, and real-time reallocations as new opportunities or risks emerge. As we will discuss in chapter 4, limiting the duration of most projects to three to six months increases focus, momentum, and accountability, making it easier to fund and deliver value incrementally. A central project investment committee or transformation office can facilitate this process, ensuring transparency, strategic alignment, and speed of execution.

In short, this is not about layering projects onto traditional operations. As we will see in chapter 7, it is about transforming operations to become enablers of continuous change.

Implementing Flexible, Rolling Budgets
Aligned with Project Timelines

Naturally, organizations must also rethink how they fund them, moving away from rigid, annual budget cycles toward more dynamic, project-aligned approaches. The budgeting cycle has been a cornerstone of organizational financial planning for over a century. In that time, companies have followed a rigorous annual process involving multiple forecasts, departmental inputs, and executive approvals. This approach served businesses well in an era dominated by operational stability and predictable market conditions.

However, as the business landscape shifts toward project-driven transformations, this demands rapid resource reallocation, swift decision-making, and the ability to pivot strategies in response to emerging opportunities or challenges. The constraints imposed by traditional budgeting cycles can hinder an organization's agility, stifle innovation, and ultimately delay or derail critical transformation efforts. As organizations grapple with the need for more flexible financial planning, it's crucial to understand the differences between fixed and rolling budgets (see table 2-2).

Recognizing these challenges, forward-thinking companies have begun to explore approaches to financial planning that better align with the needs of a project-driven, transformation-focused business environment. The Beyond Budgeting Round Table (BBRT) has advocated for more adaptive management processes and decentralized leadership. Its two core pillars—empowered teams and dynamic planning—offer a compelling alternative to rigid annual budget cycles. In particular, the BBRT principles align closely with the needs of project-driven structures, where work is organized around temporary, cross-functional initiatives rather than fixed departments. In such environments, static annual plans quickly become misaligned with reality. The BBRT ap-

TABLE 2-2

Fixed budgets versus rolling budgets

Feature	Fixed budgets	Rolling budgets
Time horizon	Set for a defined period, typically twelve months, with only limited adjustments allowed during that time to maintain overall fiscal discipline	Are continuously updated, usually monthly, always maintaining a twelve-month (or other predetermined period) outlook
Adaptability	Adjustments are time-consuming and require lengthy formal approvals, making it hard to respond promptly to unexpected changes or new opportunities	Designed for flexibility, allowing rapid adaptation to changes such as shifts in customer demand, competitive pressures, supply chain disruptions, or revised strategic goals
Resource allocation	Tend to lock in resource allocations for the requested period, making it hard to adjust to new requirements or unexpected demands	Allow for more dynamic resource reallocation based on emerging needs and new opportunities
Forecasting accuracy	Rely on projections made far in advance that can quickly become outdated	Provide more up-to-date and accurate forecasts by regularly incorporating the latest data and trends
Decision-making	Often result in delayed or suboptimal decisions due to reliance on outdated information	Support faster informed decision-making by providing up-to-date data, trends, and revised forecasts

proach enables organizations to plan and fund projects in shorter cycles, based on strategic relevance and real-time performance, not historical allocations.

By replacing fixed targets with relative goals and encouraging decentralized accountability, project teams can adapt their plans based on evolving conditions and still stay aligned with overarching business goals. The result is a financial system that supports—not constrains—transformation, enabling organizations to move at the speed of change.

Coloplast, a global medical device company, provides an excellent example of the benefits of moving beyond traditional budgeting practices.[7] In 2009, Coloplast implemented a new planning model called "Turning Ambition into Action," which replaced its annual budget with more dynamic processes. Coloplast now prepares quarterly rolling forecasts covering the subsequent five quarters. These forecasts contain far fewer details than previous budgets, increasing agility and providing a better overview of the company's financial outlook.

The approach also emphasizes relative targets rather than fixed budget figures. It focuses on KPIs that are meaningful to its industry and strategic objectives. This allows the company to adjust its strategies and resource allocation based on market conditions and competitive dynamics rather than being constrained by predetermined budget figures.

Coloplast's capital allocation process has been particularly impactful. An investment committee meets monthly to evaluate investment proposals, accepting or rejecting them based on their contribution to the strategic agenda, potential for value creation, and available cash flow. This approach has increased agility and improved decision-making, allowing the company to allocate resources where they create the most value quickly.

Coloplast's transition to this more flexible approach has yielded impressive results. Since implementing the new model ten years ago, it has been one of the most successful and value-creating companies listed on the Nasdaq Copenhagen. Its turnover has doubled, and it has maintained an EBIT margin of 30 to 34 percent for several years, the highest in the industry. Moreover, Coloplast's customer and patient satisfaction ranks at the top of recent surveys, and the company is considered one of the most innovative companies in its field.

Despite these successes, Coloplast acknowledges that the transition is an ongoing process and continues to refine its model. Current focus areas include digitalization to improve reporting and data analysis and optimizing production and supply chain planning.

While transitioning away from traditional budgeting practices may present challenges such as resistance from finance teams, uncertainty in forecasting, and the need to overhaul long-standing approval processes, the potential benefits of increased agility, improved resource allocation, and enhanced ability to execute transformational projects make it a consideration worthy of exploration for PDOs.

Staffing Projects for Peak Performance

Even with the right vision and strategic initiatives, transformation efforts stall when project teams are stretched too thin, split between

competing priorities, multitasking, or operating without full commitment. In a project-driven structure, how you staff projects becomes just
as important as which projects you prioritize.

About 95 percent of the companies I work with dramatically underestimate their true capacity for project delivery. They launch too many initiatives simultaneously, overload their people, and create hidden
bottlenecks that quietly paralyze the organization. Without deliberate,
realistic capacity modeling, even the most promising projects risk collapsing under the weight of divided attention and operational distractions. To build a strong foundation for autonomy and transformation,
organizations must structure project staffing intentionally:

- Senior leadership and HQ functions should dedicate around
  75 percent of their available time to leading and sponsoring
  critical projects.

- Business units and divisional leaders should target 50 percent
  project engagement.

- Site operations, plants, and frontline teams may realistically
  allocate around 25 percent to transformation and innovation
  work.

These are starting points—each company must refine them based on
its maturity and strategic goals. But without clear capacity thresholds,
autonomy becomes hollow, burnout rises, and transformation slows to a
crawl.

Understanding capacity is just the first step. To unlock peak project
performance, organizations must also rethink how they assign their
people –not splitting attention across dozens of competing demands
but building fully dedicated teams committed to transformational
outcomes.

A recent article by McKinsey highlights the importance of having the
right number of people involved in transformation projects.[8] It finds
that successful transformations typically involve 5 to 10 percent of the
organization's workforce. This means that for a company with ten thousand employees, between five hundred and a thousand should be fully
dedicated to transformation efforts. This level of commitment guaran-
tees that the project has the necessary focus and resources to succeed.

The Pitfalls in Building a Project-Driven Structure

Shifting from a traditional hierarchy to a project-driven structure promises greater agility, accountability, and innovation—but the journey is not easy and rarely straightforward. Many organizations underestimate the deeply embedded habits, legacy systems, and structural rigidities that can undermine even the most well-intentioned transformations. Redesigning your structure isn't just about new reporting lines—it's about changing how work flows, how decisions are made, and how teams are resourced and empowered.

Here are three structural pitfalls organizations often suffer when building their project-driven structure.

Superficial Flattening without Real Empowerment

Organizations frequently reduce layers and introduce cross-functional teams to boost agility, but unless these teams are granted absolute authority and autonomy, the flattening remains cosmetic. Roles may change on paper, but decision-making still flows upward, and progress slows under the weight of approvals and ambiguity.

This half-measure frustrates employees, who are asked to act with agility but are constrained by outdated governance and control mechanisms. True empowerment means shifting decision rights closer to the action, backed by trust, clarity of mandate, and accountability.

Overcommitting to Projects without Strategic Filters

In their enthusiasm to "run everything as a project," organizations often try to do too much at once. Without a disciplined approach to project

It's clear that both role-specific time allocations and overall workforce dedication are crucial. While senior leaders and managers integrate transformation into their roles, a dedicated cohort of employees focuses exclusively on driving change. This balanced approach ensures that transformation efforts are both integrated into daily operations and receive the attention necessary for success.

selection and prioritization, resources become stretched and the organization loses focus.

The result is a proliferation of initiatives—many of them marginal or
misaligned—competing for limited time, talent, and attention. Strategic
projects become just one item among many, rather than the driving
force of organizational focus. To avoid this, companies need strong
portfolio governance that ruthlessly filters, prioritizes, and sequences
work based on impact, urgency, and alignment with strategic goals.

Structural Inertia That Locks Resources in Traditional Roles

One of the most significant barriers to project execution is the inability
to free people from their operational responsibilities. Most organizations
still rely heavily on part-time contributors for their most important
initiatives—individuals expected to lead or support transformation projects while continuing to fulfill their day-to-day roles.

This model is unsustainable. Divided focus leads to slower progress,
diluted accountability, and diminished energy. The underlying problem
is structural. Employees are locked into legacy functions, and organizations struggle to decouple them for full-time project work. Until leaders
are willing to reallocate talent and invest in dedicated capacity for projects, even the most promising structures will underperform.

Each of these pitfalls stems from a disconnect between intention and
execution. Becoming a PDO requires more than structural tweaks—it
demands a rethinking of how work is organized, how authority is distributed, and how transformation is resourced. Without addressing the barriers, the shift toward a project-first structure risks becoming just
another initiative—rather than the foundation for lasting change.

Allocating Fully Dedicated Project Teams

Organizations increasingly realize the impact that fully dedicated project teams can have on all aspects of their projects' performance. This
approach minimizes distractions, eliminates the inefficiencies of multitasking, and allows team members to focus entirely on the project, leading to higher-quality outputs and faster completion rates.

Research by the American Psychological Association shows that multitasking can reduce productivity by as much as 40 percent, largely due to the cognitive cost of switching between tasks.[9] In project-driven environments, where success depends on sustained focus and seamless execution, constant project-switching creates friction that delays outcomes, lowers quality, and increases the risk of failure. Structurally dedicating teams to a single project minimizes these inefficiencies, enabling deeper engagement, faster iteration, and stronger collective ownership of results.

Aerospace company SpaceX allocates fully dedicated teams to each project and credits this approach as the key factor in its success. This structure has enabled the company to achieve remarkable milestones, such as the successful launch, landing, and reusability of orbital-class rockets. Rather than spreading employees across multiple initiatives, SpaceX forms tight, focused teams that are assigned exclusively to a single mission or engineering objective—whether that's developing the Falcon 9 reusable rocket, the Dragon spacecraft, or the Starlink satellite constellation.

These teams operate almost like startups within the company, with engineering, manufacturing, testing, and launch operations all integrated into a single, autonomous unit. This deep focus allows them to iterate faster, make real-time decisions, and maintain intense alignment on mission objectives without the distractions of competing priorities.

SpaceX leaders, including Elon Musk, have emphasized that the company's ability to rapidly prototype, test, and fail forward is directly tied to their choice to allocate small, fully committed teams that are structurally shielded from dilution. It has been critical to achieving milestones that many industry veterans thought would take decades.

Ten Steps for Implementing a Transformation Pilot with Fully Dedicated Resources. While organizational transformation implies a universal change initiative, attempting to change everything simultaneously can lead to chaos and resistance. A more effective approach is to start with a single, strategically chosen, fully staffed transformation project, which can serve as a proving ground for new ways of working and demonstrate the value of complete resource dedication. By starting here, organizations can demonstrate the power of dedicated resources in driving change, build a cadre of employees with hands-on transformation experience, create a model for future transformation initiatives, and generate quick wins that build momentum for broader organizational change.

Here are ten steps to take to run a transformation pilot with dedicated staffing:

1. *Select a high-impact, visible project.* Choose a transformation initiative that has the potential to deliver significant value and is visible across the organization. This visibility will help build momentum and support for future transformation efforts.

2. *Fully staff the project.* Allocate dedicated resources to the project and ask the cross-functional team members to step away from their regular operational duties. This may seem daunting, as operational work often provides a sense of stability and security. However, it's crucial for the success of the transformation initiative.

3. *Involve HR in the process.* Work closely with HR to develop policies that support temporary reassignment of staff to transformation projects; create incentives for employees who volunteer for these projects; and ensure that participating in transformation initiatives is recognized in performance reviews and career development plans.

4. *Reward volunteers.* Recognize and reward those who step up to participate in the transformation project. This could include public recognition from senior leadership, priority consideration for future leadership roles, or special development opportunities or training programs.

5. *Embrace diverse participation.* Don't shy away from involving senior managers or those managing large teams. Their participation can lend credibility to the project and help break down silos. Moreover, they stand to gain valuable hands-on experience that can shape their leadership approach in the future

6. *Create learning opportunities.* Frame the transformation project as a unique learning experience. Participants will gain new skills,

broaden their perspective, and potentially position themselves for future leadership roles. This can be a powerful motivator for volunteers.

7. *Backfill critical operational roles.* For roles that cannot be left vacant, consider temporary backfills, promotions, or job rotations. This creates opportunities for other employees to step up and gain new experiences as well.

8. *Communicate the importance.* Clearly articulate why this approach is being taken and how it aligns with the organization's long-term goals. This helps build understanding and support across the organization.

9. *Share learnings.* As the pilot project progresses, capture lessons learned and share them widely. This helps build organizational knowledge and paves the way for future transformation initiatives.

10. *Plan for reintegration.* Have a clear plan for how team members will transition back to their regular roles (or into new roles) after the project. This helps alleviate anxiety and ensures the organization can benefit from their new skills and perspectives.

This approach can be a powerful catalyst for organizational transformation. It sends a clear message about the initiative's importance and the organization's commitment to radically changing its decades-old project staffing practices. Moreover, it creates a unique opportunity for employees and future leaders to grow, learn, and potentially reshape their careers. What happens next is a self-reinforcing cycle: as employees take ownership of transformational projects, they accelerate the initiative's success, and the success of the projects in turn reinforces the organization's ability to take on even more ambitious change. Transformation becomes embedded not as a onetime push, but as a continuous capability built through empowered project ownership at every level.

Harnessing the Power of Volunteerism in Project Staffing

The engagement level of team members is another critical aspect of project success. Traditional staffing by appointing or assigning individuals to projects can lead to varying levels of commitment. Our recent research highlights just how pervasive this issue is: 62 percent of project teams are staffed by management, while only 6 percent of roles are filled by volunteers. While a top-down approach may work well in stable operational contexts, it often falls short in the dynamic, interdependent environment of transformation work.

This gap reveals a significant opportunity. Embracing a volunteer-based model for project staffing can dramatically increase engagement, motivation, and ultimately outcomes. When individuals raise their hands to join a project rather than being directed, they bring energy, purpose, and often a personal connection to the mission. Volunteer participation leads to:

- *Increased engagement.* Volunteers who choose to participate in a project are typically more engaged and motivated. They see something in the project that resonates with them—whether it's the purpose, the challenge, or the leadership involved.

- *Alignment with personal interests.* When employees and managers volunteer for projects, they're more likely to select initiatives that align with their skills, interests, and career aspirations. This alignment can lead to higher job satisfaction and better performance.

- *Sense of ownership.* Volunteers often feel a stronger sense of ownership over the project's success, leading to increased dedication and effort.

- *Diverse perspectives.* Encouraging volunteerism can unite individuals from various departments and backgrounds, fostering creativity and innovation.

Organizations can create internal project marketplaces to showcase upcoming initiatives and encourage volunteerism. Employees and managers may explore and opt in to projects that excite them. Communicating a project's purpose and potential impact taps into their intrinsic motivation, while emphasizing skill development opportunities attracts those looking to grow professionally. Participation can be further boosted by recognizing and rewarding employees who volunteer for projects beyond their regular roles and by offering flexible time allocations—similar to Google's famous "20 percent time"—so that volunteering fits sustainably within normal work rhythms.

Staffing projects for peak performance is not simply about assigning people—it is about structuring the organization to protect focus, accelerate completion, and unleash the full capacity of engaged teams to drive continuous transformation.

Conclusion

Effective project-driven structures require foundational shifts. Shimizu's story demonstrates how speed, autonomy, and collaboration can be structurally enabled by flattening hierarchies and empowering dynamic, cross-functional teams. By prioritizing transformational projects, leaders such as GM's Mary Barra show how focused investment drives momentum where it matters most. And by staffing projects for peak performance—assigning fully dedicated teams rather than stretching resources thin—SpaceX proves that concentration of talent accelerates execution and unlocks breakthrough results.

However, redesigning the organizational structure is only part of the equation. Without reimagining governance, outdated decision-making and control systems can slow even the best project-driven structures. In the next chapter, we turn to project-driven governance, where we will explore why traditional governance models struggle to support continuous transformation—and how modern organizations redesign governance to enable speed, alignment, and strategic resilience.

CHAPTER 3

Project-Driven Governance

At the heart of Haier's governance philosophy is the principle of decentralization. Decision-making authority is vested in MEs, allowing teams closest to the user to make critical strategic and operational decisions. This autonomy is supported by Haier's "three powers" framework, which *delegates authority* over business decisions, talent management, and compensation to the MEs. Leaders within these units function as CEOs of their projects, fully empowered to steer initiatives based on user needs. This decentralized approach eliminates bottlenecks that often plague traditional project management. Haier also uses AI-powered analytics to track real-time consumer trends, enabling its MEs to respond quickly to changes in market demand. Rather than waiting for centralized directives, MEs can autonomously make strategic decisions based on AI-driven insights.

Haier's commitment to *reducing bureaucracy and eliminating bottlenecks* that often plague projects is another critical pillar of its governance model. The company dismantled its hierarchical structure, removing layers of middle management that often stifle innovation and slow down decision-making. In their place, Haier established a platform-based organization where MEs operate independently while drawing on shared resources as needed. This shift accelerates project implementation and fosters a culture of accountability and ownership.

By eliminating traditional silos, Haier has minimized delays associated with hierarchical approvals. Haier also uses AI-powered analytics to track real-time consumer trends, enabling its MEs to respond quickly to changes in market demand. For example, in developing its internet of things (IoT)–based COSMOPlat platform, project teams had the autonomy to collaborate directly with external stakeholders, reducing the lead time for decision-making. The result was a platform that quickly evolved into a global standard for mass customization, underscoring the benefits of streamlined governance.

Haier's governance model is designed to be both lean and effective, with a focus on transparency and agility. Instead of relying on complex committee structures, Haier has implemented *minimal yet impactful governance mechanisms*. These include clear mandates for project governance and a reliance on digital tools to facilitate real-time tracking and reporting. Transparency is further enhanced by Haier's value-sharing mechanisms, which link the rewards earned by team members directly to the success of each project. These mechanisms motivate teams to excel and ensure that governance processes remain visible and easily understood across the organization. For instance, EMC contracts define roles, responsibilities, and performance metrics in advance, creating clarity and trust among all stakeholders.

Governance at Haier is also inherently adaptive, allowing teams to pivot quickly when user needs or market conditions change. The flexibility of its governance structures was particularly evident during the height of the Covid-19 pandemic when Haier rapidly redirected resources to support health-care initiatives, including the production of smart vaccine-storage solutions. This ability to adapt governance in real time ensured that Haier could deliver impactful solutions at critical moments.

The concept of organizational governance has evolved significantly since its inception in the early twentieth century. Initially focused on hierarchical control and rigid decision-making processes, governance has gradually shifted toward more flexible and responsive models. This evolution has been driven by the increasing complexity of business environments, the rapid pace of technological change, and the growing recognition of the value of cocreation, employee empowerment, and agility.

One of the most frequent challenges I encounter with senior leaders is the persistent disconnect between corporate headquarters and local business units, especially when executing transformational projects. Global strategies often look compelling on paper, but when implementation begins, they get mired in slow approvals, conflicting priorities, and rigid control processes that paralyze local action.

This rigidity is one of the most common, and most costly, reasons why large transformation programs fail to deliver their intended impact. The reality is simple: transformation does not happen at headquarters—it occurs on the ground. Unless decision-making authority and cocreation are deliberately delegated to the teams closest to where the execution happens, even the best strategies will stall. Modern governance must empower, not control.

Today's organizations face an urgent challenge: balancing the need for oversight and control with the growing imperative for speed, flexibility, and frontline empowerment. In transformation environments, traditional governance models designed for stability and predictability often become liabilities. Instead of enabling success, they create bottlenecks, stifle innovation, and slow decision-making at exactly the moment when adaptability matters most.

To truly thrive in the transformation age, governance must be reimagined for speed, ownership, and real-time learning. We will examine three critical shifts that enable this—delegating authority for faster local decisions and unlocking cocreation, streamlining processes to eliminate bottlenecks, and designing lean, effective governance bodies.

These shifts fundamentally rethink how power, process, and oversight are distributed. Project-driven governance enables faster execution, more transparent accountability, and greater alignment with strategic goals in an era where speed and adaptability are everything (see figure 3-1.)

Delegating Authority for Faster Local Decisions

One of the defining characteristics of traditional, operations-driven organizations is that decisions are made at the top. In day-to-day

FIGURE 3-1

Project-driven governance

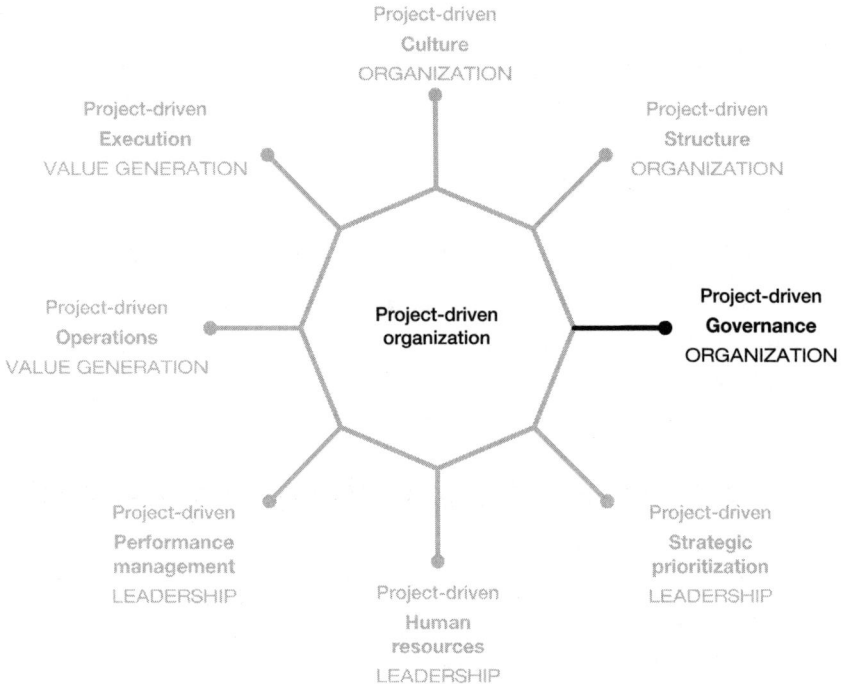

Project-driven
Culture
ORGANIZATION

Project-driven
Execution
VALUE GENERATION

Project-driven
Structure
ORGANIZATION

Project-driven
Operations
VALUE GENERATION

Project-driven
organization

**Project-driven
Governance
ORGANIZATION**

Project-driven
Performance
management
LEADERSHIP

Project-driven
Human
resources
LEADERSHIP

Project-driven
Strategic
prioritization
LEADERSHIP

operations, this centralized model can offer consistency and control. However, it becomes a significant obstacle in transformation initiatives and project-driven environments. When key decisions must always escalate back to corporate headquarters or senior leadership, projects lose speed, agility, and frontline ownership. Instead of empowering those closest to the work, organizations paralyze them, forcing delays, creating bottlenecks, and missing opportunities for adaptive execution.

Our research on governance highlights how widespread this issue remains. Only 5 percent of organizations report fully localized decision-making, where the project team makes all decisions. Meanwhile, 19 percent have mostly decentralized structures, with only a few decisions, such as scope changes, made centrally. The largest group, 42 percent, operates with somewhat localized models, where some decisions, like budget changes, are centrally decided. In contrast, 25 percent maintain primarily centralized decision-making and 8 percent operate under completely centralized models, where all project changes are decided and approved outside the project team.

Empowering Frontline Decision-Makers

In project-driven organizations, accelerating decision-making demands delegating authority to project teams and frontline leaders. Without this shift, even the most agile structures will stall under old habits of centralized control. Delegating authority closer to the work accelerates execution, empowers ownership, and builds the momentum essential for transformation.

When Jesper Brodin, CEO of INGKA Group, which holds the vast majority of IKEA's stores, accelerated the company's sustainability transformation, he quickly ran into a familiar roadblock: slow, centralized decision-making. Even straightforward projects, like switching to LED lighting or reducing packaging waste, were delayed by complex approval processes. Innovation stalled and local teams felt disconnected from the company's ambitious green goals.

To fix this, Brodin and his leadership team made a bold move: they delegated authority to those closest to the work. Store and country-level managers were appointed as chief sustainability officers, empowered to lead local initiatives with clear decision rights. Within predefined financial and sustainability parameters, they could implement energy upgrades, redesign supply chains, and reduce waste without waiting for corporate sign-off. Procurement teams also gained autonomy to make supplier changes that aligned with strategic goals.

The impact was swift. Projects that once took months were executed in weeks. Local teams tailored solutions to their specific needs, and accountability increased as they owned both the decisions and the outcomes. Within a few years, IKEA had converted all of its lighting to LED, cut landfill waste by over 50 percent, and sourced more than 98 percent of its wood sustainably.[1] Just as significantly, employee engagement surged as teams saw their ideas translate into real environmental impact, showing that empowerment breeds ownership and ownership drives results.

Delegating authority does not mean abandoning oversight. It means setting clear guardrails, defining decision rights at the correct level, and trusting capable teams to act within them. In PDOs, speed is not just about working faster but about deciding faster. And fast, well-placed decisions start with deliberate authority delegation at every level.

Building Local Decision-Making into the Project DNA

Local decentralized decision-making has become a powerful lever for project-driven organizations' quest for greater agility and innovation. This approach goes beyond simply moving decision rights; it shifts control closer to where real work and customer interactions happen—embedding speed, adaptability, and cocreation into the execution fabric.

Delegating authority locally delivers multiple benefits. Teams can find solutions and respond quickly to changes without waiting for top-down approval. Entrepreneurship and innovation flourish because employees are empowered to propose and implement creative solutions. Engagement improves when team members see a direct connection between their decisions and tangible outcomes.

Chris Rufer founded Morning Star, a global leader in tomato processing, without traditional managers, titles, or hierarchical structures.[2] Every employee negotiates their own Colleague Letter of Understanding (CLOU) annually, setting performance expectations directly with peers. Individuals can issue purchase orders, initiate hiring, acquire tools, and even set compensation through peer-driven processes. Morning Star's model shows that radical decentralization and decision-making autonomy with clear expectations and peer accountability can produce extraordinary business results—the company has sustained double-digit growth for more than two decades.

Reducing Hierarchical Approval Requirements for Project Initiatives

While empowering local decision-makers and decentralizing control are critical first steps, one of the most persistent practical challenges remains: finding lean, effective alternatives to traditional hierarchical approval chains. Simply removing layers is not enough—organizations must actively design new mechanisms that allow project teams to move quickly without sacrificing alignment or accountability.

Several innovative approaches are emerging to meet this need. One method is the creation of *innovation hubs* with explicit autonomy to make rapid decisions outside the day-to-day organization. These hubs operate as protected spaces where experimental ideas can be tested, iterated, and scaled without being dragged through cumbersome approval processes. For instance, a sustainability-focused hub might pilot new energy-efficient lighting systems in a handful of retail locations and, based on rapid feedback, roll out successful solutions company-wide, bypassing conventional top-down bottlenecks.

Another approach involves *internal crowdsourcing* for decision-making. Rather than routing proposals through layers of managers, organizations increasingly leverage collective intelligence platforms to cocreate solutions, source input, and make collaborative decisions at the team or community level. This cocreation can take many forms—from translating a project's broader purpose into locally relevant narratives, defining measurable, localized benefits, and crafting customized solutions to organizing activities that strengthen team spirit and engagement. This democratizes decision-making, speeds up consensus, and builds stronger buy-in among those tasked with implementation.

Flexible funding models also play a powerful role in reducing bureaucratic drag. Instead of locking projects into rigid annual budget cycles, organizations allocate pools of resources tied to specific project milestones. As we explored in chapter 2, rolling budgets support this approach by allowing teams to access funds dynamically as they deliver agreed-on outcomes, minimizing the need for repeated executive approvals. For example, a retail chain undertaking a green transformation might release additional budget tranches once a team proves it has reduced energy consumption by 10 percent, enabling faster scaling of successful initiatives.

Of course, decentralized decision-making brings challenges. Potential misalignment, inconsistent quality, and varying skill levels across teams must be actively managed. Organizations must invest in clear communication systems, robust quality standards, intensive training programs, and cultural transformation initiatives to support true autonomy at scale.

Tracking key metrics such as time-to-market, project success, employee engagement, customer satisfaction, and innovation rates helps refine the model and sustain stakeholder confidence.

Streamlining Processes to Eliminate Bottlenecks

Ultimately, local decision-making lays the foundation for more effective project execution. Empowering teams to act quickly and confidently eliminates bottlenecks at the source and transforms organizational speed, resilience, and adaptability from isolated ambitions into everyday habits. Bureaucracy, excessive reports, meeting overload, and unnecessary paperwork slow down project execution, create frustration, and stifle creativity.

Our research highlights both progress and remaining gaps. While 18 percent of organizations have significantly reduced bureaucracy, minimizing documentation and streamlining approval processes, most still struggle to adapt fully. A further 57 percent report only moderate or minor improvements, and 16 percent have yet to take any meaningful steps.

Organization experts Gary Hamel and Michele Zanini found that managers spend 40 percent of their time writing reports and 30 percent to 60 percent of it in coordination meetings. This leaves only 10 percent to 30 percent of their time for the work they were actually hired to do. Such excessive bureaucracy hampers productivity and erodes employee morale and innovation.[3]

Identifying and Clearing Structural Bottlenecks

The ability to proactively identify and eliminate bottlenecks often separates successful transformations from those that stumble. Too often, leaders focus heavily on strategy but underestimate the execution barriers hidden within their own organizational systems. If left unaddressed, these barriers sap momentum and undermine even the most ambitious change efforts.

Some of the most critical obstacles are structural bottlenecks, particularly those rooted in outdated or overly complex processes. These include fragmented workflows with excessive handoffs, inconsistent data standards, slow approval chains focused more on compliance than speed, redundant meetings, and legacy reporting that pulls teams away from actual delivery. Addressing these bottlenecks often requires rethinking how value flows through the organization—not just optimizing tasks, but redesigning end-to-end processes for speed, clarity, and learning.

TechCorp United, a multinational technology company, faced widespread issues: data silos, inefficient decision-making, fragmented project execution, and a lack of data-driven culture.[4] Under the leadership of CEO Sarah Chen, TechCorp embarked on a major digital reinvention. Despite initial enthusiasm, the company's traditional management structures quickly began to choke progress. Recognizing the risk, Chen and her executive team moved rapidly to build a systemic response by:

- Streamlining *slow, compliance-heavy approval processes* by empowering midlevel project managers to handle operational decisions independently, without constant executive sign-off.

- Resolving *inconsistent data standards* through a unified data governance framework, supporting faster decisions and eliminating duplication.

- Eliminating *redundant meetings* by introducing collaborative workspaces and structured rituals like sprint reviews that focus on outcomes, not status updates.

- Modernizing *legacy reporting* through real-time dashboards and lean performance tracking, freeing teams to focus on delivery rather than documentation.

- Bridging *skill gaps* through targeted upskilling programs that combine external expertise with internal mentorship, fostering just-in-time learning embedded within project delivery.

- *Controlling scope changes* by tightening project charters and enforcing disciplined change control protocols, while allowing for rapid adjustments when justified by shifting priorities or new insights.

By systematically clearing these bottlenecks, TechCorp United accelerated project delivery and reignited organizational momentum across its entire transformation portfolio, turning stalled initiatives into compounding wins.

Beyond operational fixes, forward-looking companies are now building execution clarity structurally. They deploy models like *single-threaded leadership*—assigning one dedicated leader to each major initiative with full accountability, no competing priorities, and a clear, singular mandate to drive results. These leaders are responsible not only for setting the vision but for securing resources, removing barriers, maintaining strategic alignment, and ensuring day-to-day momentum. They are not pulled across multiple projects, functional distractions, or shifting short-term demands.

By eliminating fragmented ownership, single-threaded leadership dramatically increases execution speed, clarifies decision-making, and builds a deep sense of personal responsibility for outcomes. This model ensures that initiatives are not just launched with enthusiasm—they are sustained with relentless focus until they deliver tangible impact. Organizations that master the discipline of clearing structural bottlenecks and reinforcing leadership focus on building more than momentum; they establish the capacity to sustain transformation consistently and at scale.

Zero-Based Processes for Transformations

Once structural bottlenecks are addressed, the next critical step is redesigning processes to increase execution speed without sacrificing strategic control. In large transformation efforts, the tension between agility and discipline is one of the most significant organizational challenges.

Stripping all existing processes back to zero is a strong starting point for any transformation. Rather than tweaking legacy workflows, organizations must adopt a zero-based design mindset: assume no process is sacred—start from scratch and deliberately rebuild only those processes that are absolutely necessary to drive execution and deliver transformational outcomes.

Four simple but powerful questions should guide decision-making when evaluating whether a process deserves to be rebuilt:

- *Does this process accelerate project execution or transformation outcomes?* For instance, a monthly transformation review focused purely on strategic milestones and risk-adjusted forecasting can sharpen executive decision-making and accelerate investment allocation. This process should be preserved. In contrast, a mandatory monthly reporting deck requiring hundreds of KPIs, many outdated or irrelevant, consumes time and energy without advancing execution—and should be eliminated.

- *Does this process clarify accountability, ownership, or risk management?* A brief executive steering review that assigns clear owners to cross-functional, high-priority risks, such as supply chain disruptions or regulatory hurdles, helps lock in responsibility and prevent costly blind spots. Meanwhile, requiring multiple sign-offs for internal schedule adjustments, where risks are minor, only clogs the system without strengthening oversight.

- *Does this process provide critical insight that enables better, faster decisions?* An integrated dashboard that highlights at-risk initiatives, tracks value realization against strategic assumptions, and flags urgent decision points directly informs better governance actions. Conversely, retrospective variance reports that analyze closed fiscal quarters, without real-time relevance, simply add reporting noise without improving agility.

- *Could this process be automated or enhanced through AI or intelligent technologies?* Increasingly, AI-driven tools can automate compliance checks, monitor project health dynamically, and even predict emerging risks. If a workflow can be reliably accelerated through real-time dashboards, intelligent escalation triggers, or predictive analytics, senior leaders must question whether manual process overhead is still justified.

Designing Processes for Speed without Losing Control

Organizations should not treat zero-based design as a onetime exercise. In high-velocity transformation environments, execution processes must be challenged and refined on a regular basis. Applying the four core questions to critical workflows every ninety days ensures that processes remain aligned with dynamic realities, not institutional habits. With this stripped-down foundation, companies can rebuild execution systems that balance speed and control.

The first priority is radical simplicity. Project workflows focus only on activities that create direct value, while necessary complexity (such as compliance demands) is isolated rather than spread across every initiative. Real-time information replaces static reporting cycles. Dashboards, predictive analytics, and live project-health reviews enable course correction based on immediate insights, rather than lagging data. Smart processes also embed risk-based checkpoints. Instead of requiring approvals at every phase, escalation is triggered only when clearly defined thresholds—budget variance, regulatory exposure, customer impact—are crossed.

Owning closure criteria is equally critical. Clear definitions of "done," tied to business value milestones, prevent projects from dragging endlessly and enable faster reallocation of scarce resources.

Finally, project-related processes must be designed for continuous evolution, not rigid perfection. Short feedback loops, retrospectives, and frontline learning cycles ensure that execution workflows stay responsive to changing realities and emerging risks.

A strong example of this approach was Walmart's Store No. 8 innovation hub.[5] Created in 2017, Store No. 8 was designed as a semi-independent incubator to explore disruptive technologies like conversational commerce, autonomous shopping platforms, and virtual reality retail. Unlike traditional corporate R&D teams, Store No. 8 was structured to move at startup speed: teams were empowered to pursue rapid experimentation cycles, launch minimally viable pilots, and adapt quickly to market feedback—without waiting for standard corporate approval chains. Lightweight governance models ensured that critical risks and learnings were surfaced in real time through direct executive touchpoints, rather than buried in bureaucratic layers.

Walmart's decision to dismantle the initiative in early 2024 reflected not a failure but a strategic transition.[6] The company announced that the innovation capabilities developed within Store No. 8 had matured and were now embedded across its broader global technology, product, and design organizations. Several of its initiatives—such as voice-based shopping, intelligent fulfillment technologies, and early ventures into AI-enhanced retail experiences—have since been scaled and integrated into Walmart's mainstream operations.

In practice, Store No. 8 laid the groundwork for a more distributed, project-driven model of innovation, in which a central governance function maintained strategic alignment without stifling speed or creativity, and processes were designed for speed without loss of control. Its legacy is the diffusion of its mindset and methods throughout the organization, a hallmark of the PDO.

Designing Lean, Effective Governance Bodies

Creating lean, effective governance bodies is essential for organizations seeking to scale transformation without losing strategic control. Many current governance bodies—such as steering committees, project boards, and portfolio councils—were built for a different era. With their rigid hierarchies, formal reporting structures, and sequential decision cycles, they often slow down rather than support the pace of modern execution.

These bodies tend to focus too much on risk avoidance and compliance, which then become barriers rather than strategic enablers. As a result, even well-intentioned transformations get caught in loops of approvals, unclear ownership, and delayed action.

Earlier in this chapter, we explored how delegating decision authority and streamlining execution processes are fundamental to building PDOs. However, without rethinking governance bodies themselves, these gains will eventually stall. Governance must evolve in parallel, redesigned not to control every move but to amplify speed, ownership, and transparency while safeguarding value creation. It must be responsive and adaptive—able to sense shifts in the external environment and recalibrate priorities in real time.

The Pitfalls in Building Project-Driven Governance

Governance is the backbone of any successful project-driven organization, but traditional models are often too slow, too complex, and too disconnected from where the real work happens. While governance is meant to enable strategic alignment and risk management, it often becomes a source of friction that stalls execution. In the transformation age, where speed and adaptability are essential, governance must evolve to support, not stifle, projects. Yet as organizations attempt to modernize their governance models, they often fall into traps that undercut progress. Here are three common pitfalls that can hinder the shift toward project-driven governance:

Keeping Decision-Making Centralized and Slow

Many organizations retain centralized governance structures where critical project decisions require executive sign-off, even on routine matters. This slows execution, undermines ownership, stifles cocreation, and keeps teams waiting instead of delivering.

A global consumer goods company attempted to accelerate digital transformation by forming agile product teams. However, all decisions budgeted for over $50,000 still required review by senior executives in a monthly committee. This created delays of four to six weeks—crippling momentum and frustrating teams. The agile structure couldn't deliver on its promise until decision rights were delegated to empowered local leaders.

Overengineering Processes with Too Many Layers of Approval

Many organizations build governance models with multiple approval steps, redundant reporting, and overlapping oversight bodies. While well-intentioned, these complex systems become bottlenecks that drain energy from execution.

The BBC launched its Digital Media Initiative (DMI) in 2008 to modernize its video production and archiving systems. Despite its ambitious goals, the project was plagued by governance and management oversight failures. A PwC report highlighted how the BBC failed to identify the signs— evident as early as July 2011—of DMI's impending failure. The project was abandoned in May 2013—costing license-fee payers nearly £100 million.

The report cited inadequate project management, lack of business change focus, and piecemeal assurance arrangements as contributing factors.[a]

Creating Oversized, Ineffective Governance Bodies

Steering committees and review boards are often overloaded with stakeholders, many lacking the context or authority to make decisions. The goal is inclusion, but the outcome is indecision, and when too many people are involved, accountability disappears and decisions stall.

A multinational bank created a transformation oversight board comprising eighteen senior executives from every primary function. Meetings often devolved into irrelevant status updates rather than decision-making on relevant matters, and conflicting priorities led to repeated rework. When a leaner, cross-functional task force replaced the board with a clear mandate and decision rights, execution improved dramatically.

These pitfalls highlight a familiar pattern: traditional governance mindsets applied to modern challenges. Becoming project-driven doesn't mean abandoning governance—it means redesigning it for clarity, speed, and effectiveness. When governance becomes an enabler rather than a gatekeeper, organizations unlock their projects' and people's full potential.

NOTE

a. Mark Sweney and Tara Conlan, "BBC 'Took Too Long to Realise DMI Project Was in Trouble,'" *The Guardian*, December 18, 2013, https://www.theguardian.com/media/2013/dec/18/bbc-dmi-project-pwc-report.

The first critical shift is toward *lean governance*. Rather than applying a uniform level of scrutiny across all initiatives, governance intensity should align with the actual level of uncertainty, risk, and strategic importance.

Lower-risk initiatives typically don't require formal governance bodies. Instead, they should be guided by lightweight oversight mechanisms—such as empowered team leads operating within clearly defined boundaries—to maintain speed and agility. Formal governance in these cases often adds unnecessary friction without commensurate benefit. On the other hand, high-stakes transformation programs should be supported by actively engaged governance bodies. Their active presence signals the strategic importance of the initiative, fosters a sense of urgency, and drives prioritization at all levels. The more frequently these bodies meet and interact with project teams, the greater the visibility and momentum they create across the organization.

The second critical shift is empowering leadership through *explicit delegation of decision rights*. Leaders must take the initiative to align governance rhythms to the actual speed of project execution, moving away from rigid quarterly cycles toward more responsive, initiative-driven cadences. They must also set strategic intent early and unambiguously, providing the direction and guardrails that teams need to execute with confidence and accountability.

The third critical shift is *real-time, automated monitoring and compliance*. AI, predictive analytics, and dynamic dashboards allow project health, risks, and value realization to be tracked continuously—not simply through lagging quarterly updates. Well-designed real-time governance systems highlight emerging issues early, trigger lightweight escalations when needed, and enable interventions before small problems escalate into major failures.

When governance bodies are equipped with live insights and are empowered to act on them, they move from being procedural gatekeepers to dynamic enablers of transformation. In doing so, organizations replace cumbersome bureaucracy with living, responsive transparency—making governance not just faster, but smarter and more strategic.

NASA's Streamlined Governance Model

NASA's approach to project management offers valuable lessons in simplifying governance for speed and transparency. The agency's *Systems Engineering Handbook* provides a framework that balances rigorous oversight with the flexibility required for complex, high-stakes projects.[7]

One of the key elements of NASA's governance model is the use of integrated project teams (IPTs). These cross-functional teams bring together experts from various disciplines to work collaboratively on projects. Unlike traditional siloed structures, NASA's IPTs are empowered to make real-time decisions within their technical domains, without waiting for constant escalation to senior leadership.

This model proved critical during the Mars *Perseverance* rover missions. When engineers detected unexpected vibrations during the final stages of testing the rover's descent stage, it was an IPT—not a top-down committee—that rapidly analyzed telemetry, simulated possible landing scenarios, and determined on-the-fly adjustments to the Sky Crane deployment sequence. Because the IPT included propulsion specialists, systems engineers, and flight dynamics experts working side by side, the team made critical refinements in real time, avoiding schedule delays and mitigating potential mission risks. By empowering these teams with both the authority and the trust to resolve challenges locally, NASA was able to maintain project momentum and adapt to new challenges as they arose.

Another critical aspect of NASA's governance model is the tiered review process. This process categorizes reviews based on the project's phase and risk level, allowing for flexibility and ensuring that resources are focused where they are most needed. Early-stage projects undergo less frequent and less intensive reviews, while high-risk or critical projects receive more rigorous oversight.

The agency's governance structure includes checks and balances between the management of the program and independent technical authorities. This structure helps ensure that decisions benefit from diverse perspectives and are not made in isolation, a lesson hard learned from past incidents like the *Challenger* and *Columbia* disasters.

In recent years, NASA has adapted its approach to accommodate more public-private partnerships, such as those in the Commercial Crew program. This has required new ways of thinking about project governance, risk sharing, and performance metrics. The success of projects like SpaceX's crewed missions to the International Space Station demonstrates the potential of these new models, highlighting the need for NASA to continue evolving its project management practices.

The Transformation of MTN Group

MTN Group, a leading telecommunications company in Africa, provides another example of effective governance in a complex, high-stakes environment. The company has undergone a significant transformation to enhance its agility and innovation capabilities, focusing on overhauling its governance structures.

This transformation began in earnest around 2020, as part of MTN's Ambition 2025 strategy—a multiyear road map aimed at repositioning the company as a leading digital operator across Africa.[8] MTN's transformation was driven by the need to respond swiftly to Africa's rapidly changing telecommunications landscape.[9] The company faced challenges such as regulatory changes, market competition, and the need to expand its digital services. To address these challenges, MTN implemented several innovative governance strategies.

Agile governance committees were established to operate with minimal bureaucracy. These committees are composed of cross-functional leaders who meet regularly to review and approve project initiatives. The focus is on making swift, data-driven decisions that align with the company's strategic goals. Project managers at MTN are given significant autonomy to make decisions within their projects. Clear guidelines and a robust framework for accountability support this empowerment. They can respond quickly to challenges and opportunities by reducing the need for constant higher-level approvals.

MTN's governance model emphasized outcomes rather than processes. The company sets clear objectives for each project and measures success based on achieving these objectives. This outcome-focused approach ensured that governance efforts are aligned with the company's strategic priorities and drive meaningful results.

This new approach also enabled the company to launch its mobile money platform MoMo across multiple African markets in record time, capturing a substantial market share and expanding access to digital financial services in previously underserved regions. By the end of 2024, the MoMo platform had contributed more than 25 percent of MTN's overall fintech turnover.

MTN's strong business performance shows the impact of these simplified structures. In 2024, the company reported fintech revenue growth of 28.5 percent and service revenue growth of 13.8 percent, with its mobile money platform MoMo surpassing 60 million active users.[10]

Conclusion

Critical governance shifts are required to make project-driven organizations successful. By delegating decision-making authority, streamlining overly complex processes, and establishing lean, focused governance bodies, organizations can unlock innovation, accelerate execution, and foster a culture of ownership, cocreation, and entrepreneurial problem-solving. These changes do not eliminate governance—they redefine it as a dynamic enabler of responsiveness, clarity, and momentum. New technologies, from real-time analytics to AI-driven decision support, are making this evolution possible and essential. Modern governance must harness these tools to enhance visibility, accelerate feedback loops, and ensure more imaginative, faster execution across the project portfolio.

Yet the culture, structure, and governance discussed in these first three chapters are not enough to succeed in the transformation age. As we move into the second part of this book, our focus shifts from organizational mechanics to personal leadership responsibility.

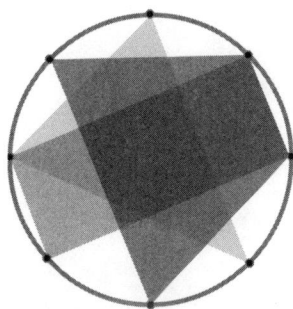

PART TWO

PROJECT-DRIVEN LEADERSHIP

n part 2, we move from organizational aspects to examining leadership's critical role in enabling and accelerating a project-driven organization.

In the project economy, leadership is not defined by long-term vision statements or charismatic strategy launches; it is measured by the ability to prioritize ruthlessly, empower teams, remove obstacles, and deliver faster results through projects. For many senior leaders, the comfort zone lies in managing day-to-day operations, where they can rely on experience, routines, and existing authority. But the real challenge—and opportunity— lies in stepping into unfamiliar territory: sponsoring strategic projects, shaping cross-functional priorities, and building capabilities that don't yet exist. Project-driven leadership is hands-on. It's about making critical resource bets early, having teams with measurable benefits, getting results, and staying deeply engaged in transformation efforts without reverting to top-down control.

Look at the pivotal role that BioNTech CEO Uğur Şahin played in actively sponsoring the development of the Pfizer-BioNTech Covid-19 vaccine and the transformation of British Telecom (BT) following its acquisition of EE. In this new era, the most effective leaders aren't those who only set direction; they are those who roll up their sleeves, build momentum and engagement through projects, and lead transformation by example, one initiative at a time.

CHAPTER 4

Project-Driven Strategic Prioritization

At Haier, purpose is at the core of every project. Each ME or EMC leader is tasked with developing a *compelling purpose tied directly to specific benefits*. This alignment ensures that projects are strategically relevant and resonate with both global and local contexts.

For example, Haier Biomedical transitioned from manufacturing ultra-low-temperature storage equipment to creating life sciences ecosystems. This shift was driven by leaders articulating a clear purpose: addressing unmet needs in health-care scenarios, such as automating hospital pharmacy operations. By defining its purpose around user value and societal impact, Haier was able to drive both business growth and transformative benefits in critical sectors.

This clarity of purpose extends to defining measurable benefits on a global and local scale. Haier ensures that its projects contribute to broader organizational objectives while addressing specific market challenges. Its "zero distance" model empowers MEs to propose and pursue initiatives aligned directly with customer needs and strategic goals. At the heart of this approach is leadership clarity. Senior leaders set the expectation that every project must link clearly to the defined benefits and they reinforce this alignment at every major decision point.

Haier also exemplifies the principle of *ruthless prioritization*, focusing its resources on projects that promise the greatest value. Leadership discipline is key here: executives know that saying no is as important as saying yes. Leaders rigorously evaluate initiatives, with an emphasis on aligning efforts with the company's overarching strategy and user-centric mission. Projects that fail to demonstrate measurable impact are quickly discontinued, allowing resources to be reallocated to higher-priority initiatives.

One example is Haier's Smart Medical EMC, which identified inefficiencies in hospital pharmacy workflows and developed automated solutions to address them. Rather than spreading resources across multiple initiatives, Haier concentrated on addressing this critical pain point, resulting in significant improvements in efficiency and safety for health-care providers. Through such prioritization, Haier ensures that its projects deliver maximum impact while minimizing waste.

Leaders championed this laser focus. Senior leadership plays an integral role in Haier's project success. Executive involvement in projects is often symbolic, but Haier assigns *senior executives as active sponsors* for strategic initiatives. Leaders protect the team from distractions and ensure they have the resources and autonomy needed to develop and scale the solution rapidly, remove roadblocks, and ensure alignment with the company's vision. More importantly, their involvement signals the project's importance to the organization, fostering engagement from the team and buy-in from broader stakeholders.

Founder Zhang Ruimin exemplified the role of an active sponsor by championing the RenDanHeYi transformation and directly engaging with project teams to provide guidance and support. This hands-on approach extends to Haier's EMCs, where leaders are empowered to sponsor and oversee initiatives within their domains.

Haier's sponsorship model also emphasizes accountability. Sponsors are evaluated based on the success of the initiatives they oversee, aligning their incentives with project outcomes. This accountability ensures that sponsorship remains a dynamic and impactful component of Haier's project-driven strategy.

n my workshops with senior leaders, I often begin with a simple test: "How often do you launch new projects?" Many proudly respond, "About once a month." Then I follow up with, "And how often do you finish or kill projects?" At this point, the responses falter. Some say, "Maybe one every six months," while others can't recall a recent project completion or cancellation.

At this point, I explain that they have a serious issue if they start projects faster than they finish them. Launching new initiatives without completing or closing others creates a growing backlog that dilutes focus, strains resources, and hinders the organization's ability to achieve its goals.

In a world of competing demands and constant transformation, the ability to prioritize is a defining capability. As the Haier example shows, effective prioritization is foundational to thriving in a project-driven environment. It's not just about launching more initiatives—it's about choosing the right ones, aligning them with purpose, and backing them with commitment and clarity.

This chapter addresses one of the most critical responsibilities of project-driven leadership: selecting the right projects and ensuring they deliver strategic value. While many organizations fall into the trap of doing too much, leading organizations are learning to focus—investing their time, capital, and talent in fewer, more meaningful initiatives. In my experience, most companies carry far more projects than they have the capacity to manage or execute effectively. I often challenge senior leaders to cancel 50 percent of their active projects within a week. Those few who take this bold step see immediate improvements in alignment, speed, and impact.

To achieve this sharper focus, leaders must master three essential leadership disciplines that define effective strategic prioritization (see figure 4-1): defining purpose and measurable benefits from the start, ruthlessly prioritizing a few high-value initiatives, and activating sponsors to champion execution.

These disciplines are more than management techniques—they represent a new leadership mindset. In this chapter, we will break down

FIGURE 4-1

Project-driven strategic prioritization

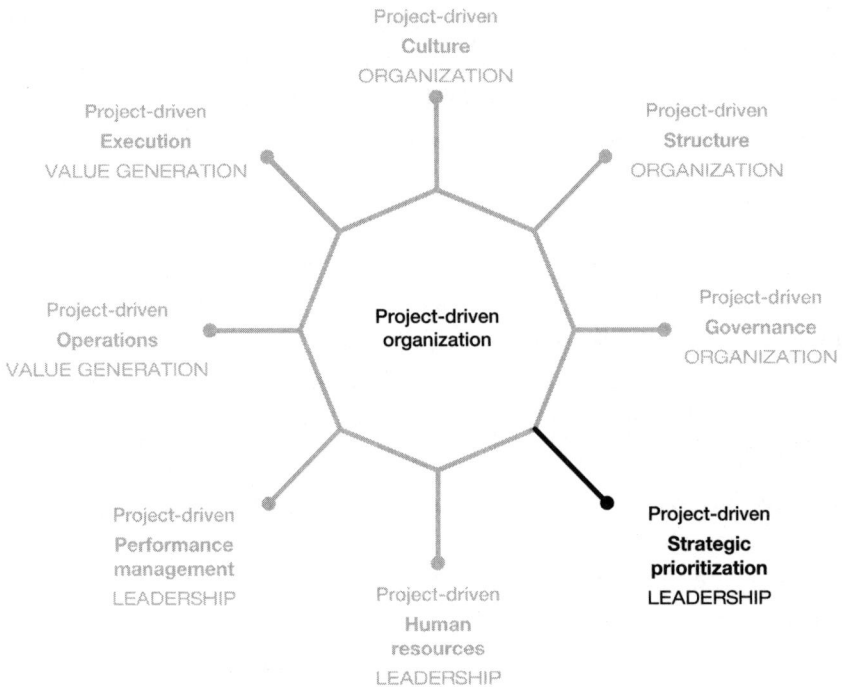

how leaders can master these disciplines and use strategic prioritization as a true lever for building the future.

Developing a Compelling Purpose and Measurable Benefits for Projects

One compelling example of purpose comes from Akio Morita, cofounder and longtime CEO of Sony. When he launched Sony onto the global stage in the 1950s and 1960s, Morita didn't simply declare that it would become a successful company. He framed a larger purpose: that Japan itself would become known worldwide for the quality of its products. His leadership instilled a sense of national pride and ambition across Sony's teams, driving innovations like the transistor radio, the Walkman, and early video technology. And the company transformed global perceptions of Japanese manufacturing in just a generation.

Leaders must initiate their key transformational project by anchoring it in a well-defined, compelling purpose. As a leader, the time you spend articulating the intent and the consequences will be well repaid. Teams will operate more confidently, need fewer course corrections, and stay focused. Remember, project purpose isn't just something you define at the start and forget. As execution progresses, the momentum and demands of delivery can easily pull teams away from the original intent. That's why leaders must regularly reinforce the "why"—or risk letting the project's output drive the purpose, instead of purpose guiding the outcome.

Establishing purpose is the foundation of impactful projects. When leaders can clearly communicate why a project matters within the larger organizational strategy, they create a shared sense of ownership and commitment that enhances both focus and resilience. This clarity around purpose is especially critical for PDOs, where employees are increasingly engaged simultaneously in multiple initiatives. Purpose not only aligns efforts but also establishes a sense of direction that can sustain momentum, even through challenging phases of a project.

The other essential part of any transformation is defining benefits: measurable outcomes that connect work directly to strategic impacts, whether revenue growth, sustainability milestones, market expansion, or social value. Purpose and benefits create a robust leadership framework that ensures projects aren't just creating activity—they are building the organization's future.

Purpose: The "Why" of Your Transformations

Our recent research underscores organizations' challenges in aligning projects with a defined purpose and long-term goals. Only 19 percent of organizations reported that all their projects are fully aligned with strategic road maps, while 49 percent indicated that most projects generally support the organization's purpose with some exceptions for immediate needs. Meanwhile, 21 percent admitted that projects often require adjustments to align with organizational goals, reflecting a reactive rather than proactive approach to project planning. Shockingly, 8 percent stated that project selection is mostly ad hoc, with alignment occurring more by chance than design, and 3 percent acknowledged projects are selected without consideration of the organization's purpose or long-term strategic direction. This data highlights the need for leaders to establish a clear, purpose-driven approach to avoid wasted resources and ensure meaningful contributions to strategic goals.

To define the true purpose of a project or transformation, leaders can use the simple but powerful technique of repeating the question "Why?"—typically three to five times. This practice uncovers the deeper motivations behind a project, helping to move from surface-level, tactical reasons to a higher purpose that resonates with employees. Leaders can dig into the project's fundamental rationale, revealing connections to the organization's mission and values. This process helps ensure that each project is not just a short-term fix or isolated task but is meaningfully aligned with strategic goals.

The Golden Rule of Getting to Purpose. If, after asking your "whys," you cannot arrive at a compelling, meaningful purpose, it might signal that the project lacks strategic value and should not proceed. This prevents resources from being allocated to initiatives that don't genuinely support the organization's mission or deliver meaningful benefits.

Consider a project aimed at improving operational efficiency in a manufacturing company. The purpose may initially seem straightforward, but by using the "Why?" approach, leaders can explore deeper motivations that give the project a more compelling and strategic purpose:

- *Why do we need to improve operational efficiency?* To reduce production costs.

- *Why is reducing production costs important?* To increase profitability and ensure we remain competitive in the market.

- *Why is competitiveness critical for us right now?* Because we need to protect our market share as new players enter with more cost-effective solutions.

- *Why do we need to protect our market share in this industry?* To secure employee jobs and sustain growth, allowing us to continue serving our customers and supporting the community.

Through this drill-down, the initial goal of improving operational efficiency evolves into a higher purpose. It turns a vague cost-cutting initiative into a mission-driven project that aligns with corporate goals and resonates with employees.

Leaders have a critical role in ensuring this reflective process for two reasons. First, asking "Why?" is a useful way of learning more about the initiatives your organization is championing. The answers will help you prioritize between different investments and also provide a useful early warning for a project that may need to be stopped because it no longer aligns with your strategy. Second, while everyone on the project team is encouraged to be a *reflective practitioner,* the pressure of delivery means few have time to reflect and even fewer feel empowered to suggest stopping the project altogether. Leaders can guide the team back to the larger perspective.

SMART Purpose. After defining the deeper purpose, leaders should add "By when?" and "How much?" to make the purpose SMART—specific, measurable, achievable, relevant, and time-bound. This ensures that the purpose isn't just inspiring but also actionable and trackable, with clear deadlines and measurable outcomes.

In the manufacturing example, a SMART purpose might be refined as follows: "To secure employee jobs, maintain our market competitiveness, and sustain community support by achieving a 15 percent reduction in production costs within the next twelve months." This final statement goes beyond the initial cost-cutting objective, providing a time-bound and measurable target that all stakeholders can work toward. By combining the "Why?" questioning technique with specific goals for "By when?" and "How much?" leaders can craft a purpose that is both compelling and grounded, giving employees a clear vision and measurable milestones that align with the company's strategic objectives.

Benefits: The Core Reason for Every Project

Although the importance of benefits realization has gained visibility, many organizations still struggle to embed it as a leadership discipline. Too often, projects are initiated around deliverables—an asset built, a system installed, a product launched—without connecting these outputs to measurable outcomes. Leaders must close this gap. Shifting the organizational mindset from "delivering outputs" to "realizing benefits" is one of the most critical steps in becoming a truly project-driven enterprise.

Effective leadership involvement in benefits realization is essential from the start. Senior sponsors must champion both the stakeholder-driven and the bottom-up articulation of benefits—not only easily quantifiable financial returns but also harder-to-measure strategic shifts like enhanced resilience, improved public trust, or future-readiness. As we will see later, a critical early step is to develop a clear and shared benefits plan that outlines intended outcomes, assigns ownership, and defines how value will be measured over time. Leaders must act as arbiters of value during project execution, making conscious trade-offs when resources, timelines, or strategic needs evolve. In moments of pressure, the leader's role is to keep the organization anchored in impact, ensuring that delivery choices serve the ultimate purpose—not just short-term convenience.

As OpenStrategies cofounder Phil Driver insightfully framed it, "Projects create assets or results, which citizens use to create benefits for themselves and others."[1] Benefits are not guaranteed by project closure—they only materialize when people engage with and leverage the project's outcomes. Leaders must internalize this truth: their job is not just to deliver assets but to ensure that assets lead to adoption, use, and measurable impact.

Positive impact—whether financial, operational, social, or environmental—is the real scoreboard. Success is not ticking off milestones; it's leaving behind a reality where stakeholders, employees, or customers can clearly say, "This is better because of what we did."

SMART Benefits. As with strategic purpose, benefits must be specific, measurable, and time-bound; otherwise, they cannot guide decision-making, resource allocation, or course correction during a project's execution.

Our research shows how much progress still needs to be made: only 18 percent of organizations require mandatory, quantifiable benefit plans for every project. The rest either impose such discipline only for major programs or operate with informal expectations at best. But without a formal benefits framework, organizations run the risk of projects that consume resources but deliver little of the promised impact.

Leaders must therefore insist on three nonnegotiables when defining their benefit plan:

- *Clear metrics.* What exactly will improve (revenue, costs, satisfaction scores, carbon emissions, etc.)?

- *Timelines.* When will these benefits be realized, and what interim signals will indicate progress?

- *Accountability.* Who owns the realization of benefits, not just the delivery of outputs?

At the same time, leaders must avoid two traps: overstating vague, unprovable benefits or ignoring strategic value simply because it is hard to measure. Benefit plans should not be afterthoughts or check-box artifacts. If your transformation benefits are not measurable and time-bound, they are just aspirations—not real outcomes.

OpenSky Data Systems—a digital transformation firm that works primarily with public-sector organizations to deliver data-driven, citizen-focused solutions—exemplifies how close contact with end users during project design and delivery helps ensure that benefits remain grounded in real-world needs.[2] In its work with the Dublin Region Homeless Executive, OpenSky, which defines benefits as tangible, measurable improvements tied directly to strategic and operational outcomes, developed the PASS system to streamline bed allocation and case management across eighty-plus agencies, enabling faster service delivery and improving coordination. By shaping benefit definitions with the insights and expectations of those who will ultimately live with the results, OpenSky's approach increases the likelihood that projects will produce true, sustained value.

From Top-Down to Bottom-Up Benefit Setting: A Four-Stage Leadership Framework. In a PDO, leaders must shift the definition of the project's benefits from a top-down setting to a bottom-up, participatory approach. When benefits are imposed from above without engaging those closest to execution or end users, misalignment and frustration are inevitable. Local teams may perceive benefits as irrelevant, impractical, or unachievable, sapping motivation and weakening project traction.

A structured, four-stage framework allows leaders to institutionalize benefit realization, accelerate impact, and build stronger connections between strategy and execution.

1. *Identify and align.* Leaders must drive early, inclusive conversations to collaboratively define intended benefits with key stakeholders, connecting them clearly to strategic ambitions and local operational realities. Tools like benefits cards—a checklist I developed to collaboratively identify the primary quantifiable benefits of a project with key stakeholders—can help you clearly visualize the connection between project activities and their intended outcomes. When a global food company launched a project to redesign its packaging for sustainability, senior leaders didn't dictate the benefit from headquarters. Instead, they involved local plant managers, marketing teams, and sustainability officers. Together, they defined two measurable benefits: a 30 percent reduction in plastic use within eighteen months and a 10 percent boost in brand trust scores among eco-conscious consumers.

2. *Plan and commit.* Benefit planning must be treated with the same rigor as delivery planning. Leaders should ensure that every major project has a formal benefit plan, detailing milestones, responsible owners, measurement approaches, and assumptions about external factors. One regional health-care provider launching a telemedicine project created a benefit plan identifying measurable improvements: reducing patient wait times by 20 percent and increasing patient satisfaction by 15 percent within the first year. These benefits were tied to specific KPIs, tracked monthly, and reviewed by the executive steering committee.

3. *Track and adapt.* Leaders must treat benefit tracking as a central, ongoing part of project governance—not just a box to tick at the end of a project. Steering committees should prioritize discussing benefits, progress, and ways to accelerate impact. While traditional metrics like budget, time, and risk remain important, a focus on outcomes keeps stakeholders engaged. Celebrating

achieved benefits builds pride and reinforces a culture of execution. In a smart-city pilot project, leaders initially expected that adding e-bike stations would increase public transit ridership by 10 percent. Six months into execution, usage data showed slower-than-expected uptake. Leadership quickly intervened, reallocating marketing resources to promote first-mile/last-mile connectivity and adjusting the benefit targets realistically based on real-world behavior.

4. *Accelerate and amplify.* Transformational leaders must continually ask: "How can we accelerate impact and scale the success of benefits?" This requires activating an exponential mindset (introduced in chapter 1)—challenging teams to find ways to achieve greater benefits faster, remove internal bottlenecks, and extend successful initiatives more broadly across the enterprise. For example, after piloting a successful paperless claims process that cut turnaround time by 50 percent, an insurance company's leadership immediately prioritized expanding the model across all business units within six months rather than waiting for slow sequential rollouts.

The Golden Rule on Benefits. If you and your key contributors cannot define measurable, time-bound benefits for the project, it's a clear signal that the case for value isn't strong enough. It's often better to delay—or even cancel—the launch until the benefits are clarified and owned. Without this foundation, alignment will be weak, engagement will fade, and execution will drift.

Ruthless Prioritization of a Few High-Level Initiatives

Not every idea deserves to become a project. One of the defining leadership capabilities in PDOs is the ability to say no to initiatives, ideas, and projects that do not meet the highest strategic threshold. Without this discipline, organizations risk scattering their focus across too many parallel efforts, diluting impact and slowing transformational progress.

Many projects start too early—before the idea has matured, before the environment is ready, or before the organization has built the necessary capabilities to succeed. In a *Harvard Business Review* article, Whitney Johnson and I argued that one of the most overlooked leadership disciplines is knowing when *not* to start a project.[3] Giving ideas time to evolve, gather internal support, and develop proof points increases the chances that projects launched will actually deliver transformational outcomes.

Steve Jobs showed this disciplined leadership approach in the development of the iPhone. The original idea for a smartphone was discussed with Jobs as early as 2001. While he acknowledged it was a brilliant idea, he made a critical leadership decision: he said no to launching a project immediately. Apple needed first to win the music battle with the iPod and iTunes—and focus was paramount. Instead of starting a formal project, Jobs authorized a small, dedicated team to quietly explore the idea, build internal know-how, and push the technology boundaries. Only in 2004, after Apple had secured its leadership in digital music, did Jobs give the green light to what became known as the Purple Project— the code name for the first iPhone development.

The way Jobs drove the iPhone project embodies many of the project-driven leadership principles discussed in this book—focus on a few critical priorities, fully dedicated teams, ruthless resource protection, and top-level sponsorship—remains one of the most remarkable examples of strategic prioritization and project-driven execution in modern business history. It also exemplifies the new role of CEOs in project-driven organizations. (See the sidebar, "The Role of the Chief Executive Officer.")

Consequences of Poor Prioritization:
A Strain on Middle Managers and Employees

Our recent research highlights significant gaps in how organizations approach prioritization in their project-driven transformations. Only 12 percent of respondents reported practicing extreme prioritization by focusing on a select few strategic initiatives—typically up to three

The Role of the Chief Executive Officer

In a PDO, the role of the CEO undergoes a profound transformation. Traditionally seen as the guardian of long-term strategy and shareholder value, the CEO must now also serve as the chief architect of organizational focus—ensuring that strategy is executed through a coherent, dynamic portfolio of projects. In this new model, vision alone is not enough; CEOs must take active ownership of how strategic priorities are translated into action through projects.

The CEO's role complements that of other C-suite leaders: while COOs ensure operational alignment, CFOs oversee project-based resource allocation and performance management, and CHROs shape the project-ready workforce, the CEO is uniquely positioned to orchestrate these capabilities around a unifying vision and enterprise-wide priorities. In a world of finite resources and limitless ambition, the CEO's ability to say "no" is as critical as their ability to inspire. Without clear prioritization from the top, organizations risk fragmentation, project overload, and a disconnect between vision and execution.

A critical partnership emerges between the CEO and the chief project officer (CPO)—a role designed to oversee enterprise-level project governance, portfolio integration, and strategic alignment. The CPO acts as the CEO's execution partner, ensuring that the project portfolio reflects real strategic intent and that resources, capabilities, and leadership attention are consistently aligned with top priorities. When this partnership functions effectively, it transforms the CEO's vision into tangible, high-impact outcomes across the organization.

In a PDO, the CEO must:

- **Redesign the organization for project-driven execution.** CEOs lead the transition from operations- or agile-centric models to a fully project-driven enterprise. This means embedding projects at the center of structure, decision-making, and strategy execution— breaking down silos and aligning governance and culture to support cross-functional delivery at scale.

(continued)

- **Drive the shift from operations- to project-focused work.** CEOs champion the transformation of core business operations to align with project-based delivery. This is one of the most challenging yet necessary shifts: moving the organization away from a hierarchical, top-down culture, legacy processes, and efficiency-driven models. The goal is to build flexible, outcome-oriented operations that support strategic initiatives and cross-functional teams while enabling both projects and operations to deliver continuous and measurable value.

- **Prioritize with strategic discipline.** To ensure focus on what truly matters, CEOs must establish and uphold enterprise-wide prioritization systems. Just as critically, they must lead by example—regularly stopping or defunding lower-impact initiatives to reinforce the strategic clarity and agility that define project-driven leadership.

- **Sponsor with time and visibility.** Rather than standing apart, project-driven CEOs devote a significant portion of their own time—at least half—to personally sponsoring the most important transformation initiatives. This sponsorship involves sustained engagement with project teams, intervention to remove obstacles, and consistent reinforcement of urgency and value delivery.

- **Build a high-performing executive team.** CEOs must create a cohesive C-suite where each leader owns a key enabler of the PDO. Every C-suite member should sponsor and actively drive at least one strategic project. They must foster mutual accountability, cross-functional collaboration, and unified leadership across all major initiatives.

- **Empower and reward project teams.** CEOs push authority, benefit ownership, and decision-making to the edge—where work happens. At the same time, they build systems that recognize and reward team performance based on value delivered, not hierarchy or effort alone.

- **Anchor transformation in value creation.** CEOs will ensure that every strategic project contributes measurable value—whether growth, innovation, or operational excellence—and track that value continuously. Leveraging AI-powered insights, CEOs can shift from relying on lagging reports to predictive, real-time decision-making, reinforcing focus and responsiveness.

In the project economy, CEOs are not just visionaries—they are orchestrators of transformation. By focusing their time, leadership, and attention on enabling strategy execution, they make project success not the exception, but the expectation.

projects at any time—to maximize impact. Meanwhile, 32 percent reported high prioritization, managing around ten initiatives while attempting to maintain focus. The majority, 37 percent, operate with a broader project scope, juggling more than ten strategic initiatives, which can lead to diluted attention and resources. A further 16 percent indicated minimal prioritization, selecting projects without a strict limit, largely based on immediate needs rather than strategic alignment. Alarmingly, 2 percent admitted to having no prioritization process at all, approving all proposed projects regardless of strategic focus. These findings reveal a substantial opportunity for organizations to refine their approach to prioritization.

The lack of prioritization has cascading effects throughout an organization, particularly impacting middle management and employees. When leaders constantly launch new projects without a corresponding effort to finish or eliminate others, it results in a flood of initiatives, each competing for limited time, attention, and resources. This environment of project overload has several negative consequences:

- *Fragmented focus.* Middle managers and employees often find themselves stretched thin, juggling corporate and local initiatives with competing priorities. This fragmented focus reduces their effectiveness and leads to subpar project outcomes.

- *Decreased engagement and morale.* A constant influx of projects with unclear priorities can lead to burnout and disengagement. Employees feel that their efforts are spread too thin to make a real impact, leading to a sense of frustration and futility.

- *Lack of cross-departmental collaboration.* Critical expertise, insights, and resources are not shared across teams, resulting in duplicated work, conflicting goals, and wasted opportunities.

- *Diluted strategy execution.* When too many projects are launched without rigorous prioritization, the organization's capacity to execute effectively is compromised. This leads to a fragmented portfolio where even high-value initiatives struggle to gain traction, draining resources and weakening overall strategic delivery.

Only a high level of disciplined prioritization ensures that every project undertaken truly earns its place by advancing the organization's most critical strategic goals.

The Hierarchy of Purpose: A Framework for Ruthless Prioritization

To help leaders prioritize effectively, a *hierarchy of purpose* provides a structured approach by assessing each project across five critical dimensions—*purpose, priorities, projects, people,* and *performance.*[4] By using these dimensions, leaders can ensure that every project is aligned with the organization's strategic objectives and worthy of the resources it requires.

Repsol is a global energy company headquartered in Spain, operating across more than twenty-five countries and engaged in the exploration, production, refining, and distribution of oil, natural gas, and low-carbon energy solutions. Faced with the challenge of remaining competitive in a rapidly evolving industry, Repsol launched an ambitious digital program to drive operational efficiency, innovation, and sustainability across its operations.[5] The program, forecasted to generate €1 billion (later adjusted to €800 million) in additional cash flow by 2022, demonstrates how a purpose-centered approach to project management can lead to remarkable outcomes.

Applying the hierarchy of purpose, Repsol structured the program to align with corporate goals, help scale projects effectively, and generate substantial financial returns. This framework helped the company allocate resources, build engagement, and drive strategic impact across its portfolio of initiatives.

First, Repsol's digital transformation was driven by a clear purpose: to enhance operational efficiency, foster innovation, and secure a competitive advantage in the energy sector. This purpose was directly tied to the company's vision of sustainability and resilience in an industry facing significant technological and regulatory changes. By setting a purpose-driven financial target, Repsol motivated stakeholders across the organization, ensuring that each digital initiative aligned with the company's vision for a sustainable and profitable future.

Repsol also established clear priorities within its digital program, concentrating on initiatives that could drive significant cost savings and operational improvements. With a five-stage funding model, Repsol carefully allocated resources to high-potential projects, prioritizing initiatives that offered substantial strategic and financial returns, ensuring that Repsol's resources were focused on projects with the greatest impact and enhancing the program's efficiency and effectiveness.

The digital transformation comprised a portfolio of over 450 projects, each strategically designed to advance Repsol's goals. By defining each project clearly within the digital program framework, the company ensured that initiatives in areas like data analytics, AI, and process optimization were aligned with broader strategic objectives. The establishment of a Digital Product Factory (DPF) enabled seamless collaboration between development and deployment teams, allowing projects to move efficiently from concept to implementation. This structured approach ensured that Repsol's digital projects contributed cohesively to the overall transformation.

One prominent example is Waylet, Repsol's mobile payment and loyalty app, which scaled rapidly to reach over seven million users, exemplifying how cross-functional collaboration and digital platforms can generate real customer and business value.[6]

Understanding that successful transformation depends on both technology and talent, Repsol invested in people—building a digitally skilled workforce. It established dedicated teams and fostered a culture of innovation, providing employees with training in areas like data analytics and AI. Centralized technology hubs and the DPF facilitated knowledge sharing, empowering employees to actively contribute to the program's success. The Waylet initiative reinforced this approach by embedding innovation into frontline operations, sustaining momentum through strong team engagement and user-centric design.

Finally, Repsol's commitment to performance was fundamental to its digital program. Each project was monitored against specific performance metrics, with regular evaluations to ensure alignment with the €800 million cash flow target. Waylet alone delivered over €100 million in customer savings in the first nine months of 2023, with fuel discounts reaching €0.40 per liter—clear indicators of its tangible impact. By establishing clear benchmarks for success, Repsol was able to assess which projects were delivering value and make timely adjustments as needed. This focus on performance ensured accountability and helped Repsol achieve its ambitious financial goals, demonstrating the tangible impact of its digital initiatives.

By applying the five Ps of the hierarchy of purpose, Repsol structured its digital transformation to drive strategic alignment, foster employee engagement, and deliver substantial financial returns. This approach enabled Repsol to focus on high-impact initiatives, ensuring that every project contributed meaningfully to the company's overarching goals of innovation, efficiency, and sustainability.

Prioritizing Project Capacity Using a Balanced Portfolio Approach

Not all projects are created equal—and neither should they be treated as such when allocating your organization's finite resources. One of the most effective ways to strategically manage your project portfolio is by classifying projects into three main types—efficiency, sustaining, and transformative—and then aligning your capacity (resources, number of initiatives, budgets, and leadership attention) accordingly.[7]

Recommended Capacity Allocation. A practical and proven rule of thumb is to distribute your project capacity as follows:

- *Efficiency projects: 50 percent of capacity.* These projects form the operational backbone of the organization. They are typically lower in complexity and uncertainty, covering areas such as process improvements, compliance, IT upgrades, and other incremental enhancements. Because they are vital to keeping the organization running smoothly, they should dominate your portfolio, but not crowd it out. These are your operations projects and should be executed with a high success rate.

- *Sustaining projects: 30 percent of capacity.* These initiatives help grow and evolve your business. They include the development of new products, services, and business capabilities. Sustaining projects require more investment in planning, stakeholder alignment, and risk management. Their success rate will be lower than efficiency projects by design, as they stretch the organization into new areas.

- *Transformative projects: 10 percent of capacity.* These are your moon shots—the bold bets that aim to redefine the future of the business. They involve high levels of uncertainty and complexity, such as launching disruptive business models or experimenting with breakthrough technologies. Their success rate should be low by nature (around 30 percent), but their potential payoff is enormous. They also demand a different mindset: a culture of experimentation, learning, and rapid iteration.

- *Reserved capacity: 10 percent.* Importantly, leaving 10 percent of your capacity uncommitted allows your organization to remain agile and responsive. This buffer enables you to act on unforeseen opportunities or urgent challenges without derailing existing priorities or overwhelming teams.

Using the typology shown in figure 4-2, you can balance your portfolio across different levels of complexity and uncertainty, ensuring that your organization runs efficiently today while preparing for growth and innovation tomorrow.

The Risks of an Unbalanced Portfolio. When a portfolio skews too heavily toward one project type, risks emerge:

- *Too many efficiency projects can lead to stagnation.* The organization becomes overly focused on short-term, incremental

FIGURE 4-2

Prioritizing project capacity using a balanced portfolio approach

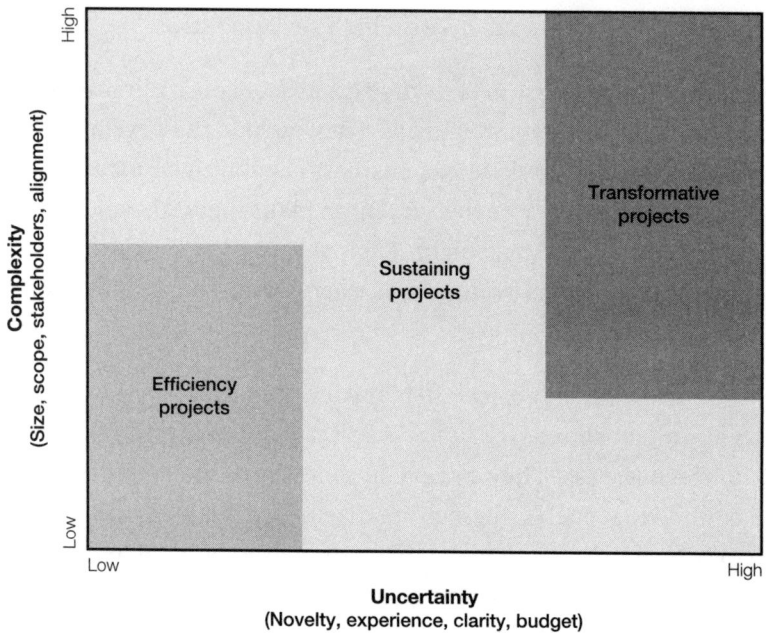

Source: Antonio Nieto-Rodriguez, *Harvard Business Review Project Management Handbook: How to Launch, Lead, and Sponsor Successful Projects* (Boston: Harvard Business Review Press, 2021).

improvements and operational stability, often at the expense of innovation and long-term strategic growth.

- *Too many sustaining projects can stretch the organization's focus and dilute execution.* With too many growth initiatives competing for attention, resources may be spread too thin, resulting in lackluster performance, missed synergies, and strategic drift.

- *Too many transformative projects can destabilize the organization.* These high-risk, high-reward initiatives require experimentation, patience, and a tolerance for failure—conditions that are difficult to sustain at scale. When overemphasized, they can create confusion, strategic inconsistency, and misalignment with current capabilities.

- *Overcommitting overall capacity—pushing beyond 90–100 percent utilization—creates systemic risk.* With no slack in the system, the organization loses its ability to absorb shocks, pivot quickly, or address emerging priorities. This often results in project delays, quality erosion, and employee burnout or disengagement.

By actively managing your project mix and aligning capacity with strategic intent, you create a portfolio that is both resilient and future-focused. This disciplined approach ensures your organization can continue to perform today while building what it needs for tomorrow.

Accelerating Project Completion to Drive Ruthless Prioritization

Ruthless prioritization isn't just about choosing the right projects—it's about finishing them decisively. Leadership focus cannot scale if strategic initiatives linger endlessly, draining attention and resources that should fuel the next wave of transformation. (See the sidebar, "Seven Steps for Performing an Effective Project Closure for Executive Sponsors.")

As we saw in chapter 1, building the habit of stopping low-value projects quickly is vital. But at the leadership level, the discipline must go further: ensuring that the most critical, strategic initiatives are completed thoroughly and at speed. Otherwise, even the best prioritization frameworks falter, and the organization's momentum stalls.

Accelerating project completion does not mean rushing deliverables or sacrificing quality. It's about embedding structural clarity around what "finished" means, ensuring that benefits are realized, and freeing up leadership attention for other transformational initiatives. The gains from faster closure are critical:

- *Sharper strategic focus.* Resources stay concentrated where they create the greatest value, rather than being diluted across too many initiatives.

- *Enhanced organizational agility.* Leaders can pivot faster in response to market shifts, new technologies, or competitive threats.

- *Increased transformation velocity.* Momentum compounds when projects are finished cleanly, lessons are absorbed rapidly, and new waves of strategic work are launched with renewed energy.

- *Strengthened organizational credibility.* Consistently delivering on promises builds trust internally with employees and externally with customers, investors, and partners.

Seven Steps for Performing an Effective Project Closure for Executive Sponsors

Leaders who want to drive faster closure of high-priority projects must embed seven practical behaviors into their leadership playbook:

- **Define completion in terms of value, not tasks.** Closure isn't about ticking off deliverables—it's about confirming that the project's intended benefits have been achieved.

- **Embed exit strategies from the beginning.** Even the most critical initiatives must have built-in decision checkpoints. Leaders should deliberately include "off-ramps" to reassess strategic fit, market shifts, or internal capability gaps.

- **Structure projects for shorter, value-driven cycles.** Break major initiatives into smaller, focused projects lasting three to six months. This time-bounded approach promotes urgency, sharpens focus on value creation, and makes project closure more visible and manageable.

- **Prioritize smaller, value-centric deliverables.** Instead of long timelines with deferred value, structure major initiatives into focused, high-impact phases. Deliver value early and often, and maintain momentum through visible results.

- **Host a visible, high-energy closure meeting.** Use closure meetings to publicly recognize success, connect project outcomes to strategic goals, and reinforce that transformation is tangible.

- **Capture and share lessons at speed.** Don't delay learning. Facilitate concise, forward-looking reflections that capture what can be applied to future projects, turning every closure into a launchpad for faster, better execution next time.

- **Celebrate team contributions and future potential.** Teams that deliver prioritized projects on time, realize benefits, and formally close initiatives should be celebrated. Rewards tied to closure reinforce accountability and sharpen future execution speed.

- **Redeploy resources deliberately.** Release people, budgets, and assets thoughtfully and visibly, linking the redeployment to new priorities.

Activating Sponsors to Champion Execution

Prioritization and closing projects faster alone aren't enough to drive successful transformation initiatives. Turning strategy into results requires leaders to fully step into their role as project sponsors—instilling an entrepreneurship mindset, actively championing execution, clearing roadblocks, and keeping teams aligned through complexity.

In my experience, around 25 percent of a project's success is directly tied to the involvement of a committed executive sponsor. And this level of engagement is particularly crucial for large-scale, cross-functional, and cross-regional projects—those that have the potential to shape the organization's future and require sustained support from the top.

Throughout my project management career, I've observed that having an effective sponsor was likely to be a matter of luck. In rare instances, I've had the privilege of working with highly involved sponsors who regularly engaged with the team, facilitated decision-making, and proactively removed barriers, greatly accelerating project momentum. However, more often than not, I found myself leading projects with limited or inconsistent sponsor involvement. This was rarely due to a lack of commitment. Many senior leaders are deeply dedicated to their organizations, but their daily operational responsibilities make it challenging to dedicate time and attention to transformative projects.

The Pitfalls in Building Project-Driven Strategic Prioritization

Strategic prioritization is one of the most critical acts of leadership in a project-driven organization—it shapes where time, talent, and capital flow. However, in practice, prioritization is often vague, political, or inconsistent. Leaders fail to provide strategic clarity, projects are launched without measurable benefits, organizations try to do too much at once, and executive sponsors fail to actively support the work they champion on paper. These breakdowns not only waste time and re-sources, they also erode trust in the very idea of strategic focus. Let's look at three of the most common pitfalls that prevent prioritization from becoming a true driver of transformation:

Launching Projects without a Clear Purpose or Measurable Benefits

Leaders often greenlight projects based on ambition, buzzwords, or peer pressure without establishing clarity around purpose and measurable outcomes. Teams may feel energized early on, but enthusiasm quickly fades when misalignment grows, stakeholders lose confidence, and mea-suring success becomes nearly impossible.

A global financial firm launched a major customer experience initiative to "reinvent service delivery," but leadership failed to define clear out-comes up front. As teams pushed forward, conflicting priorities emerged and resources were spread across unrelated activities. The effort eventu-ally stalled due to a lack of traction and executive support.

Spreading Resources Too Thin by Prioritizing Everything

Project-driven leadership demands saying no more than yes, yet leaders often struggle to make hard trade-offs, leading to an "everything matters" culture. The result is overloaded teams, shallow execution, and underper-formance across the board.

WeWork, a coworking space provider, experienced rapid global expan-sion in the late 2010s.[a] Fueled by substantial venture capital investments, it aggressively opened new locations worldwide, reaching 777 sites across 39 countries by mid-2019. However, this rapid growth outpaced sustain-able demand and strained the company's resources. The lack of disciplined prioritization and overcommitment to expansion without thorough evaluation of project viability led to significant financial challenges that were compounded by the Covid-19 pandemic. In November 2023, it filed for bankruptcy.

Treating Sponsorship as Symbolic Rather Than Strategic

Many leaders treat project sponsorship ceremonially—appearing at kickoffs or steering committees and then stepping away. But without consistent executive engagement, teams struggle to escalate key issues, remove critical bottlenecks, or secure resources.

A major retailer launched a digital transformation program with high-level executive backing. However, the sponsor rarely engaged beyond the formal monthly checkpoints. When a vendor integration roadblock emerged, the lack of executive support delayed resolution for months, derailing the overall timeline.

These pitfalls reflect a more profound leadership challenge: applying old leadership habits to a new reality. Becoming truly project-driven requires a fundamental shift in how leaders prioritize, commit, and execute. When prioritization is clear, focused, and actively supported, it becomes a powerful transformation engine, turning strategy into results.

NOTE

a. David Love, "WeWork's Bankruptcy: A Tale of Rapid Expansion and Unfulfilled Profitability," Quiver Quantitative, November 7, 2023, https://www.quiverquant.com/news/WeWork%27s%20Bankruptcy%3A%20A%20Tale%20of%20Rapid%20Expansion%20and%20Unfulfilled%20Profitability.

Our recent research highlights the reality of this challenge: 31 percent of sponsors dedicate less than half a day each week to their projects, while only 14 percent invest more than two days weekly. This discrepancy indicates a significant gap between the level of sponsorship needed and the amount of time executives can realistically provide. Transformation leaders must address this gap by advocating for stronger executive engagement and by building mechanisms to sustain sponsor involvement over the course of high-stakes projects.

When I spoke with Kate Duchene, CEO of RGP, about their multiyear technology transformation, her reflections really stayed with me. She emphasized that strong project leadership alone isn't enough—you need relentless senior executive involvement all the way through. "You have to show up," she told me. "Not just at the kickoff, but over and over, at every critical point, especially when things get tough."[8]

At RGP, leaders kept the transformation alive by celebrating milestones, being radically transparent about progress, and constantly reinforcing the strategic purpose behind the change. They weren't afraid to pivot, refine priorities, and even close projects that no longer served the larger goal—all decisions that required visible, courageous leadership. Duchene's experience is a powerful reminder: real sponsorship is not about lending your name to a steering committee; it's about lending your energy, your voice, and your presence when it matters most. (See the sidebar, "Eleven Tough Questions to Ask Yourself as an Executive Sponsor.")

Roger Martin, a prominent business thinker, explored the essential role of senior executives in project leadership in his influential article, "Rethinking the Decision Factory."[9] He argued that almost all corporate and head office roles are fundamentally about leading projects. Strategic transformations, in particular, require more than passive oversight; they need dedicated time, attention, and decision-making from the top.

Why Active Sponsorship Matters

Active sponsorship provides several critical advantages to transformation projects. First, actively involved sponsors bring decision-making agility to their teams. They can make timely, impactful decisions that keep the project moving forward. Without senior input, projects can become bogged down, awaiting approval or facing conflicting priorities that delay progress. Sponsors who are present and engaged can address issues immediately, prevent roadblocks, and align resources swiftly.

As sponsors, senior executives align and focus the project. They bring an understanding of the broader organizational strategy, ensuring that

Eleven Tough Questions to Ask Yourself as an Executive Sponsor

Projects that have the potential to shape the organization's future cannot succeed if they are not supported by strong executive sponsors. As a sponsor, you need to ask:

- **Accountability.** Who's responsible for the transformation?

- **Competencies.** Do I have the competencies to sponsor the project?

- **Commitment.** Can I dedicate enough time to support the team (two to four hours per week)? If not, why?

- **Alignment.** Is the executive team 100 percent supportive of the project? If not, why not?

- **Purpose.** Is it clear to me why we are doing this project and can I explain it compellingly?

- **Benefits.** Have the key benefits been defined jointly with the key contributors and impacted stakeholders?

- **Value.** Have the transformation benefits been quantified? If not, why not?

- **Belief.** Am I certain the transformation will be successful and deliver the benefits—or, if doubts persist while it's underway, am I prepared to terminate it promptly if that is in the organization's best interest?

- **Prioritization.** Is the transformation treated as the top priority across the organization—above other projects and daily operations—and has that priority been explicitly communicated?

- **Project manager.** Have I appointed a fully committed project leader who is empowered to challenge me and drive the initiative forward? If not, why not?

- **Resources.** Have we dedicated enough fully dedicated resources the transformation? If not, why not?

projects align with long-term goals. This alignment is essential for transformational projects, as it provides clarity and direction for teams who may otherwise struggle to understand the project's impact on the larger corporate mission.

Sponsors can also leverage their influence to secure necessary resources, whether financial, technological, or human. They are also in a position to remove barriers, breaking down organizational silos or bypassing bureaucratic hurdles that would otherwise impede project progress.

Finally, strong sponsorship brings enhanced accountability to teams. Active sponsors can hold project teams accountable for achieving milestones and meeting timelines. This accountability is vital for maintaining momentum, especially on complex projects with multiple stakeholders. It signals to all involved that the project is a top priority and that support from the highest levels of the organization is present.

A Sponsor's Time Commitment in Project Success

One of the most effective ways a leader can accelerate transformation is by dedicating focused time to it. Even allocating one full day each week to a strategic initiative can significantly influence its trajectory. When a CEO or senior executive consistently shows up for a project, participating in updates, addressing obstacles, and reinforcing priorities, the visibility, motivation, and support it generates within the team are profound. People feel their work matters. They stay more focused, aligned, and energized by the sense that leadership is walking the path with them.

Steve Jobs famously exemplified this during the development of the first iPhone. Despite his role as Apple's CEO, he devoted up to two days a week to the project. When asked why, he replied, "Running the business is easy. Building the future of Apple is where a CEO should spend most of their time." His commitment galvanized the team, removing barriers and clarifying priorities in a way that contributed directly to one of the most transformative products in technology history.

I've seen firsthand how consistent leadership involvement drives results. In one organization I advised, the CEO set aside Fridays exclusively for transformation work. This steady engagement led to sharper execution and faster progress, as teams prepared to deliver meaningful updates each week. When leaders visibly invest their time in transformation, they send a powerful signal: this work matters. And in doing so, they help embed a project-driven mindset throughout the organization.

In essence, when leaders actively invest their time in transformation initiatives, they not only drive results but also set a precedent. So the real question is: *How much time are you really spending on your most important projects, and are you prepared to invest more?*

Challenges to Securing Active Sponsorship

While the benefits of active sponsorship are clear, securing it remains a challenge. Many executives are caught in the demands of daily operations, making it difficult for them to commit time to transformation efforts. Additionally, the role of a project sponsor is not always clearly defined, leading to inconsistent levels of engagement. Some sponsors may not fully understand their responsibilities or underestimate their involvement's impact on the project's outcome.

To address this, organizations should formalize the project sponsor's role, outlining specific responsibilities and expectations. Sponsors should understand that their role goes beyond simply approving budgets or attending occasional updates. Their active participation is crucial for resolving issues, aligning stakeholders, and ensuring that the project remains strategically relevant. Providing training or mentorship on effective sponsorship can also help leaders understand the importance of their role and equip them with the tools to fulfill it effectively.

Becoming a Top-Performing Sponsor

Truly effective sponsors are genuinely committed to a project's success. They engage actively and bring a strategic mindset to accelerating benefits and championing execution. According to the Project Management Institute, sponsors who actively advocate for their teams and secure critical resources see project success rates increase by up to 40 percent compared to hands-off sponsors.[10]

Here are essential actions that senior leaders can take to maximize their impact and drive transformation projects toward successful outcomes:

- *Master the strategic purpose and benefits of the project.* Top-performing sponsors understand the project's purpose and core goals and how they align with the organization's broader strategic objectives. This deep understanding enables sponsors to provide informed support, prioritize resources effectively, and clearly communicate the project's purpose to other stakeholders.

- *Show up consistently with visible, active sponsorship.* Visibility and consistent engagement are fundamental to effective sponsorship. A top-performing sponsor attends regular updates, provides feedback, and participates in critical decisions. This visibility signals the project's importance, motivating team members to remain committed.

- *Clear the path for execution.* Exceptional sponsors go beyond providing resources—they proactively eliminate the organizational friction that can stall execution. Whether it's navigating bureaucracy, securing cross-functional buy-in, or making swift decisions during escalations, sponsors who act as advocates clear the path so teams can focus on delivery.

- *Encourage cocreation and flatten hierarchies.* High-performing project environments thrive on collaboration, not command-and-control. Instead of imposing top-down directives, sponsors cocreate project scopes, goals, and benefits alongside their teams. By structuring projects where the best ideas win—regardless of rank—organizations unlock creativity and significantly improve the likelihood of breakthrough outcomes.

- *Drive a culture of ownership, responsibility, and results.* Top-performing sponsors foster a culture of accountability by setting clear expectations and holding both the team and themselves accountable for meeting milestones. At Tata Steel's Phase II Kalinganagar expansion—where capacity was increased from three million tons a year to eight million—this was supported by structured milestone reviews and cross-functional coordination, ensuring transparency and on-schedule delivery.[11]

- *Lead clear, credible communication and stakeholder alignment.* Effective communication is a cornerstone of successful sponsorship. Top sponsors provide transparent, consistent updates to both the project team and other senior stakeholders. A study by McKinsey found that projects with strong sponsor communication had a 25 percent higher success rate. In PDOs, clear communication from the sponsor fosters alignment and helps to avoid misunderstandings that could derail progress.[12]

- *Take a long-term view to sustain momentum.* Top sponsors focus not only on achieving immediate project goals but also on sustaining long-term benefits. They actively work to integrate the project's outcomes into the organization's operational framework to ensure lasting value. Involvement in the handover process and ensuring accountability for post-project benefits are crucial for avoiding "zombie projects" and maximizing the project's long-term impact.

By understanding the project's purpose, staying visible, empowering teams, fostering accountability, communicating effectively, and taking a long-term perspective, senior executives can move beyond passive oversight and become true enablers of transformative change. In a project-driven world, such sponsorship is essential for organizations striving to achieve sustainable growth, agility, and innovation.

Conclusion

In this chapter, we explored the leadership disciplines required to drive effective project prioritization in the transformation age. Clear and courageous leadership in defining purpose and measurable benefits help teams stay aligned and engaged. Ruthlessly focusing leadership attention on high-value initiatives ensures that resources are concentrated where they can deliver the most significant impact. And engaged sponsors—those who show their commitment with daily action—provide the momentum and support necessary to turn strategic ambitions into results.

Together, these practices form the foundation of a more focused, accountable, and outcome-driven organization. When prioritization becomes a continuous, strategic discipline—not a once-a-year exercise—leaders unlock greater clarity, faster execution, and more meaningful results from their transformation efforts.

In the next chapter, we build further on this leadership foundation by turning to project-driven human resources.

CHAPTER 5

Project-Driven Human Resources

Haier's decentralized structure has dissolved traditional distinctions between project and operational roles. The company operates through over four thousand MEs, each functioning autonomously with the agility to allocate resources swiftly to strategic projects. This approach exemplifies a new distributed leadership model, where decision rights and accountability are pushed as close to the customer as possible. This *dynamic resource allocation* enables Haier to respond promptly to market changes and user needs, ensuring that resources are directed where they can create the most value. For instance, in 2024, they introduced ninety-day project cycles and a "marketplace of opportunities," allowing talent to flow to the most impactful initiatives, ensuring that people, not just funding, are allocated where they create the most value.[1]

Haier places a strong emphasis on transforming groups of individuals into *cohesive, high-performing project teams*. Central to this is the concept of psychological safety, which Haier fosters by empowering employees to act as entrepreneurs within their MEs. Leadership at Haier is defined by enabling others—building a system where team leaders at every level feel ownership over outcomes, not just tasks. This practice encourages open communication, risk-taking, and innovation, as team members feel secure in sharing ideas without fear of retribution. The company's culture promotes collaboration and mutual accountability, enhancing team performance and engagement.

Recognizing the rapid pace of change in the modern business environment, Haier is also committed to *upskilling its workforce to ensure future readiness*. The company encourages all employees to develop skills that enhance agility and entrepreneurship, essential traits in any project-driven model. Middle management is reimagined not as a layer of control, but as an accelerant to transformation. Acting as coaches, managers support their teams in navigating complex projects, foster a culture of continuous learning and adaptation, and guide teams to project success.

A s project work becomes the primary vehicle for value creation, traditional HR models—built for predictability and static roles—are being reimagined. A chief transformation officer at one of Europe's largest energy companies recently shared with me a painfully honest truth: if she could, she would need to fire forty-five thousand employees and start over with talent equipped with strong transformation capabilities. Of course, that's neither feasible nor responsible—but it starkly illustrates the dramatic challenge many leaders are now facing. The only viable path forward is to upskill and reorient the existing workforce to meet the demands of today's project-driven organization.

Similarly, a client in the high-end spirits industry approached me after I trained sixty of its top transformation and project leaders. They asked if I could extend this training to eleven thousand employees across the entire organization. They recognized that middle managers and employees increasingly spend more time working on projects yet lack training or a shared language for such work across their global network.

In this chapter, we explore how leaders are reshaping their approach to talent to thrive in the transformation age. Haier's ME model shows what's possible when employees are empowered to act like entrepreneurs. Meanwhile, leading companies across industries—from energy to consumer goods—are recognizing that transformation isn't about replacing their workforce but equipping it. Whether it's retraining those forty-five thousand employees or creating a shared project language for eleven thousand people across a global network, the message is clear: to lead through transformation, organizations must build a workforce that is flexible, future-ready, and deeply connected to the mission of each initiative.

We will also examine the evolving roles of senior leaders in a project-driven organization. The COO, CFO, and CHRO are no longer just stewards of operations, finance, and people—they are transformation enablers. Their ability to collaboratively direct talent, investment, and attention toward strategic initiatives is critical. Alongside them, a new leadership role is emerging: the chief project officer (CPO). Tasked with aligning project execution with enterprise strategy, the CPO becomes a central figure in orchestrating how work gets done. This shift in leadership mindset is essential, as to move fast and adapt continuously, organizations need not only structural agility but also leaders who can connect people, strategy, and execution at scale.

With this context in mind, we explore three critical shifts required to build a high-performing, project-ready workforce (see figure 5-1): adopting dynamic resource allocation models, building high-performing, collaborative project teams, and upskilling for the future of work and leadership.

These shifts are not just about HR practices—as we are seeing, they are about culture, leadership, and an organization's capacity to adapt and execute. In a project-driven world, your people are your edge—but only if you create the conditions for them to lead, learn, and thrive.

Dynamic Resource Allocation in a Project-Driven Organization

The best transformations I've been part of—and the most effective project-driven organizations I've studied—share one powerful trait: they commit fully dedicated people to their strategic projects. These organizations understand that transformation isn't a side task—it's the main event, and it demands focused, capable teams.

Yet, it's astonishing how rare this level of commitment remains. How is it possible that a global corporation with more than fifty thousand

FIGURE 5-1

Project-driven human resources

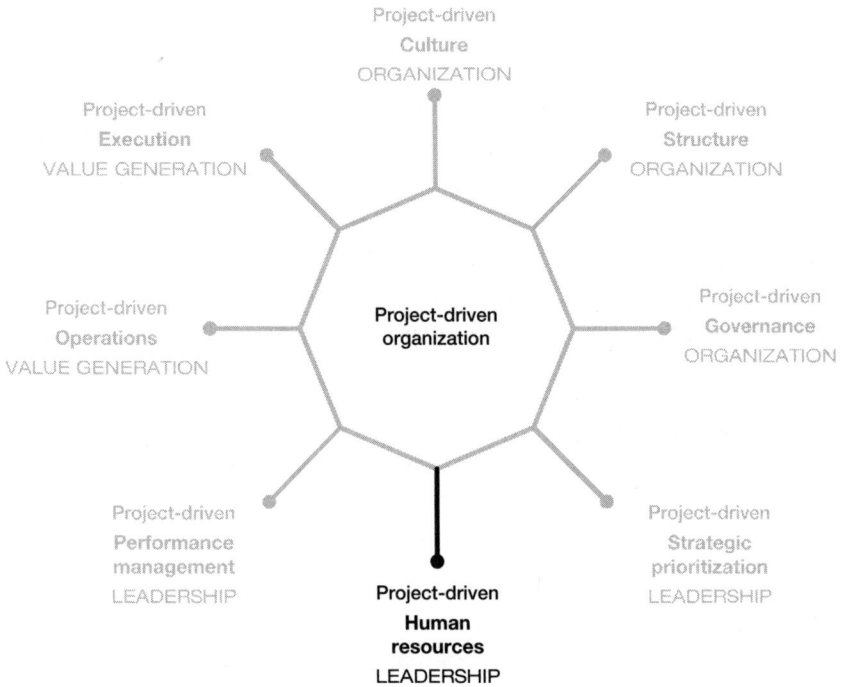

Project-driven
Culture
ORGANIZATION

Project-driven
Execution
VALUE GENERATION

Project-driven
Structure
ORGANIZATION

Project-driven
Operations
VALUE GENERATION

**Project-driven
organization**

Project-driven
Governance
ORGANIZATION

Project-driven
Performance
management
LEADERSHIP

**Project-driven
Human
resources
LEADERSHIP**

Project-driven
Strategic
prioritization
LEADERSHIP

employees struggles to fully dedicate just thirty people—including a senior leader—to drive a critical strategic initiative? Instead, it falls back on part-time contributors or external consultants, diluting any attempt to create a high-performing team.

This common challenge points to a deeper issue: outdated and inflexible resource allocation models. Most organizations are still built for static planning and functional staffing—not for the fluid, rapid deployment of talent required in the transformation age. Adopting dynamic resource allocation models—where people are assigned quickly and flexibly to strategic priorities—is essential to closing this gap and turning project ambition into reality.

According to our survey, only 19 percent of organizations can allocate resources "immediately" (within days) to strategic projects, while an additional 27 percent can do so "quickly" (within weeks). However, a significant portion still needs to catch up, with 28 percent reporting that it takes up to a month to allocate resources, and 25 percent indicating that the process takes several months or more. And only 6 percent of organizations reported that they could not allocate resources dynamically, underscoring the substantial barriers that organizations face in achieving true agility in their resource management.

Resource allocation remains a neglected but essential component of transformation success. In many organizations, projects are treated as part-time responsibilities, with employees still deeply committed to daily operational duties. This fragmented approach often leads to delays, diluted accountability, and weakened team cohesion. Building momentum and sustaining progress becomes challenging without a clear focus as employees struggle to balance competing priorities. Research consistently shows that projects staffed with fully dedicated resources perform far better and deliver more impactful results faster, yet many organizations resist this model.

The irony is that organizations often have vast workforces but hesitate to commit even a small number of employees exclusively to high-stakes projects. Research by McKinsey suggests that the great majority of organizations understand the imperative of dynamic resource allocation but organizational inertia—stemming from cognitive bias, risk aversion, and corporate politics, among others—means that they rarely implement it effectively. The report said that one technique for unsticking the process is by implementing rules that effectively automate a level of reallocation:

> When Lee Raymond was CEO of ExxonMobil, he required the corporate-planning team to identify 3 to 5 percent of the company's assets for potential disposal every year. The company's divisions were allowed to retain assets placed in this group only if they could demonstrate a tangible and compelling turnaround program. In essence, the burden on the business units was to prove that an asset should be retained, rather than the other way around. The net effect was accelerated portfolio upgrading and healthy turnover in the face of executives' natural desire to hang on to underperforming assets.[2]

This feels particularly relevant at the moment, as leaders look to AI to help accelerate decisions. Achieving dynamic resource allocation in a PDO requires a systemic shift in how resources are managed. For this shift to succeed, HR plays a crucial role, requiring rethinking how resources are structured, incentivized, and transitioned between operations and projects. (See the sidebar, "The Role of the Chief Human Resources Officer.") Leaders in a PDO must adopt a real-time resourcing model, ensuring that employees can be assigned full-time to strategic projects when needed, with a clear pathway to transition back to operational roles if required. This flexibility not only fosters the ownership and accountability needed for successful transformation but also aligns the workforce with the organization's most strategic goals.

Balancing Project and Operations Roles in a Project-Driven Organization

In a PDO, projects—not routine operations—are at the heart of value creation. This shift redefines the organization's core, making project work the central focus and operations a supportive framework. This doesn't mean that all employees must transition to project roles—many may not wish to. But nearly all will be involved in the transformation work.

Jonathan Smart, head of Ways of Working at Barclays, shared a story to explain what inspired the company's new approach to operations: "David Marquet was the commander of a US Navy submarine. Put in charge of the worst-performing vessel in the fleet, he realized that his team needed to work very differently to turn things around. 'Leadership,' he said, 'should mean giving control rather than taking control and creating leaders rather than forging followers.'"[3]

Within twelve months, Marquet's submarine went from being the worst- to the best-performing in the navy, and in that year he didn't issue a single command. Locked up for six months at a time with 130 people, he created a culture where the people working on the submarine said: "I intend to do this, and I've checked these things," and he would reply: "Did you check that?" or "Well, go ahead," but he would do it without forcing orders. Each member of the project team was aware of the mission, became engaged by assuming responsibility, and developed new expertise.

The Role of the Chief Human Resources Officer

As explored in chapter 1, one of the most difficult shifts in the transformation age is accepting that there is no "back to normal." Yet many employees—and even many managers—still hope for a return to stability after each wave of change. It's the CHRO's responsibility to lead the organization beyond this mindset. They must build lasting transformation capabilities within the workforce—capabilities that can no longer be outsourced to consultants or treated as temporary fixes.

This mindset shift is foundational, but it must be paired with action. Successfully shifting toward dynamic resource allocation is a leadership test for the CHRO. In an environment where projects are the primary vehicle for execution, the CHRO must drive, not just support, this transformation. Key actions to achieve this transformation include:

- **Champion structural flexibility.** Instead of merely adjusting organizational charts, CHROs must lead a visible shift away from rigid departmental structures toward fluid, real-time models. By proactively designing cross-functional pathways and enabling fast, project-based deployment, HR becomes a key catalyst for transformation, not just a back-end enabler.

- **Redefine careers around impact, not tenure.** Traditional career ladders are misaligned with the pace of transformation. CHROs should build systems that tie compensation and advancement to real project outcomes, the ability to shift between roles and teams, and leading cross-functional work. Career progression must be linked to delivering measurable impact to the organization and individuals, not just years of service within a department.

- **Create internal transformation talent marketplaces.** Instead of simply filling project roles reactively, HR leaders should create internal transformation talent marketplaces—dynamic platforms that match strategic initiatives with employees who have the right skills, availability, and readiness. These are not generic resource pools; they should be treated as the organization's transformation

(continued)

backbone—a curated group of high-impact, project-ready talent capable of being deployed quickly to critical initiatives. To work effectively, these marketplaces require active talent management, visibility into the skill sets available within the company, and alignment with the organization's strategic priorities.

- **Steward the transition to a dual operating model.** As project work becomes the organization's core engine and operations increasingly shift to automated platforms, CHROs must lead employees through the change. Those remaining in operational roles must focus on human oversight, judgment, and continual improvement. Continuous upskilling, psychological safety, and resilience-building are essential for those transitioning to project roles.

The CHRO's leadership role is not simply managing change but shaping it. This includes driving critical shifts like dynamic resource allocation and building internal transformation capabilities. Those who embrace this new mandate will not only future-proof their organizations but also elevate the strategic influence of the HR function to unprecedented levels.

It's a big mindset shift, requiring a new perspective at all levels—from leadership, middle management, and the teams doing the work.

This approach to cocreating and distributing change, rather than driving new practice by decree, has informed the scope of what's been achieved across Barclays' business. The focus on modern ways of working at a 327-year-old company that was not born agile includes HR, legal, sourcing, real estate, audit, and other core functions of the bank.[4] Within a year, more than eight hundred teams adopted agile methods, delivering three times as much work in one-third the time, with twenty-three times fewer production incidents and record-high employee engagement.[5]

Creating Dual Talent-Management Models. To address this transition, HR must develop two talent management models: one for project-based work and another for operational roles that support day-to-day continuity. Each model should have its own structures for career progression, skill development, and incentives to ensure alignment with the organization's strategic direction.

In the project model, employees are assigned to transformation initiatives, strategic projects, or other critical change efforts. This model focuses on agility, cross-functional collaboration, and rapid skills development. Career paths should prioritize exposure to diverse projects, learning opportunities, and advancement through project successes. For employees, middle managers, and executives, transitioning between projects or moving from project to project becomes the primary career path, with rewards tied to project impact and the successful delivery of strategic outcomes.

The operations model should cater to employees who prefer the routines of operations or whose roles involve business-as-usual activities that may not translate easily to project work. While many operational tasks will continue to be automated or phased out—particularly through AI—critical roles will remain, especially those focused on overseeing automation systems, managing customer interactions, and driving continuous improvement. Career growth in this space can focus on building deep expertise in automation technologies, robotics, and the governance of AI-enabled systems. At the same time, these employees will increasingly need to develop foundational skills in transformation and project-based work, as even operational roles will intersect more often with change initiatives. (The operating model is covered in more detail in chapter 7.)

As organizations evolve into dual talent-management models, HR must facilitate smooth transitions for employees who wish to move between project and operations roles. For employees, middle management, and executives, these transitions allow for diversified career growth and enable the organization to deploy resources where they are most needed. To facilitate the transitions, HR should establish:

- *Defined transition pathways.* HR can create structured pathways that enable employees to shift from operations to project roles as strategic needs arise or as employees express interest in project-based work. These pathways should provide clarity on the skills required for project roles and offer training programs to build these skills, creating a bridge between competencies.

- *Skill development for both models.* For project roles, HR must invest in developing competencies in modern project management, cross-functional collaboration, and strategic thinking. For operations roles, skills in managing AI-driven systems, intelligent process automation, human-robot collaboration, data-driven decision-making, and real-time performance optimization will be crucial. Employees in operations should have access to training that helps them prepare for possible contributions or transitions to transformation initiatives, should they choose to pursue it.

- *Incentives aligned with strategic goals.* Incentives should be adapted to reflect the organization's priorities. For project-based roles, rewards and recognition should be linked to successful project delivery, innovation, and contribution to strategic goals. In contrast, operations roles could be incentivized based on efficiency metrics, quality improvement, and successful integration with automated systems. For both models, HR should encourage a culture of continuous learning, enabling employees to stay relevant in an environment where skills requirements are rapidly changing.

As organizations shift to dynamic resource models, CHROs, CFOs, and CPOs must align people, priorities, and funding with greater speed and precision. Structure alone is no longer enough. True success depends on building high-performing, engaged teams to deliver continuous transformation at scale.

Developing High-Performing and Engaged Teams

Imagine a sports team that meets only briefly each week—just enough to discuss a few plays—and then disperses until the next game. The players juggle other jobs, practice independently, and rarely have the opportunity to develop trust, teamwork, or a shared sense of purpose. Such a team would struggle to achieve cohesion, momentum, or real success.

In my experience, a stunning 95 percent of projects are carried out by groups of individuals—not real teams. Yet successful transformations are delivered by teams, not loosely associated contributors. This disconnect lies at the heart of many project failures.

Despite this evidence, this is precisely how many transformation projects are structured today. Projects are often staffed with groups of individuals appointed by management who must juggle project responsibilities alongside their day-to-day roles. Team members may come together only for short, sporadic meetings each week before returning to their regular duties, with little opportunity to build team cohesion, trust, or a collective mission. This fragmented, part-time approach undermines accountability, makes it difficult to build momentum, and often leads to disengagement.

According to Neri Karra, founder of Moda Métiers and recognized in the Thinkers50 Radar 2024, building resilient, high-performing project teams is fundamentally a leadership act.[6] Drawing from her family's entrepreneurial journey—rebuilding their lives after fleeing their home country—Karra shared with me how true leadership is about creating environments of trust, purpose, and emotional connection. In her own organization, she fosters a culture where project teams are not just operational units, but communities with shared meaning and ambition. This leadership mindset transforms team building from a process of assigning resources into a deliberate act of inspiring commitment.

Across many organizations today, project team selection still varies widely in maturity. Some companies rely on top-down appointments without strategic matching of talent, risking frustration when teams are assembled through politics rather than purpose. More evolved organizations use hybrid approaches, combining leadership nominations with voluntary participation based on skills and motivation. The most mature environments go further, using transparent, competency-based assessments to match capabilities and personal drive to project demands. However, without leadership setting the tone for transparency and trust, even the best selection processes can falter. As Karra's insights powerfully remind us, building great project teams isn't just about the right skills—it's about the right spirit, cultivated by leaders who know how to connect people to a larger mission.

In a PDO, building a high-performing team should be seen as essential from the outset. Too often, the initial focus is on the technical details of the transformation without the necessary investment in team dynamics and cohesion. Every transformation leader should begin with a clear objective: to cultivate a cohesive, high-performing team, rather than assuming such a team will naturally emerge.

The Challenges of Fragmented Teams

A study by leadership and innovation scholar David Burkus highlights that team members working together full-time are more productive and innovative than those splitting time between multiple projects.[7] Burkus notes that members of part-time teams frequently experience "cognitive overload," as they struggle to balance competing priorities. This fragmentation not only slows project progress but also reduces engagement, making it challenging to sustain momentum and reach project milestones.

The Risks of Low Engagement and the Importance of Commitment

When employees are only partially involved in a project, they are less likely to feel invested in its outcomes, and their performance tends to suffer. Gallup research shows that companies with highly engaged employees are 21 percent more profitable and experience 41 percent lower absenteeism.[8] However, in a project environment where people are constantly shifting focus between different tasks, maintaining engagement is challenging.

Low engagement affects the project in numerous ways: team members may be slower to respond to project needs, overlook critical details, or fail to anticipate potential issues. This leads to delayed timelines, missed opportunities, and ultimately, less successful project outcomes. For transformation projects to succeed, team members need to be fully committed and engaged with the project goals, which requires dedicated time and focus.

To counteract low engagement, PDOs should focus on creating environments where team members are not only accountable for their roles but are also personally invested in the project's success. High engagement must be fostered through deliberate actions such as involving employees in defining the project's purpose, recognizing achievements, and ensuring that team members have clarity on how their contributions impact the broader organizational mission. (For an example, see the sidebar, "Team-Building Lessons from GSK's Sustainability Transformation.")

Many project organizations are currently rushing to use the latest data revolution as a means of automating processes and are using AI to accelerate—or in some cases, replace—human decision-making. The benefits in terms of speed and productivity are undeniable, but there are associated risks. Removing human agency from projects may feel efficient, but there's also the very real risk that we'll overlook the social needs of employees who need to feel involved, consulted, and valuable (beyond the paycheck) if they are to be engaged and motivated by their projects.

New workplace rituals may be needed to ensure this continued oversight and engagement.[9] Continual, anonymous, near real-time feedback to trigger reflection and conversation among the delivery team is a good example of this. The feedback process is hardwired into the regular weekly cycle of progress meetings and consequently becomes part of the accepted ritual of the project.

Team-Building Lessons from GSK's Sustainability Transformation

In 2021, Emma Walmsley, CEO of GSK, launched GSK's sustainability transformation initiative, setting ambitious goals to integrate sustainable practices across every facet of the organization—from R&D to manufacturing to distribution. Walmsley didn't just endorse the initiative from afar; she was a driving force behind it, bringing a sense of purpose and urgency that energized the entire organization. She dedicated a significant portion of her time to its launch and follow-up, reinforcing its priority through consistent engagement and visible leadership. She made GSK's sustainability goals a matter of public commitment, aligning

(continued)

them with the company's long-term vision and brand promise. This public announcement was a critical moment, solidifying the importance of the transformation both internally and externally, and setting clear expectations across all teams and business units.

By embedding these principles of high-performing teams throughout its organization, GSK has achieved substantial progress in its sustainability goals. As a program director from the beginning until October 2024, I witnessed firsthand how Walmsley's commitment to building high-performing teams transformed GSK's approach to this initiative. This focus helped the organization's transformation initiatives gain momentum, with each project team motivated not just by deadlines, but by a collective drive to contribute to GSK's overarching vision of sustainability. Let's look at how we created this high-performing team:

- **Shared purpose.** High-performing teams don't just understand their tasks; they understand why their work matters and how it contributes to a larger mission. At GSK, the purpose of the sustainability transformation was clear: to position the company as a leader in sustainable health care by reducing environmental impact across all operations. This common purpose connected employees at every level—scientists, engineers, managers, and support staff—who all saw how their contributions directly aligned with the sustainability goals. By communicating this purpose widely, GSK fostered a culture where team members across functions felt that their work had a significant, positive impact beyond immediate business goals.

- **Clear roles and responsibilities.** GSK ensured that each team member understood their specific role in the sustainability journey, whether it was reducing emissions in production, enhancing sustainable sourcing in supply chains, or innovating in product design. This clarity helped employees work more effectively, knowing their unique contributions were part of a cohesive, organization-wide effort. With a clear structure in place, teams could execute tasks more efficiently, and everyone knew exactly how they were contributing to the overall goal.

- **Strong communication and collaboration across functions.** For instance, the production plants worked closely with the supply chain teams to identify and implement sustainable practices that reduced waste and improved energy efficiency. Regular cross-functional meetings, supported by robust digital communication platforms, allowed teams across different regions and functions to share best practices and align their efforts. This collaborative approach created a sense of unity and cohesion, ensuring that the sustainability goals were embedded into daily operational decisions across the entire organization, not just within specialized "sustainability" teams.

- **Mutual accountability.** Each function and business unit had specific sustainability targets tied to their operational realities, whether it involved water usage, carbon emissions, or waste reduction. By setting measurable targets, tracking progress rigorously, and encouraging mutual accountability, GSK ensured that each part of the organization took responsibility for contributing to the transformation. Regular reviews allowed teams to assess their progress, address setbacks, and keep momentum, fostering a culture that held everyone to a high standard.

- **Continuous learning and improvement.** Employees across departments were offered training in sustainable practices relevant to their specific roles, from energy-efficient manufacturing processes to sustainable sourcing methods. For example, data insights on energy usage in production facilities led to adjustments that significantly reduced overall consumption. This commitment to learning empowered teams to innovate within their roles, ensuring that the transformation program evolved in line with the latest advancements and industry standards. As team members continuously developed their skills, they became more agile and effective in driving the transformation forward.

Psychological Safety in Projects: Leading outside the Comfort Zone

Psychological safety—a "shared belief that the team is safe for interpersonal risk-taking"—is a foundational element for helping individuals step outside their comfort zones, enabling the agility, innovation, and resilience that project work demands in the transformation age.

Amy Edmondson, a Harvard Business School professor known for her groundbreaking work on team dynamics, coined the term in 1999, and it was popularized in her 2019 book, *The Fearless Organization*.[10] She introduced the concept after observing health-care teams and noticing that high-performing teams were not those that avoided mistakes, but those that openly discussed them, learned from them, and moved forward together. This insight was later validated by Google's Project Aristotle, a study examining over 180 Google teams to identify what makes teams effective. The study found that psychological safety was the single most critical factor for team success. Teams that felt safe to share their perspectives consistently outperformed those that did not.[11] This finding underscores the essential role of psychological safety in enabling open dialogue, innovative thinking, and productive collaboration.

Psychological safety is critical for project teams, where uncertainty, change, and experimentation are the norm. Unlike operational work, projects involve navigating unfamiliar territory, testing new ideas, adapting rapidly, and making decisions without guaranteed outcomes—all of which heighten the risks of failure and exposure. Because projects challenge the status quo and push people to work out of their comfort zones most of the time, team members must feel safe to voice concerns, question assumptions, and propose new solutions. Without psychological safety, teams risk falling into groupthink, missing opportunities, and letting critical errors go unaddressed—each capable of derailing the project's success.

In a PDO, psychological safety allows teams to:

- *Challenge assumptions.* Project teams often work with uncertain data or untested ideas. Encouraging team members to question assumptions helps avoid blind spots and surface potential risks early.

- *Adapt quickly.* Psychological safety enables rapid learning and iteration, allowing teams to pivot without fear of blame when initial approaches don't work out.

- *Promote cross-functional collaboration.* Projects often bring together individuals from different functions or backgrounds. A psychologically safe environment allows them to bridge their differences and work toward common goals, fostering unity and trust.

In a PDO, psychological safety is the foundation upon which high-performing teams are built. By establishing this environment, leaders not only improve team morale and performance but also ensure that their organizations are ready to adapt to continuous transformation.

Upskilling Competencies for the Transformation Age

As organizations pivot to project-centric ways of working, leaders must equip the entire workforce with competencies that support agile, dynamic project environments. Upskilling at scale isn't just about individual professional development; it's an urgent strategic imperative to ensure organizations remain competitive and resilient in the transformation age.

One of the most significant shifts facing leaders in the transformation age is the need to provide employees with future-ready skills as they are increasingly required to move beyond traditional operational tasks and instead focus on contributing meaningfully to strategic projects. This shift calls for a workforce skilled in analytical thinking, agility, collaboration, and digital literacy. These skills enable employees to engage fully in projects, drive innovation, and adapt to the rapidly evolving needs of project-based work.

In recent years, the demand for future-ready skills has been highlighted by various reports, including the World Economic Forum's *Future of Jobs Report 2023*, which predicts that by 2027, six in ten workers will require upskilling in areas such as analytical and creative thinking, as well as digital competencies like AI and big data.[12]

This shift reflects a broader trend as organizations pivot toward project-driven structures, meaning that all employees—not just those in technical roles—must acquire skills that support transformation. As the boundaries between traditional operational roles and project roles are blurring, future-ready skills enable employees to contribute to projects effectively, regardless of their primary role. Unlike day-to-day operational work, which often involves repetitive tasks and stability, projects are dynamic and require employees to adapt to changing objectives, collaborate with diverse teams, and think critically to solve complex

The Pitfalls in Building Project-Driven Human Resources

Redesigning how leaders manage people in a project-driven world is one of the most important—and most difficult—transformation challenges. While many companies recognize the need to become more agile, empowered, and flexible, they often fall into familiar traps that undermine their progress. Old habits persist, legacy systems dominate, and workforce strategies lag behind transformation demands.

Here are three common pitfalls that can prevent HR from becoming a true driver of transformation:

Keeping Rigid, Function-Based Resource Allocation

Most organizations still allocate people based on functional departments and static job roles, even as their strategic priorities demand cross-functional execution and dynamic project staffing. As a result, critical initiatives suffer from resource bottlenecks and high-performing talent remains locked in traditional silos. This system also frustrates employees eager to contribute beyond their narrow role, reducing engagement and adaptability.

Take, for example, a global B2B firm that launched a salesforce rollout across five business units. Part-time staff from sales, IT, and operations juggled project tasks with daily work. Without dedicated ownership, delays and misalignment across units led to a six-month slip and poor adoption—exposing the limits of fragmented, function-based resourcing.

Treating Project Teams as Temporary Task Groups

Too often, organizations assemble project teams based solely on expertise and availability, overlooking the importance of team dynamics, trust, and cohesion. These teams end up functioning as disconnected task groups rather than high-performing units. Without psychological safety and shared ownership, collaboration suffers, innovation stalls, and conflict goes unaddressed—especially under pressure.

One global tech firm assembled a cross-functional team to develop a new AI-powered service. While the members were top performers in their domains, they had no prior experience working together. Meetings were tense, feedback was withheld, and team members hesitated to challenge flawed assumptions. The project missed key deadlines and required multiple reworks—delays that could have been avoided with a stronger focus on team culture and trust-building from the start.

Treating Upskilling as a One-Off or Optional Effort

Many companies still approach learning as just a box-ticking exercise, if they invest in it at all. Upskilling remains an HR formality rather than a business necessity, leaving employees and middle managers—who spend a growing share of their time on projects and transformation initiatives—without the skills, mindset, or tools needed to succeed. Treating upskilling as optional not only slows execution but also fuels frustration and disengagement across the organization.

When candy maker Haribo implemented a new SAP enterprise resource planning system to modernize its supply chain, the rollout suffered major setbacks.[a] Employees lacked adequate training, resulting in operational confusion, inventory issues, and unmet customer demand. The disruption led to empty shelves and a sharp dip in sales. The core issue wasn't the technology—it was the failure to embed upskilling as a central, ongoing part of the transformation process.

In a project-driven organization, people are the core enabler of transformation. Fluid resource allocation, high-performing teams built on trust, and continuous upskilling are strategic imperatives for executing change and staying competitive.

NOTE

a. Bill Baumann, "Lessons Learned from the Haribo ERP Failure," Panorama Consulting Group, January 6, 2021, https://www.panorama-consulting.com/haribo-erp-failure/.

problems. Without these competencies, employees may struggle to keep pace with project demands, limiting the organization's ability to execute transformation initiatives successfully.

Prepare Your Team

The leadership imperative is clear: invest in upskilling existing employees now. In a fierce talent market, retaining and transforming the workforce that already holds critical know-how is essential to sustaining both performance and culture through change.

The shift also demands a new skills profile across the organization. Table 5-1 outlines how workforce capabilities must evolve from traditional operational roles to transformation-ready project roles.

Best-in-class organizations have already begun upskilling efforts to build a workforce equipped for the future. For example, L'Oréal has invested in large-scale training initiatives to equip employees with data literacy, digital skills, and modern project management, especially as project-based work has become more central to the company's growth strategy. By aligning its learning and development programs with strategic goals, L'Oréal has enhanced the ability of teams across its global network to adapt and innovate. Programs focused on developing critical competencies have created a workforce that is both project-ready and capable of leading in its highly competitive industry.

Key Future-Ready Skills for All Employees

As organizations shift to project-driven structures, equipping employees with competencies for flexible, collaborative, and dynamic project roles becomes critical. Below are six skills that project-driven organizations must foster to survive:

- *Data-driven thinking and problem-solving.* In transformation projects, ambiguity is the norm and clarity comes from insight. Employees must be able to interpret data, spot patterns, and apply structured thinking to complex challenges. Analytical skills enable faster, more informed decisions, while problem-solving capabilities turn uncertainty into progress. These abilities are essential for delivering meaningful results in fast-changing environments.

- *Modern project management for the transformation age.* Today's project environments demand a modern approach that moves beyond rigid methodologies. It emphasizes hybrid methods tailored to each project, simplified tools, a focus on measurable benefits, and a clear sense of purpose. At its core, modern project management fosters cocreation, real team formation, and an

TABLE 5-1

Top ten skills for operations-driven organizations versus project-driven organizations

Operations-driven organizations (past)	Project-driven organizations (future)
Process optimization: Improving and standardizing processes for consistency and efficiency	**Strategic adaptability:** Adjusting or stopping projects as strategic priorities evolve
Customer service orientation: Delivering consistent service within operational frameworks	**Purpose-driven leadership:** Inspiring teams with a vision aligned with transformative and measurable benefits
Risk management and compliance: Minimizing risk and adhering to regulations and standards	**Digital and analytical fluency:** Applying AI and data tools to automate low-value tasks and focus on high-impact work
Resource management: Efficiently allocating and managing resources for steady output	**High-performing collaboration:** Establishing high-performing teams across departments, business units, and geographies
Quality assurance: Maintaining consistent quality within operational standards	**Innovation and entrepreneurship:** Developing novel solutions with an entrepreneurship drive
Cost management: Reducing costs and managing budgets for operational efficiency	**Stakeholder engagement:** Aligning project benefits and key stakeholders to maximize engagement and impact
Time management: Managing time effectively within a controlled environment	**Resilience and change management:** Guiding teams through change and thriving on uncertainty
Analytical problem-solving: Addressing operational issues with established data analysis techniques	**Autonomous decision-making:** Empowering project teams to make timely decisions without relying on hierarchical approval structures
Routine task proficiency: Executing repetitive tasks with high accuracy	**Modern project management:** Developing proficiency in hybrid methods that increase alignment, engagement, and acceleration of benefits
Team supervision and hierarchical leadership: Supervising effectively within a hierarchy to maintain productivity	**Continuous learning and upskilling:** Being committed to establishing frequent learning habits to keep up with the speed of change

entrepreneurial mindset, encouraging individuals to innovate, take ownership, make decisions, and drive outcomes.

- *Digital literacy and tech readiness.* As project work becomes increasingly digital, employees must be fluent in using AI-enabled project tools, data analytics, and collaborative platforms. This fluency supports real-time tracking, faster decision-making, and seamless communication—key to accelerating execution and adapting quickly to change.

- *Agility beyond flexibility.* In fast-moving environments, project plans rarely stay static. Employees must be able to pivot quickly—adjusting scope, timelines, or resources in response to shifting priorities or challenges. It also means recognizing when a project is no longer viable and having the discipline to pause or stop it. Teams that develop this mindset stay focused on impact, not just execution, and are better equipped to navigate uncertainty and deliver meaningful results.

- *High-impact collaboration and communication.* Project success depends on more than just working together—it requires high-quality collaboration and clear, consistent communication across functions, locations, and time zones. Employees must navigate diverse perspectives, share information openly, and align quickly around shared goals. These skills are essential for reducing misunderstandings, enabling faster decisions, and keeping projects on track from start to finish.

- *Resilience and growth through continuous learning.* Transformation projects are demanding—setbacks, shifting priorities, and uncertainty are part of the journey. To thrive, employees must build resilience and stay open to learning in real time. This means treating each project as a development opportunity: gaining new skills, adjusting strategies, and staying engaged, even when challenges arise. Continuous learning is not optional; it's how individuals and organizations stay relevant and effective.

Implementing a Future-Ready Skills Development Program

Leading a transformation toward a project-driven organization requires nothing short of a full commitment from the CEO, supported strategically by the CHRO. This shift calls for a comprehensive, top-down approach to upskilling that aligns resources, policies, and incentives with the organization's new direction.

Building future-ready skills across an organization is challenging but essential for thriving in a transformation age. The first step is to map the evolving demands of project roles against current capabilities in real time. A dynamic skills intelligence approach replaces traditional gap analyses by utilizing tools such as employee self-assessments, project performance data, and AI-enabled learning diagnostics. This enables HR and transformation leaders to identify emerging skill needs, anticipate future gaps, and adjust learning strategies accordingly. The result: a workforce equipped to evolve alongside the organization's priorities, project by project.

Unlike traditional operational roles, project roles demand a variety of dynamic skills, and a one-size-fits-all approach will not suffice. By creating a *customized learning framework*, organizations can cater to the unique needs of each role. Foundational skills like digital fluency or modern project management should be cultivated across the workforce. Meanwhile, more advanced skills, like high-impact collaboration and data-driven problem-solving, can be offered to specific project teams or leaders. A customized approach ensures that employees receive relevant training that they can apply directly in their roles.

The third step is to *foster a culture of continuous learning habits*, essential in a PDO where skills must evolve alongside project demands. It's not just about providing access to training, but also about helping people form lasting habits around learning and development. Encouraging employees to integrate learning into their regular routines— whether through short daily modules, goal tracking, or peer-based accountability—creates consistency and ownership. This can be achieved by offering access to e-learning platforms, incentivizing skill achievement with rewards or recognition, and embedding learning opportunities in employees' daily routines. A culture that values and rewards these habits ensures that employees remain adaptable, resilient, and prepared for future projects.

PDOs must also *leverage technology for scalable learning*. In a large organization, scaling training across all employees requires an efficient and flexible system. AI-driven learning platforms offer tailored content, track progress, and adjust learning paths based on individual performance, making them ideal for project-driven environments. For example, AI can analyze skill gaps in real time, offering employees personalized training that evolves as they gain expertise. The scalability of these platforms is invaluable, as they provide just-in-time training and insights that meet the demands of ongoing transformation.

Finally, organizations need smarter ways to measure the impact of skills development—both to prove value and to continuously optimize. Beyond traditional KPIs, companies should implement real-time learning analytics that track how skill acquisition translates into project performance. This could include project velocity, quality of team collaboration, learning adoption rates, or how quickly employees apply new skills in live project settings. Pulse surveys, skill verification tools, and feedback loops built into project workflows can provide richer and faster insights than annual reviews can. These dynamic metrics enable HR leaders to adapt learning programs in near real time, making upskilling a core engine of the PDO.

The New Role of Middle Management

One serious risk in the transition to a project-driven organization is stagnant middle management. Traditionally responsible for coordinating day-to-day operations and managing staff, middle managers now face an existential challenge as organizations increasingly shift to project-based structures. Companies like Haier and X (formerly Twitter) have already taken radical steps to overhaul or even eliminate middle management layers, underscoring the urgency for change.

In an organization centered on projects, the value of a middle manager lies in driving transformation initiatives, fostering collaboration, and contributing to strategic objectives. This new model requires middle managers to evolve from traditional roles into ones focused on flexibility, impact, and entrepreneurial thinking. This plays out in a number of ways.

"All Different, All Equal" Management for a Hybrid Workforce. As we have seen, in the transformation age, a significant portion of operational work is or will be automated or supported by AI, reducing the need for human oversight in routine tasks. Fewer middle managers will be needed to supervise daily activities. Instead, middle managers must learn to lead hybrid teams composed of human employees, AI, and soon, even robots.

For example, a middle manager might oversee a project team where AI agents handle data analysis, while human team members focus on creative problem-solving and client interactions. This hybrid approach requires managers to understand how to leverage technology for optimal team performance, blending human skills with machine capabilities. To adapt successfully, middle managers must cultivate digital literacy, strategic thinking, and a deep understanding of project fundamentals.

Building Cross-Functional Collaboration. In traditional operational roles, middle managers often work within their functional silos. However, in PDOs, their role shifts to one that requires extensive cross-functional collaboration. They must now act as bridges between various departments, fostering teamwork and ensuring that all project components are aligned with organizational goals. This is essential for achieving coherence in complex projects, where different functions may have conflicting priorities or perspectives.

For example, a project-driven middle manager overseeing a product development initiative may need to collaborate closely with marketing, engineering, and customer service teams to ensure that all elements of the project are cohesive and aligned with market needs. This shift from a siloed to a collaborative approach enables organizations to deliver faster and more effective results on strategic projects, enhancing the overall agility of the organization.

Developing an Entrepreneurial Mindset. In a PDO, middle managers must adopt an entrepreneurial mindset, focusing on value creation and innovation. They are expected to lead projects with a clear objective of delivering measurable results, whether through revenue generation, cost savings, or process improvements. This mindset shift is crucial in transformation initiatives, where traditional metrics like productivity or compliance are less relevant than metrics tied to project impact and strategic contribution.

To achieve this, middle managers need training in entrepreneurial skills, including strategic decision-making, exponential thinking, and financial literacy. They must learn to approach projects with a profit-driven focus, understanding the financial implications of their decisions and seeking ways to maximize project ROI. This shift allows them to add tangible value to the organization.

Leading Transformation. As middle managers transition into project-driven roles, they also become champions for change, actively promoting the transformation goals of the organization. They are responsible for communicating the purpose and importance of projects to their teams, helping to build buy-in and align their team's efforts with organizational objectives. This requires strong communication skills, emotional intelligence, and the ability to inspire others—a marked departure from the traditional, often bureaucratic role of middle management.

Middle managers who embrace this role as transformation champions help build a culture of adaptability, resilience, and commitment within their teams. Their influence is particularly crucial in large-scale transformations, where engagement and alignment across the organization can make the difference between success and failure. In effect, they become pivotal figures who drive the organization forward in its transformation journey.

I n a project-driven organization, the future middle manager will be a cross-functional facilitator and an entrepreneurial thinker: essentially, a project leader. The shift requires strong support and commitment from senior leaders, particularly the CEO and CHRO, who must champion the redefinition of middle management roles and provide the necessary training, tools, and incentives. By adopting a dual-track talent model—where one path emphasizes leading cross-functional transformation projects and the other focuses on optimizing core operations—organizations can define distinct development journeys for middle managers, clarifying the skills, experiences, and outcomes required to advance in either strategic execution or operational excellence. By empowering middle managers to adapt to this new paradigm, organizations can retain valuable talent and leverage it to drive strategic transformation initiatives with agility and impact.

For those middle managers who can adapt, the rewards are substantial. In a project-driven world, they can redefine their careers as pivotal drivers of transformation, moving from a role of operational oversight to one that adds strategic value. This evolution not only secures their relevance in the transformation age but also positions them as leaders in an increasingly project-oriented future.

Conclusion

Critical shifts are required to build a project-ready workforce. This means that leaders need to implement more dynamic resource allocation to allow their organizations to respond quickly to shifting priorities and ensure that key initiatives are adequately staffed. In a project economy, the workforce must evolve from loosely connected individuals to high-performing, collaborative teams, grounded in psychological safety and shared ownership—and there is an urgent need for leaders to develop continuous upskilling, not only for themselves, but also for managers, employees, and future transformation leaders. All of this demands a radical change in the role of senior leadership in this transformation. Traditional functions like HR, finance, and operations must adapt to enable more fluid, cross-functional collaboration.

In the next chapter, we'll focus on how leaders must measure and reward success in a PDO. We'll explore new approaches to performance metrics that align with project goals and the importance of recognition systems that motivate and engage employees working within this model. Together, these insights will provide a comprehensive view of sustaining momentum and driving impact in the transformation age.

CHAPTER 6

Project-Driven Performance Management

In Haier's ecosystem of MEs and EMCs, performance metrics are deeply rooted in user value. Success is not merely about meeting internal goals or adhering to timelines but about creating measurable customer impact. Each ME operates as an independent profit-and-loss center, and its leader's performance is evaluated based on how well it addresses user needs and drives market outcomes.

The emphasis on user-centric metrics is evident in Haier's Smart Home initiative, where AI-driven customer support tools were implemented to enhance service efficiency. Metrics for success were tied to tangible outcomes such as a 15 percent reduction in average conversation time with service agents and a significant drop in operator workload.[1] By *measuring success by meaningful and actionable project-focused metrics*, Haier ensured that its projects delivered real-world value for both users and the organization.

Haier employs real-time dashboards to track the performance of its MEs and EMCs, enabling transparency and agility. These dashboards emphasize metrics such as value generation, market impact, and degree of alignment with user expectations. This approach allows Haier to pivot swiftly when projects fail to meet their targets, reallocating resources to more promising initiatives.

Collaboration is also central to Haier's approach. Through *shared project and team-based reward systems*, such as EMC contracts, all members share the benefits of a successful project. Leaders play a pivotal role here: by setting clear expectations, aligning incentives with value creation, and ensuring transparency, they enable high-performing teams to focus on outcomes that matter most to users and the organization. This shared accountability encourages cross-functional teams to work cohesively, breaking down silos and promoting innovation. Teams are rewarded not only for achieving their goals but also for their ability to iterate and improve based on user feedback.

In Haier's acquisition of GE Appliances, the RenDanHeYi model replaced the traditional principal-agent incentive system (which encourages individual employees to game the system, maximizing the processes on which incentives are based; for instance, number of calls per hour) with one that rewarded employees based on their contributions to project outcomes. Previously, only a small fraction of employees participated in performance-based incentives. Under the new system, over four thousand employees were included, significantly improving engagement and productivity. Profits tripled within five years, demonstrating the transformative power of aligning rewards with project success.

Haier's performance management is built on transparency. Teams and their leaders are aware of the metrics by which they will be evaluated, and these metrics are consistently linked to the organization's broader goals. Leaders are held directly accountable. If an ME fails to meet its targets within a set time frame, it may be restructured or disbanded, ensuring that underperformance is addressed decisively.

This transparent approach fosters trust across the organization and reinforces that everyone's success is interconnected. It ensures that performance management is not an afterthought but a dynamic process that drives Haier's project-driven culture.

———————————

A few years ago, I worked with the leadership team of a Swiss biotech company whose CEO clearly understood that projects were the future of the organization. She challenged each of her eleven executive team members to design a single strategic initiative that would generate 100 million Swiss francs in new revenue over three years, with the collective goal of creating 1 billion in new value. She asked me to develop a tailored training and coaching program to support this effort, helping the executives turn bold ideas into executable transformation projects.

We introduced project-specific performance metrics to track each initiative's progress, focusing not just on milestones, but on indicators like speed, cross-functional collaboration, and value delivered. These metrics were reviewed at regular executive gatherings, sparking highly focused, outcome-driven discussions that elevated both accountability and learning. The performance data was also shared more broadly across the organization, reinforcing transparency and urgency. The result was a noticeable shift in mindset: ownership deepened, silos dissolved faster, and engagement grew—turning her vision into measurable impact.

In a world where transformation is continuous and value is created through temporary, cross-functional teams, old metrics fall short. Measuring individual output or operational performance alone no longer captures the complete picture of impact. This chapter explores how leaders are redefining the way success is measured, tracked, and rewarded to embrace a model aligned with project-driven work. That means designing systems that reflect collaboration, adaptability, and contribution to strategic outcomes- not just task completion. This shift requires new tools, new mindsets, and the courage to challenge long-held assumptions about what success looks like.

We focus on two critical areas of transformation in performance management (see figure 6-1): measuring success through project-focused metrics and providing appropriate project- and team-based rewards.

These shifts represent more than just a tweak to current systems—they require a reinvention of how performance is understood, evaluated, and rewarded. And that requires new ways of seeing, measuring, and valuing people's work. Leaders should champion this reinvention by modeling the behaviors they want to see—recognizing teams for outcomes, not effort, and reinforcing a culture where collaboration, learning, and delivering strategic value are what truly count.

FIGURE 6-1

Project-driven performance management

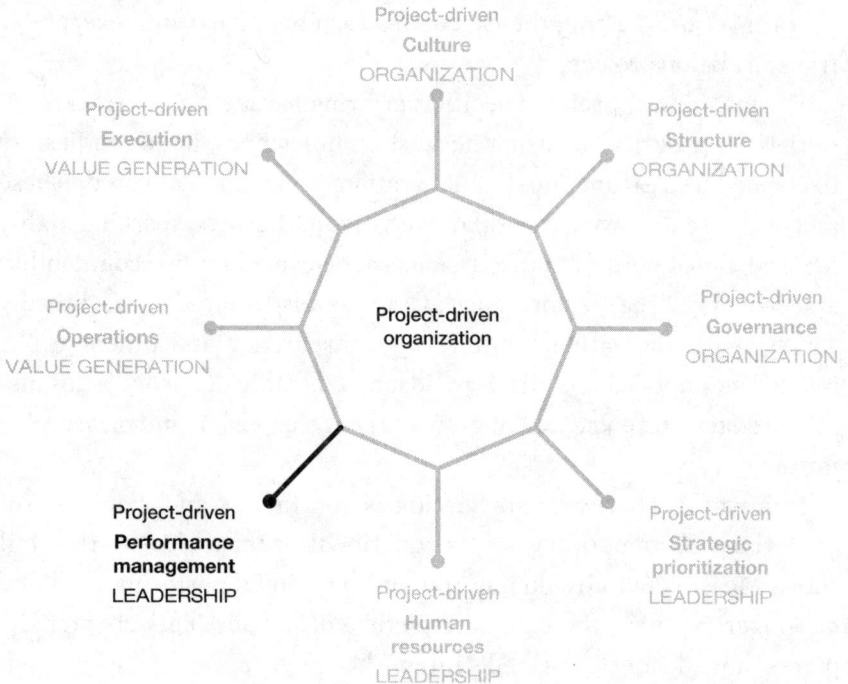

Project-driven
Culture
ORGANIZATION

Project-driven
Execution
VALUE GENERATION

Project-driven
Structure
ORGANIZATION

Project-driven
Operations
VALUE GENERATION

Project-driven
organization

Project-driven
Governance
ORGANIZATION

Project-driven
**Performance
management**
LEADERSHIP

Project-driven
Strategic
prioritization
LEADERSHIP

Project-driven
Human
resources
LEADERSHIP

Measuring Success through
Project-Focused Metrics

In the project-driven organization, traditional metrics like time, budget, and scope no longer capture the full impact of transformation initiatives. Leaders need a more holistic approach to measure the strategic value of projects and the health of the teams executing them.

In this section, we'll first examine the typical lack of visibility many leaders have in their overall portfolio of projects and highlight the importance of a high-level, portfolio-wide perspective. Then we'll focus on project dashboards that go beyond traditional metrics to capture value creation, team engagement, and impact.

Developing a Portfolio Performance Hub
for the Project-Driven Organization

Despite substantial investments of time, capital, and human resources in projects, few organizations have developed a comprehensive, dynamic system to manage their entire project portfolio with the same rigor used to oversee operational activities. As a leader, ask yourself:

- Do you know exactly how many projects your organization is currently running?

- Do you know how much value these initiatives are expected to deliver—both now and in the months and years to come?

- Are you fully aware of the resources dedicated to each one?

- Can you confidently track the real-time status of each project?

- Most importantly, do you have the insights and control needed to accelerate that value?

For many leaders, the answers to these questions are worryingly uncertain. While operational activities are typically tracked in real time through enterprise resource planning (ERP) systems, many organizations lack equivalent systems for managing projects at scale. To fully harness the power of project-driven work, leaders need a similar level of visibility and control over their project portfolios.

Our research highlights critical gaps and inconsistencies in how organizations measure project performance. Only 27 percent of respondents indicated that the performance of all strategic projects is included in their organization's top KPIs. Meanwhile, 49 percent include only some strategic projects in their top KPIs, and 20 percent do not include project performance at all. Many organizations lack a cohesive approach to measuring the impact of their project portfolio, limiting visibility into whether projects are achieving the intended value and alignment with strategic goals. For instance, some organizations rely on alternative performance metrics like objectives and key results (OKRs) instead of KPIs, or track project benefits such as learning and experience alongside financial outcomes, which can create a disconnect between project performance and organizational strategy.

These findings underscore the need for a structured, integrated approach to project performance measurement—a performance hub. By embedding project-based metrics into the organization's top KPIs, leaders can elevate project performance to the same level of visibility and accountability as other core business metrics. Some organizations are also exploring the integration of OKRs into their performance metrics to drive value in more dynamic ways, aligning project outcomes more closely with strategic goals.

Steps to Establish a Project Portfolio Performance Hub. Although some organizations may already have parts of a performance hub in place, fully realizing it as a living, dynamic system often presents challenges. Here are the foundational steps:

Map and categorize the full portfolio of projects. Leaders must begin by taking ownership of a comprehensive mapping of all active and planned projects across the organization. This critical first step creates a baseline view of the number, type, and scope of initiatives. Categorizing projects by strategic relevance, resource needs, or timelines not only supports prioritization but also enables clearer alignment with the organizational overarching goals. As emphasized in the hierarchy of purpose (chapter 4), this exercise helps leaders distinguish between core, enabling, and exploratory projects, ensuring that resources and leadership attention are directed where they deliver the highest impact. Without a complete and current inventory, organizations operate in the dark, often misallocating resources, talent, budget, and focus.

Establish centralized governance and reporting mechanisms. Establish centralized governance and reporting mechanisms—supervised by the chief project officer (CPO)—to support fast, value-driven execution. The traditional project management office (PMO) must evolve into a modern strategy implementation office that enables focus, speed, and measurable impact. This hub acts as the operational backbone for the central project investment committee, providing real-time visibility into project performance and strategic alignment across the portfolio.

This reimagined PMO becomes a transformation engine, not simply a gatekeeper.

It is critical to establish a central project investment committee as the apex decision-making body. They should meet biweekly to review, prioritize, and monitor major transformations based on their value-creation potential. Chaired by the CPO and including the full executive team, including the CEO, this committee functions much like a venture capital fund inside the organization: it allocates capital and talent based on strategic fit, potential return, and execution readiness. It has the authority to rapidly terminate underperforming projects, manage portfolio load to stay within capacity, and swiftly approve new transformation initiatives in response to shifting market or strategic demands.

Saudi Arabia's Vision 2030, a transformative plan launched in 2016 to diversify the country's economy and reduce its reliance on oil revenues, demonstrates portfolio management on a national scale. The program is unprecedented in scope and ambition, involving hundreds of initiatives across multiple sectors—tourism, infrastructure, renewable energy, and technology, to name just a few. To ensure that each initiative aligns with the kingdom's long-term goals, the government established a centralized governance and reporting structure led by the Public Investment Fund (PIF), the country's sovereign wealth fund and one of the world's largest investment funds.

The PIF established a PMO specifically to manage the vast and complex portfolio of projects associated with Vision 2030. With oversight of over a hundred local companies and numerous large-scale initiatives, the PMO plays a central role in tracking each project's progress, resource use, and alignment with strategic objectives. This approach provides real-time data on how resources are being utilized across the kingdom's projects and allows for dynamic adjustments to optimize impact. If a project requires additional resources to stay on schedule or if changing economic conditions shift priorities, the PMO can rapidly reallocate resources and adjust timelines.

Integrate real-time project data and performance dashboards. Managing a dynamic project portfolio today requires more than just static monthly reports—it demands live, AI-enhanced visibility into how every initiative is performing in the real world. Dashboards should move beyond tracking timelines and budgets to include value-based metrics like revenue impact, cost savings, innovation progress, and user satisfaction. Powered by AI agents, these platforms can surface emerging risks, predict delays, and even suggest reallocations of resources to help leaders respond proactively. When integrated across the portfolio, these data-driven systems become indispensable tools for steering transformation with precision, enabling leadership teams to make fast, informed, and high-stakes decisions in real time.

After the acquisition of several financial institutions, BNP Paribas, a large European bank, launched a multiyear strategic program to simplify processes and generate synergies across its expanded footprint.[2] This €2 billion investment encompassed over 2,700 projects spread across forty countries, with expected annual savings of €2 billion. Managing this vast portfolio required a sophisticated system to keep plans updated, track progress, and ensure strategic objectives aligned.

To support this, the bank developed a steering platform using the proPilot system, which allowed the bank's leadership to continuously monitor and coordinate these projects. The platform enabled seamless communication across various levels of the organization, from project managers to executive leaders, ensuring that reliable and consistent information was available for decision-making. Each month, project stakeholders would provide progress updates through a simplified interface, using intuitive indicators such as "weather forecasts" (sunny, cloudy, rainy) and trends (upward, stable, downward) to convey project health. More detailed reports on resources and impact were submitted quarterly, allowing leadership to track both high-level and granular data.

By consolidating project data from multiple sources, including ERP, accounting, and HR systems, the platform provided the organization with a real-time, comprehensive view of each project's status. This visibility empowered executives to stop underperforming projects and reallocate resources to high-impact ones, enabling adaptive, data-driven portfolio management. BNP Paribas took this commitment to transparency a step further by including updates on their strategic initiatives and transformations in quarterly shareholder reports—an indication of the high level of maturity and accountability the organization achieved. This practice increased internal alignment and enhanced transparency with external stakeholders, reflecting a best-in-class approach to project portfolio management in a PDO.

Assign clear accountability for portfolio performance. Responsibility for the performance of the project portfolio is shared by the executive team—with the CPO orchestrating. While the CPO ensures coherence, alignment, and execution discipline across initiatives, the true engine of transformation lies in *ensuring that every major project has a dedicated, accountable sponsor.* These sponsors are not just figureheads—they take ownership of outcomes, stay actively engaged, and drive value creation from start to finish. This shared leadership model makes clear that the project portfolio and transformation performance is a top-tier, enterprise-wide priority.

Maintain structure and discipline without bureaucracy. Effective portfolio management demands structure, but not at the cost of speed or innovation. The strategy implementation office should champion streamlined governance and lightweight processes that support execution rather than stifle it by enforcing clear and effective standards, real-time reporting, and well-defined decision-making rights that empower teams while keeping leadership informed. As we saw in chapter 3, governance must be designed for speed—lean, digital, and focused on enabling progress. When structure is built to accelerate execution and not to control it, organizations can move faster, stay aligned, and deliver greater impact.

Aligning Project Portfolio Management with Operational and Financial Reporting. For a project portfolio view to be fully effective in a PDO, it must align seamlessly with its operational and business reporting frameworks. This alignment helps ensure that project-based work remains integrated into the larger business context, supporting consistent reporting on project financial health, resource use, value delivery, and return on investment.

However, project portfolios should not be forced into traditional annual budgeting cycles. Unlike regular operations, which benefit from annual planning, projects have unique life cycles that require flexible timing and resource allocation. While financial oversight and alignment with budgeting frameworks are essential, projects should be managed on their own timelines to avoid artificial constraints. (See the sidebar, "The Role of the Chief Financial Officer.") In a PDO, this separation allows projects to follow their natural progression while maintaining financial accountability, ensuring that they contribute effectively to both short-term goals and long-term transformation efforts.

Bringing the Hub to Life. While many organizations may have some of these components, the real challenge lies in integrating them into a cohesive, responsive system that serves as a "single source of truth" for the entire project portfolio. This hub should be a living system, constantly updated and refined as projects progress, priorities shift, and new opportunities arise. Table 6-1 outlines the key elements, actions, and examples that capture the essence of how to establish this hub. By developing a robust project portfolio performance view and aligning it with operational and financial reporting, PDOs can achieve the level of agility and impact required in the transformation age. Leaders who invest in this level of visibility and control are better equipped to navigate complex environments, make data-driven decisions, and drive sustainable growth.

Emphasizing Value Generation and Impact in Project Dashboards

While portfolio oversight provides the big picture of how resources and strategic goals align across projects, project dashboards allow leaders to track the specific value and business impact of each individual initiative, such as earnings before interest, taxes, depreciation, and amortization (EBITDA) contribution; net present value (NPV); internal rate of return (IRR); revenue uplift; margin improvement; or impact on working capital. Both levels of insight are essential. Together, they enable leaders to manage projects in a way that is both agile and strategically aligned.

For over fifty years, the triple constraints of time, budget, and scope have dominated project management metrics. But while these metrics are useful for tracking project execution, they fall short in capturing two critical aspects that are increasingly essential in a PDO operating in the transformation age: the actual value generated by the project and

TABLE 6-1

Developing a portfolio performance hub in a project-driven organization

Component	What it involves	Example
Governance structure	Clear accountability led by the CPO, with oversight from the executive team	Biweekly meetings of the project investment committee, chaired by the CPO, with the CEO and executives participating
Sponsorship model	Dedicated sponsors assigned to each strategic project	A transformation initiative sponsored by the COO, with KPIs linked to business outcomes
Real-time data and dashboards	Live performance tracking tied to value metrics, in addition to timelines and budgets	An AI-enhanced dashboard showing cost savings, revenue impact, and user satisfaction in real time
AI-driven insights	Use of AI agents to monitor and flag risks and suggest optimizations across the portfolio	An AI bot that alerts the sponsor to lagging KPIs and suggests reallocating resources from low-impact projects
Lean reporting framework	Standardized, digital-first reporting focused on strategic alignment and progress	Monthly one-page updates for each project with red/yellow/green status and value-delivery summary
Project-capacity management	Project loads balanced against available delivery capacity to avoid overloading teams	CPO goal to recommend delaying or stopping 20% of projects to focus resources on top-priority work
Strategic agility	Ability to pause, pivot, or launch projects quickly based on market or competitive needs	An investment committee that fast-tracks a new AI project in response to a competitor's launch
Cultural reinforcement	Embed accountability, transparency, and continuous learning into execution culture	Project outcomes and lessons learned that are shared across teams via internal "demo days" or reviews

the human dynamics within the project team, including engagement, well-being, and dedication.

In *HBR Project Management Handbook*, I introduced two additional triple constraints to address these gaps: the value constraint and the people constraint.[3] The *value* constraint—benefits, risks, and sustainability—focuses on the project's tangible impact, ensuring that each project contributes real, measurable value to the organization's strategic objectives. The *people* constraint—dedication, commitment, and recognition—highlights the importance of team dynamics, acknowledging that highly engaged, motivated teams are foundational to project

The Role of the Chief Financial Officer

As a company shifts to a project-driven organization, the CFO is also experiencing a significant shift in responsibilities. In a PDO, the CFO moves beyond traditional financial oversight to become a central figure in funding, prioritizing, and measuring the impact of strategic initiatives. Just as COOs are tasked with operational alignment, CFOs must navigate the complexities of financial agility, ensuring that resources are allocated dynamically, that projects deliver measurable strategic outcomes, and that financial systems adapt as quickly as the business itself.

Equally important is the CFO's emerging role in project-driven performance management. In this model, success is measured not only by aggregate financial results but by how well individual projects contribute to enterprise goals. CFOs must define, track, and enforce a new set of performance metrics focused on benefit realization, time-to-impact, and alignment with strategic priorities. This shift requires finance leaders to move from backward-looking reporting to forward-looking insight generation, empowering leaders to course-correct in real time.

Key aspects of this transformation include:

- **Dynamic funding.** The CFO must responsively develop mechanisms for funding projects as priorities shift. Instead of annual budgets tied rigidly to departments, finance must enable dynamic, cross-functional resource deployment, allowing projects to be funded—and defunded—based on real-time priorities.

- **Real-time financial insights.** Financial decisions must be powered by real-time, project-level data, not lagging quarterly reports. Modern CFOs will invest heavily in digital finance platforms and analytics that provide immediate visibility into resource utilization, project health, and benefit realization—enabling faster, sharper decision-making.

- **Value-creation project funding.** Every project must contribute measurable benefits. Whether through cost savings, revenue growth, improved customer experiences, or strategic differentiation, the CFO's role is to ensure that projects deliver tangible value. This involves establishing clear metrics that capture the broader impact of projects and linking financial investments directly to strategic outcomes.

- **Cross-functional collaboration.** Siloed budgeting models break down in transformation environments. CFOs must partner with COOs, CHROs, and other C-suite leaders to synchronize financial flows with strategic execution, ensuring that projects have the right people, resources, and governance at the right time.

As COOs drive operational agility, CFOs are reshaping financial strategies to support a world where projects are the primary drivers of growth and transformation. With automation increasingly taking over operational tasks, the CFO must ensure that financial and performance management systems are designed to maximize the value derived from project activities. By embracing this broader, more strategic role, CFOs become key enablers of transformation.

success. Without these elements, project performance assessments remain incomplete, limiting an organization's ability to evaluate the true success and impact of its initiatives.

To fully embed the value and people constraints into project-driven performance management, dashboards must shift from tracking outputs to reflecting broader impact and team contribution. This evolution transforms dashboards into strategic tools—supporting leaders not only in oversight, but also in steering transformation efforts toward meaningful results. Let's explore some ways that organizations can design dashboards that emphasize value generation and impact, aligning project performance with enterprise-level outcomes.

Capturing Value Generation. To ensure project work delivers measurable impact, organizations must go beyond traditional reporting and focus on tracking actual value creation and business impact. These include financial indicators such as cost savings, revenue growth, EBITDA impact, margin improvement, and capital efficiency, as well as strategic outcomes like customer satisfaction, risk reduction, market share, and time-to-market. By aligning these metrics with business objectives, organizations demonstrate that projects are not just tasks to be completed—they are integral to building the future of the organization.

These dashboards provide the foundation for value-based decisions, allowing leaders to prioritize and scale what's working. Crucially, this approach shifts the conversation from "Are we delivering on time?" to "Are we creating value and how can we accelerate it?"—encouraging teams to think in terms of long-term impact. When used effectively, value-focused dashboards build a performance culture centered on accountability, learning, and results.

Dashboards versus Real-Time Insight. Dashboards are evolving from static displays into intelligent, interactive systems. Even so, they alone are no longer enough. The next generation of portfolio performance relies on real-time, AI-powered insight that goes beyond simply monitoring to enable decision-making on the fly. Instead of waiting for end-of-week reports, project leaders can now interact with live systems that dynamically filter, analyze, and prioritize portfolio data. AI-enabled copilots can surface what matters most to each decision-maker through tailored visualizations, voice-activated queries, and scenario modeling. Predictive and prescriptive analytics further enhance this capability, offering foresight into project trajectories and automated recommendations to mitigate risk or accelerate delivery. These capabilities shift data from a backward-looking record to a forward-driving engine of transformation.

Emphasizing the People Dimension. Alongside value generation, project dashboards should reflect the human aspects of transformations, capturing metrics that reveal project teams' health, engagement, and resilience. These might include employee satisfaction scores, team stability and turnover rates, collaboration levels, or measures of workload balance and burnout risk. Including people-focused metrics acknowledges that project success depends on the team's ability to work effectively and maintain high engagement and morale levels. Projects with low engagement or high turnover are often at risk of delays, quality issues, and failure, making it essential to track these dynamics as closely as other performance indicators.

By monitoring these team-related metrics, leaders can gain insights into the working conditions within each project, enabling them to support team well-being and address potential issues early. For example, if a project shows signs of declining team morale or increased turnover, leaders can intervene with additional resources, adjust deadlines, or implement team-building initiatives to help reset and strengthen team dynamics. This focus on people enables a more holistic view of project performance and fosters a culture where project teams feel valued, supported, and motivated to excel—an essential component of thriving in a PDO.

New KPIs for Comprehensive Project and Transformation Performance. To fully leverage dashboards as strategic tools, leaders must go beyond traditional metrics and introduce KPIs that capture the complex realities of modern transformation efforts. (See the sidebar, "Dashboards That Deliver: The KPIs behind Successful Transformations," for more information.)

Building Dashboards That Drive Strategic Decisions. When designed to reflect value creation and team performance, modern project dashboards become powerful strategic tools. They allow leaders to make faster, more informed decisions; redirect resources proactively; and reinforce alignment across the portfolio.

By emphasizing outcomes over outputs, these dashboards signal a clear shift in organizational priorities—from delivering tasks to driving transformation. They also reinforce a culture where accountability, team ownership, and impact are visible and celebrated. This not only improves execution but also strengthens engagement and strategic coherence across teams. An example of a transformation dashboard designed to track initiative-level progress, impact metrics, and team performance in real time is shown in table 6-2.

Equally important is the discipline of focusing on a small set of meaningful KPIs. Overloading dashboards with dozens of metrics can dilute focus and reduce employee autonomy. As former SAP CEO Jim Snabe observed, too many KPIs can "put brains on ice."[4] At SAP, he discovered the company was tracking over fifty thousand KPIs—an overwhelming volume that paralyzed decision-making and stifled initiative. Measurement should clarify, not constrain. Leaders should instead prioritize clarity: a few well-chosen indicators that align with purpose and guide day-to-day

Dashboards That Deliver: The KPIs behind Successful Transformations

Value-Generation Metrics

- **Benefit realization rate and time to value.** Evaluates both how much of the expected value a project delivers and how quickly that value materializes, providing a balanced view of effectiveness and speed of impact.

- **Business impact metrics.** Tracks financial outcomes such as EBITDA contribution, NPV, IRR, revenue uplift, and margin improvement, linking project execution directly to enterprise value creation.

- **Alignment with strategic objectives.** Assesses how well projects connect to the organization's strategic priorities (e.g., market expansion, digital maturity, sustainability), ensuring that resources are directed toward initiatives that drive long-term competitive advantage.

People-Centric Metrics

- **Team engagement and morale.** Monitors team motivation levels through regular surveys, providing an early indicator of productivity and project quality.

- **Team stability and retention.** Tracks turnover within project teams, identifying potential risks associated with high staff turnover.

- **Workload balance and burnout risk.** Assesses team workload to reduce burnout risk and maintain productivity, especially in intensive transformation projects.

- **Change-resistance index.** Measures the level of resistance encountered, allowing leaders to identify areas needing additional support or communication to increase buy-in and reduce friction.

Sponsor and Stakeholder Engagement

- **Sponsor engagement score.** Measures the level of involvement and support provided by the project sponsor, a critical factor in alignment, decision-making, and overall project impact.

- **Stakeholder satisfaction and engagement.** Gauges satisfaction levels among key stakeholders, reflecting the project's ability to meet expectations and secure ongoing support.

Agility and Responsiveness KPIs

- **Change adaptability.** Evaluates how effectively a project team adapts to changes in scope or priorities, a key factor in navigating complex transformation efforts.

- **Issue resolution time.** Measures the speed at which project issues are identified and resolved, ensuring that bottlenecks do not hinder progress.

- **Decision velocity.** Tracks the speed of critical decisions, providing insights into the team's empowerment and governance.

Technology and Innovation Metrics

- **Use of AI and automation.** Assesses the extent of AI and automation use, capturing the impact of advanced technologies on efficiency and decision-making.

- **Digital tool adoption rate.** Measures the integration and use of digital tools for collaboration and tracking, indicating how well the team leverages technology.

Learning and Knowledge Sharing

- **Lessons-learned implementation rate.** Tracks the application of insights from previous projects, reinforcing a culture of continuous improvement.

- **Knowledge transfer and retention.** Assesses the effectiveness of knowledge-sharing practices, crucial for ensuring that valuable insights are retained for future use.

TABLE 6-2

Example of a transformation performance dashboard

Focus area	Metric	Description	Current status	Target
Strategic intent	Purpose of transformation	Strategic rationale and SMART goal	Create $1B new revenue in 3 years to reposition the company as a biotech leader	Fully defined
Financial impact	EBITDA contribution	Value added to EBITDA	$35M	$1000M (3 years)
	Time to value	Time to first measurable benefit	4 months	≤ 6 months
	Revenue uplift	New revenue generated	$180M	$1000M
Strategic alignment	Strategic contribution	Degree of alignment with strategy	4.5/5	≥ 4.5
	Market impact potential	Potential for market expansion or disruption	Moderate	High
Execution and delivery	Benefit progress	% of benefits achieved	35%	100%
	On-time milestones	% of milestones completed on schedule	92%	≥ 90%
	Project canvas health	Review/alignment on 9 key project fundamentals	87% reviewed	100%
	Team dedication level	% of team working full-time on project	75% FT	≥ 80% FT

Category	Metric	Description	Value	Target
Team and leadership	Engagement and morale	Motivation and connection to project purpose	8.3/10	≥ 8.5
	Executive sponsor	Sponsor involvement and decision participation	Active	Active
	Collaboration and communications	Coordination, trust, and clarity	8.7/10	≥ 8.5
Organizational readiness	Learning agility	% completing digital/project upskilling	72%	≥ 85%
	AI-driven adoption	% using real-time data and AI dashboards	58%	≥ 80%
	Communication cadence	Frequency of transformation updates	Monthly	Monthly
Decision velocity	Real-time dashboard use	% of executives using dashboards weekly	65%	≥ 90%
	Transformation score	Composite score across all performance areas	7.9/10	≥ 8.5
Portfolio summary	Executive attention	Metrics/initiatives needing immediate focus	Market impact, decision velocity	N/A
	Executive actions this period	Sponsor/leadership interventions	Resource reallocation to top 3 initiatives	N/A

judgment are far more effective than an illusion of control. In this way, project dashboards become not just performance tools—but leadership instruments for shaping transformation.

Project- and Team-Based Rewards

In a project-driven organization, where teams are the foundation of strategic initiatives, the way rewards are structured can significantly impact success. Traditional, individually focused rewards often fall short in encouraging the collective efforts required for transformational projects. This section explores how organizations can design team-oriented reward systems and foster collaboration across project teams, creating a framework that aligns with both project outcomes and broader organizational goals.

The Pitfalls in Project-Driven Performance Management

As organizations transition toward a project-driven model, many attempt to modernize their performance systems—but too often, they retrofit new practices onto old assumptions. Traditional metrics and incentive structures, designed for operational stability and individual performance, fail to reflect transformation work's dynamic, team-based nature. The result? Misalignment, disengagement, and underperformance where it matters most.

Here are two common pitfalls that undermine the shift to project-driven performance:

Relying on Traditional Metrics in a Transformation-Driven World

Most performance systems are rooted in predictability and designed to track outputs, efficiencies, and individual productivity. But project work is collaborative, adaptive, and focused on delivering the future value of the organization. Using traditional metrics to evaluate project performance creates blind spots, reinforcing outdated behaviors and obscuring real progress.

A large consumer goods company tracked performance using legacy KPIs focused on volume, cost reduction, and throughput. As the company ramped up strategic transformation initiatives, these metrics failed to reflect the impact of projects aimed at customer experience and innovation. Teams delivering real value through projects were overlooked, while operational performance dominated attention and recognition.

Incentivizing Individual and Functional Performance over Team Impact

Even as organizations launch cross-functional projects to drive change, many still tie compensation and recognition to functional metrics—sales targets, departmental cost savings, or personal achievements. These incentives reward local optimization and discourage employees from investing time and effort into broader strategic initiatives.

In a global logistics firm, project teams delivered a system-wide improvement in delivery accuracy, yet bonuses were awarded based on business-unit performance metrics. Team members who led the transformation effort received no reward, while others benefited from the results. This disconnect created frustration and reduced future engagement in enterprise-wide projects.

These pitfalls reveal a fundamental misalignment between how work is structured and how success is defined. To lead in the transformation age, organizations must evolve performance management to reflect the true nature of project-based value—measuring what matters and rewarding what drives impact.

Designing Team-Oriented Reward Systems for Projects

Most reward systems in organizations today are operationally or business driven, with financial recognition often tied to operational roles and outcomes, not to projects or transformation initiatives. So while operational teams might receive bonuses for meeting sales targets or production goals, project teams that are driving significant organizational change often lack similar recognition structures. For PDOs, this is a missed opportunity. Imagine being part of a transformation project where the team, including the executive sponsor, receives a bonus based on the benefits achieved—such as revenue generated or cost savings realized. This approach would be transformative, making team members more invested in the project's success and reinforcing the importance of achieving tangible outcomes.

However, our research shows that team-based reward systems for projects remain rare. Only 10 percent of organizations reported using team-based reward systems with financial bonuses for all strategic projects, and 20 percent implemented these rewards only for some strategic projects. More commonly, 31 percent of organizations offer personalized recognition to project teams but no financial rewards, while the largest group— 39 percent—ties all rewards solely to business and operational performance.

In a project-driven environment, linking rewards to the benefits created by a project rather than just completion encourages a results-focused mindset. When project teams, project leaders, and executive sponsors are financially recognized for the value they generate, they are more likely to prioritize high-impact results. This creates a powerful alignment of incentives, where everyone involved in the project is driven not only by completion but by achieving meaningful, measurable benefits.

To design effective team-oriented rewards, leaders should consider the following approaches:

- *Anchoring rewards in clear, shared goals.* Establishing specific project goals and success metrics that all team members can align with is crucial. Clear, strategic objectives enable teams to focus collectively on achieving them. Metrics such as timely delivery, quality benchmarks, and impact assessments provide common standards for success. Involving teams in defining these metrics enhances transparency and fairness, building trust and ensuring that rewards are perceived as equitable. For example, during a company-wide ERP transformation, the implementation team co-defines success metrics—including a 90 percent adoption rate within sixty days.

- *Incorporating project benefit-based bonuses and balancing individual team-based recognition.* Rather than offering bonuses solely based on project milestones, consider linking incentives to the actual benefits achieved by the project, such as cost savings, revenue growth, or efficiency improvements. This approach not only fosters a sense of shared ownership but also reinforces the team's focus on creating real value. Extending these rewards to executive sponsors can deepen accountability across all levels and signal that project outcomes are a top organizational priority.

- *Incentivizing the right outcomes for the right teams.* Different projects and teams call for different rewards. A high-pressure innovation sprint may benefit from nonfinancial incentives like time off or development opportunities, while large-scale transformation projects may be better supported with performance-based bonuses. Understanding what motivates each team—and aligning rewards accordingly—ensures that recognition is both meaningful and motivating. Tailored incentives drive engagement and reinforce a culture where rewards reflect real impact. For example, a digital transformation team leading the rollout of a new customer engagement platform receives personalized development plans and visibility in board-level reviews.

By integrating these strategies, leaders can overcome common challenges in designing team-based rewards, ensuring that recognition systems are fair, transparent, and aligned with the organization's strategic priorities. This holistic approach enhances motivation and engagement and strengthens team cohesion and accountability. When leaders consistently recognize collective achievements and collaborative efforts that drive transformation, they reinforce a culture where teamwork becomes a cornerstone of sustainable, high-impact success.

Incentivizing Collaboration in a Project-Driven Organization

Traditional recognition programs often fall short in environments where transformation and cross-functional collaboration are the norm. High-impact projects require teamwork and alignment, yet many reward systems still focus narrowly on individual or operational accomplishments. Shifting to a project-focused reward approach means recognizing that the success of each initiative is a stepping stone toward transformation. Success must be redefined not just as individual performance, but as collective achievements.

Research supports the value of collaboration in driving organizational success. Organizations expert Heidi Gardner reports that firms earn higher margins, inspire greater client loyalty, and gain a competitive edge when specialists collaborate across functional boundaries.[5] By embedding collaboration into a project-driven reward system, organizations amplify these positive effects, building teams that are not only effective but deeply aligned with the mission and broader goals.

The following strategies help leaders design recognition systems that promote true collaboration and reinforce a culture where every project delivers value to the whole organization.

Establish Collaboration-Specific Rewards Linked to Organizational Impact. To promote a project-driven reward system, create rewards that specifically recognize collaborative actions, such as knowledge sharing, joint problem-solving, and cross-functional support—behaviors that drive both project and organizational success. For example, rewarding teams that work across departments to optimize processes or implement efficiencies ensures that collaboration benefits not only the project but the entire organization.

By linking rewards to outcomes that matter at the organizational level—like increased efficiency, reduced costs, or improved customer satisfaction—leaders reinforce the idea that every project's success contributes to the organization's strategic goals. This alignment encourages teams to think beyond their immediate objectives and consider how their efforts can create value for the organization as a whole.

Implement Peer Recognition Programs to Highlight Collaborative Contributions. In a PDO, peer recognition can be a powerful tool for highlighting the collaborative efforts that often go unseen by leadership. Often, the contributions that have the most impact on cross-functional collaboration, such as mentoring, offering insights, or bridging knowledge gaps between teams, are best appreciated by peers rather than management. Implementing a formal peer recognition program allows team members to highlight each other's efforts, acknowledging contributions that support both project and organizational goals.

Through peer recognition, employees can call out actions that align with the organization's larger mission, fostering a sense of appreciation for efforts that strengthen project execution and deliver value beyond the individual project team. For example, team members might use an online platform to celebrate colleagues who went above and beyond to support project goals. This approach ensures that contributions to organizational success are visible and valued across the organization.

Use Real-Time Feedback Loops to Recognize Collaborative Wins across Projects. In a fast-paced PDO, real-time feedback helps sustain momentum by recognizing collaborative achievements as they happen. Establish feedback mechanisms that allow for quick, frequent recognition of teamwork that impacts both project and organizational goals. Regular check-ins, project updates, or sprint reviews provide opportunities for both team leads and peers to highlight collaborative achievements that make a difference across departments.

For example, during weekly updates, project managers or team leads can set aside time to call out specific collaborative actions that advance both project objectives and organizational priorities, such as knowledge sharing or joint problem-solving sessions. Immediate recognition not only boosts morale but reinforces the connection between collaborative behaviors and their contribution to the organization's success, underscoring that project-driven work is about collective impact.

Reward Cross-Functional Partnerships to Drive Organizational Alignment. Transformation projects typically require cross-functional collaboration, with teams from diverse areas of the organization working together to solve complex challenges. Rewarding effective cross-functional partnerships signals that successful transformation relies on alignment beyond individual projects. By recognizing teams that effectively build bridges across functions, organizations ensure collaboration strengthens project outcomes and organizational objectives.

Consider offering a "cross-functional excellence" award to project teams that effectively align their efforts across departments. By publicly acknowledging successful cross-functional partnerships, organizations demonstrate that breaking down silos is essential not only for project success but for achieving larger strategic goals. This encourages teams to work collaboratively toward outcomes that drive value at the organizational level, reinforcing the importance of alignment in a project-driven reward system.

Celebrate Milestones and Project Completion as Organizational Achievements. In a PDO, every project milestone and completion should be celebrated as an achievement that strengthens the entire organization. When a project reaches a key milestone or is successfully completed, gather the team for a celebration—whether formal or informal—to recognize everyone's contribution to collective success. Celebrations can take various forms, from formal awards ceremonies to informal team lunches or shout-outs in company-wide meetings. By treating project accomplishments as shared victories, organizations foster a sense of unity and pride, reinforce the importance of unified goals, and demonstrate that every completed project drives the organization's transformation agenda forward.

Adopt Shared Risk/Reward Approaches in Your Contracts. Collaboration doesn't guarantee success, and projects will still be subject to challenges or the headwinds of external factors. Along with reward schemes, it's important to foster collective responsibility for project outcomes. When challenges such as cost overruns, rework, or delays occur, the focus should be on learning and support rather than blame. Teams should be encouraged to diagnose issues together, share accountability, and offer additional resources or guidance to lower-performing areas. This reinforces the "one-project" culture referenced earlier in the book and helps prevent siloed behaviors or tactical maneuvering that prioritize individual or departmental interests over the success of the project as a whole.

Building a reward system that prioritizes both team contributions and collaborative behaviors is essential for organizations navigating the complexities of the transformation age. Recognizing the collective efforts behind successful projects and incentivizing cross-functional collaboration elevates the organization's potential to adapt and thrive. By implementing thoughtful, project-centered rewards, leaders can inspire teams to drive strategic outcomes while reinforcing an environment where every project strengthens the organization's mission and long-term vision.

Conclusion

Performance management must evolve to support a project-driven organization. Traditional metrics and incentives—designed for individual output and operational performance—are no longer sufficient in a world defined by cross-functional collaboration and continuous transformation. By introducing project-focused metrics that emphasize value creation, outcomes, and strategic contribution, leaders can better track and accelerate what drives impact. When organizations shift rewards toward team-based achievements and shared success, they create an environment where collaboration, adaptability, and shared accountability thrive.

These shifts are not just technical adjustments—they reflect a deeper cultural evolution in how success is understood and rewarded. When performance systems mirror the realities of project work, teams feel seen, motivated, and empowered to deliver real results.

In part 3, we will build on these foundations and explore how PDOs can maximize the return on their transformation efforts.

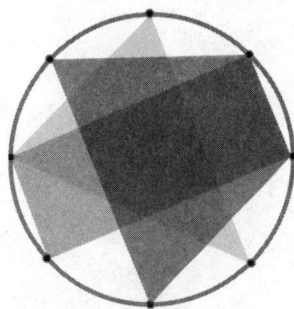

PART THREE

VALUE GENERATION IN THE TRANSFORMATION AGE

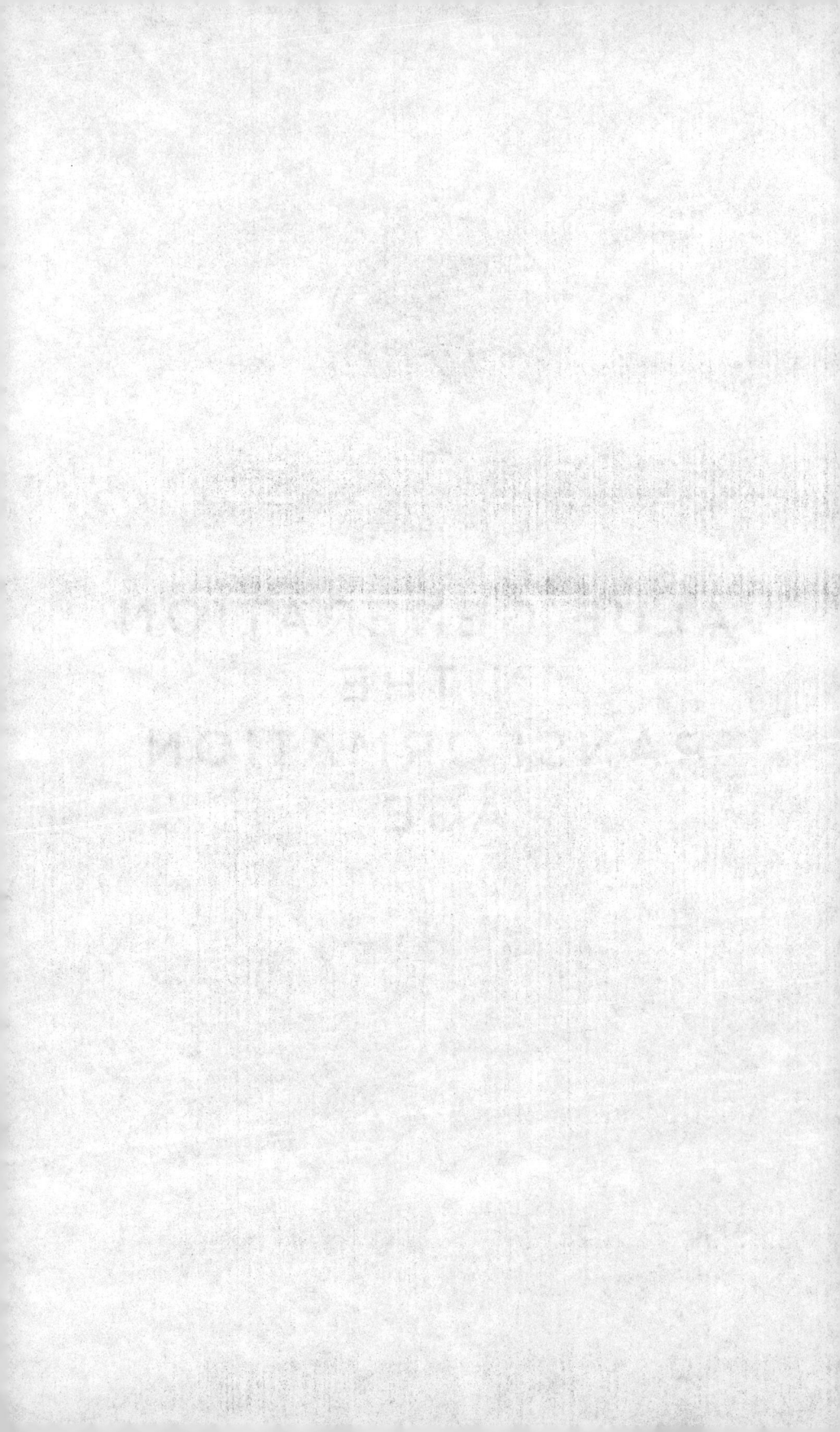

As we embark on the final section of this book, our focus turns to the ultimate purpose of every project: creating value. Parts 1 and 2 examined how to structure and lead project-driven organizations; part 3 explores how to translate that structure into sustained results by embedding project-first thinking at the core of how the business operates and delivers value.

For much of the twentieth century, value creation was operationally driven. Companies optimized supply chains, improved efficiencies, and scaled repeatable processes. Operations were the center of gravity, generating value and protecting margins. But that model is no longer enough in today's landscape of constant disruption and reinvention. The value that defines competitiveness and future growth is now created through transformation and projects.

This shift is visible on the ground. In leading organizations, operations are increasingly automated through AI, AI agents, and robots. However, responding by laying off employees and banking savings is not only shortsighted—it's contrary to the goals of a PDO. The true opportunity lies in reallocating those freed-up resources to where they matter most: projects. Initiatives that drive innovation, enter new markets, digitize experiences, or reduce carbon footprints are no longer peripheral. As long as operations consume the bulk of manpower and budget, organizations will struggle to staff their strategic priorities adequately. Projects have become the new core and need to be resourced accordingly.

As Fei-Fei Li, Stanford professor and leading advocate for human-centered AI, reminds us: "Jobs don't just provide income—they provide dignity. Our goal with any technology should be to increase overall human dignity, not reduce it."[1] Her perspective underscores a critical opportunity: to utilize automation not to displace people, but to enhance their contributions. In a truly project-driven organization, technology becomes a lever for unlocking human potential, redirecting it toward the initiatives that shape the future.

This is where modern project management comes in, as I defined in the *HBR Project Management Handbook*, as a simpler, more engaging, and hands-on discipline centered on people, stakeholders, and value creation.[2] It equips leaders with practical, human-centered tools to drive meaningful outcomes with clarity and speed. With hybrid delivery models and AI-enhanced execution, modern project management introduces a new mindset that places value at the center of every initiative. The result is not just faster delivery—it's smarter delivery, where every sprint, milestone, and decision is tied to business impact.

In the following two chapters, we'll explore two core enablers of this shift: First, operations can evolve from centers of stability to platforms that enable project execution and innovation at scale. Second, execution—including hybrid delivery models, AI-enhanced workflows, and collaborative cultures—can embed project thinking across the enterprise. Together, these capabilities demonstrate how to move beyond isolated transformation efforts and build organizations where value is created continuously through projects that matter.

CHAPTER 7

Project-Driven Operations

Haier has emerged as a global reference point in redefining the role of operations not just as engines of efficiency but as dynamic platforms for value creation through automation, strategic resourcing, and project-led innovation. At the heart of Haier's transformation lies the RenDanHeYi model, which decentralizes decision-making, empowers entrepreneurial teams, and embeds project-driven delivery deep within the organization's operational fabric.

Haier's smart manufacturing facilities showcase what it means to *lead in an era of automation and robotization.* Robots and AI tools now manage repetitive, precision-driven tasks across appliance and medical device production, freeing human employees to focus on high-value work such as oversight, data analysis, and problem-solving. Leaders are trained to manage production and orchestrate hybrid workflows—blending automation with human judgment. This human-machine collaboration extends to areas like predictive maintenance and medical supply chains, where AI helps teams anticipate issues and optimize delivery, enabling more strategic and adaptive decision-making. Unlike operations-driven organizations that may view automation primarily as a cost-cutting tool, Haier reinvests the efficiencies gained—reassigning, reskilling, and redeploying talent to project-driven initiatives that generate new forms of value.

Beyond automation, Haier has *shifted the center of its business model from operational output to project-driven growth.* What was once a manufacturing company has evolved into a network of MEs and EMCs, each responsible for initiating and executing value-generating projects. For example, Haier Biomedical's evolution into the Smart Medical EMC illustrates how project teams cocreate new health-care solutions by integrating technology, design, and user feedback. These initiatives go beyond efficiency—they generate strategic differentiation and business growth. Haier's model ensures that operations provide a stable base, while its project-led teams drive continuous waves of innovation, product development, and service expansion.

Crucially, Haier's operational transformation includes *creating shared, project-aligned service models*. Its EMC structure connects internal units with external partners, ranging from hospitals to research institutes, through EMC contracts forming a collaborative ecosystem's backbone. These hubs enable real-time resource mobilization and solution codevelopment, reducing silos and boosting responsiveness. In sectors like health care, this model accelerates the delivery of complex, scenario-based services while maintaining ethical and regulatory standards. Once isolated and standardized, operational functions are now integrated, flexible, and measured by their contribution to project outcomes and user value.

Haier's approach reveals a future-ready model in which operations are no longer defined by scale or repetition but by their ability to support and amplify the impact of strategic, project-driven execution. It is an example of operational efficiency and a blueprint for sustained value generation in the project economy.

I n my transformation workshops, one of the most thought-provoking discussions arises when I present the chart seen earlier in figure I-1, illustrating the evolution of work within organizations. Decades ago—eighty, fifty, even thirty years—most employees, managers, and senior leaders dedicated nearly all their time to operational tasks. Projects were rare, often confined to specific departments or initiated sporadically.

Today, organizations are increasingly channeling their efforts into project-based work. This transition reflects a broader trend: the automation and digitization of operational tasks. With advancements in technology, an increasing number of routine activities are now performed by machines or software, freeing human capital to focus on more complex, value-added endeavors.

Interestingly, a few executives express a clear vision for the future: a workplace where no human is involved in operational activities. They believe that human intellect and creativity are better utilized in driving change, solving complex problems, and building the future. While some traditional organizations challenge this notion, arguing that certain operations cannot be fully automated, it's essential to consider the evolving expectations of younger, digital-native generations.

For instance, would you dine at a restaurant or stay at a hotel staffed entirely by robots? Would you trust a robot to cut your hair or teach your children? While these scenarios may seem unconventional today, emerging trends suggest a growing acceptance of automation in various service sectors. Younger consumers—Millennials, Generation Z, and digital natives in particular—often value efficiency and technological integration, sometimes even preferring automated services over human interaction.

The question for leaders is this: *If your operations were built today from scratch, would they be designed to support stability—or transformation?*

This chapter explores how organizations are reimagining their operations to thrive in the transformation age, shifting from function-based, efficiency-led models to operations that enable agility, innovation, and value creation. Today, when competitive advantage depends on the speed and impact of execution, operations can no longer remain separate from transformation. They must become the engine that sustains and scales it.

Most traditional businesses have operated like cyclists on a hilly route—alternating between steep climbs of transformation and periods of steady-state operations, only to gear up again when the next hill of change appears. They periodically reorganize, digitize, or restructure in response to disruption, then revert to efficiency mode. In contrast, PDOs operate at a far more consistent cadence. They embed transformation into daily operations, ensuring that the value created by projects is not only delivered but continuously enhanced and scaled.

This shift is made possible by automation, AI, and new operating models that free up capacity, simplify execution, and allow organizations

FIGURE 7-1

Project-driven operations

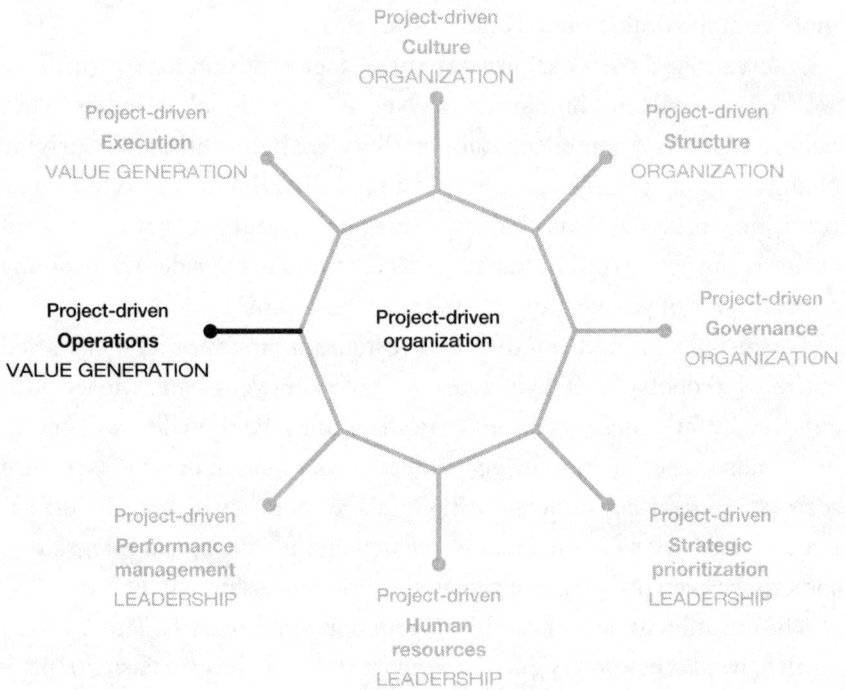

to redirect talent and resources toward strategic, project-based initiatives. According to McKinsey, AI-powered predictive maintenance tools alone could reduce downtime by up to 50 percent in asset-heavy industries like energy and transportation.[1] Collaborative robots now handle repetitive tasks, such as windshield installation, so that human workers can focus on higher-value activities like innovation, quality control, and continuous improvement. Ford is one company that has been using such systems successfully.[2]

In this chapter, we look at how leaders can develop project-driven operations by focusing on three main areas—leading in an era of automation and robotization, shifting the center of value creation from operations to projects, and orchestrating operations through project-aligned service models—all of which were visible in the examples from Haier (figure 7-1).

Leading in an Era of AI, Automation, and Robotization

As automation and artificial intelligence become deeply embedded in business operations, organizations face a pivotal choice: Will they cut staff and bank the savings or reinvest this freed-up capacity into high-impact initiatives that fuel future growth—and preserve the dignity that meaningful work provides? This decision lies at the heart of what separates operations-driven organizations from project-driven ones. In the project economy, automation is no longer just a tool for trimming costs; it's a strategic enabler for unlocking value through projects.

Across industries, automation is reshaping how work is done. Ocado Group, a British online supermarket, exemplifies how automation can revolutionize operations.[3] In its highly automated customer fulfillment centers, thousands of robots work in a synchronized grid system to pick and pack groceries with unmatched efficiency. The human workers who used to do this now focus on managing robotic systems, resolving exceptions, and maintaining equipment. Similarly, Priestley's Gourmet Delights in Brisbane has adopted an AU$53 million AI-powered smart factory.[4] This facility employs autonomous vehicles and collaborative robots, doubling production capacity while enabling employees to upskill into higher-value roles.

Where operations-driven companies often treat automation as an efficiency play, reducing labor and freezing investment, PDOs take a different path. They see automation as a release valve, freeing capacity to be strategically redirected into project portfolios. This might mean upskilling warehouse staff to become project analysts, reassigning operations leads to digital transformation teams, or investing cost savings into customer innovation pilots.

Leadership's Appetite for Disruption

This kind of reinvestment requires leadership with a high appetite for disruption. Leaders must be willing to challenge legacy assumptions, reimagine traditional job roles, and embrace the risks inherent in rapid change. Those who lead with bold intent reallocate automation gains into cross-functional teams tasked with delivering new products, expanding into new markets, or optimizing customer experiences.

Tesla's manufacturing philosophy exemplifies this mindset. Its automation initiatives are not just about cutting costs—they're designed to scale innovation. By integrating robotics, software, and design into a seamless execution engine, Tesla reinvests savings into R&D, product development, and infrastructure growth.

Similarly, IBM CEO Arvind Krishna reported that automation allowed the company to reduce its HR function from seven hundred people to just fifty while enhancing digital employee services and redeploying staff into more strategic roles. Notably, this transformation was not achieved through mass layoffs. Instead, while the company automated 90 percent of routine HR tasks such as promotions and assessments, it managed the shift primarily through attrition, allowing natural workforce changes to support reallocation.[5] The result was a leaner, more strategic HR function focused on high-value support and analytics.

The difference isn't technological—it's cultural. While every organization can adopt automation, not everyone is prepared to embrace its enabling function: the reinvention of work.

Leading in Automated Workplaces

Leaders increasingly manage *human-AI hybrid teams*—workforces composed of both people and intelligent systems working in tandem. This evolution requires a transformation in leadership approaches, focusing less on supervising individuals and more on orchestrating collaboration between human talent and AI capabilities. Tasks are often categorized as follows:

- *Task substitution.* AI systems take over repetitive tasks previously performed by humans, such as virtual assistants handling customer inquiries.

- *Task augmentation.* Humans and AI collaborate, with AI providing data-driven insights to enhance human decision-making. For instance, AI-powered design tools in manufacturing can suggest optimizations that engineers evaluate and implement.

- *Task assemblage.* Humans and AI work together dynamically, each contributing their strengths to complete tasks. For example, AI may assist in analyzing medical images in health care, while doctors make final diagnoses and treatment decisions.

Leading such teams requires a blend of technical proficiency and interpersonal skills. Leaders must understand AI systems' capabilities and limitations to integrate them effectively into workflows.

In any work with AI, ethical considerations become paramount. Leaders are responsible for ensuring that AI systems operate transparently and fairly, safeguarding against biases and protecting data privacy. They must also address employee concerns about job displacement, emphasizing the role of AI as a tool to augment human capabilities rather than replace them.

A pertinent example is the Crossrail project in the UK, which employed system architecture models and AI-enhanced tools to manage the design and delivery of its complex railway infrastructure.[6] They developed more than seven hundred architecture diagrams—ranging from simple concept views to multilayered metadata-rich models—to visualize and integrate components from concept design to commissioning. These models provided a holistic view of the railway system, illustrating various components and their interrelationships, facilitating effective communication among stakeholders, and streamlining the integration of diverse systems throughout the project's life cycle. Additionally, AI-driven predictive analytics were utilized to anticipate potential project delays, budget overruns, and resource shortages, supporting decision-making and risk management. Integrating AI in dynamic resource allocation, such as optimizing refueling operations for construction equipment, exemplified the project's commitment to leveraging AI for improved operational effectiveness.

A Modern Framework for Human-Robot Collaboration

In traditional operations, automation was rigid and narrowly applied. Robotic arms in assembly lines performed repetitive tasks like fastening a door on a specific car model. If the product changed, the robot often became obsolete, requiring costly reprogramming or replacement. These systems prioritized efficiency but offered little flexibility, limiting their value in dynamic environments.

Today, that paradigm has changed. Thanks to advances in AI, robots are no longer confined to static roles. They can adapt to new instructions, reconfigure for different products, and even learn from previous actions. A robotic arm once limited to car doors might now pivot to install components on a bicycle or assist in assembling a medical device. This adaptability unlocks a new era of value generation—what we might call the "projectification" of robots—where these tools contribute to innovation, experimentation, and transformation.

Collaboration between humans and robots must evolve as organizations shift toward project-driven operations. This means moving beyond basic task delegation to building systems where human and robotic team members work together dynamically, each enhancing the capabilities of the other. To support this, organizations need a modern framework for human-robot collaboration that reflects the technological and strategic realities of the transformation age.

- *Real-time coworking platforms.* Organizations should invest in platforms that enable seamless, real-time coordination between humans and robots. For example, AI-powered orchestration tools can assign and reassign tasks dynamically based on shifting priorities. In operations, this might mean rerouting robot workflows to accommodate a spike in demand. In a project setting like a critical infrastructure rollout, it could mean redirecting drones or automated sensors to gather real-time data when unexpected conditions arise.

- *Proactive workflow transparency.* Predictive analytics can monitor and flag potential bottlenecks in human-robot workflow. For instance, Ocado's fulfillment centers rely on AI algorithms to forecast robot performance degradation, allowing teams to intervene early. This same principle can be applied in project contexts, anticipating delays in resource allocation or task execution and enabling preemptive adjustments that keep transformation initiatives on track.

- *Enhanced communication interfaces.* As robots become more embedded in workflows, intuitive communication is critical.

Augmented reality (AR), voice commands, and haptic feedback tools allow workers to interact with robotic systems more naturally. Imagine a technician wearing AR glasses that display the intended motion path of a robotic arm, allowing them to coordinate movements in tight spaces with greater precision and safety.

- *Robot-coached training.* Robots equipped with AI can support human learning by demonstrating complex procedures and offering real-time feedback. This might involve training a new technician on a machine's maintenance protocol in operations. In projects, it could mean guiding team members through new digital platforms or prototyping tools, ensuring that employees are supported by technology and actively learning from it.

- *Role customization and personalization.* Humans' ability to tailor robotic behavior enhances productivity and engagement. For example, a project manager might configure a construction robot to generate status updates in a preferred format or frequency. At the same time, an operations supervisor might adjust a robot's interaction parameters to better fit their team's workflow style. This personalization increases alignment and reduces friction across collaborative workstreams.

- *Adaptive collaboration models.* Organizations should adopt models where the human-robot relationship evolves dynamically across project stages. For instance, robots might lead high-throughput data collection in the early discovery phase of a pharmaceutical R&D project. Human scientists would interpret findings, design tests, and shape final recommendations as the project matures. This fluidity ensures that human creativity and robotic efficiency are applied immediately for maximum value.

By implementing these advanced collaboration practices, PDOs position themselves to thrive. This is not merely about doing work faster—it's about unlocking new types of work that were previously too complex, resource-intensive, or unpredictable. As automation continues to accelerate, the organizations that will lead recognize robots not as replacements, but as reinforcements. When human ingenuity and robotic capability are aligned, the potential for breakthrough performance expands exponentially.

Unlocking this potential also requires rethinking how we prepare people to work in these new environments. It's not enough to teach employees how to operate or supervise automation—they must be empowered to use automation to drive strategic change. In PDOs, that means building training programs beyond technical instruction, equipping employees to extract insights from AI systems, optimizing workflows, and translating data into transformative action.

This effort begins by listening, but also by actively encouraging employees to experiment with AI. In many organizations, employees are already exploring AI tools to improve efficiency, yet leadership remains unaware. A 2025 KPMG–University of Melbourne study of forty-eight thousand workers across forty-seven countries found that 57 percent conceal their AI use from employers, and 58 percent say they use it intentionally, with about a third using it weekly.[7] This silent innovation presents a powerful opportunity.

However, enabling safe experimentation must be paired with structured development. Organizations should remove restrictive policies on third-party tools—despite the challenges around cybersecurity and confidential data—by implementing ring-fenced test environments where employees can innovate freely without compromising core systems. This creates a controlled sandbox for AI experimentation, preserving safety while uncovering valuable use cases.

In parallel, leadership must set expectations. For example, Shopify's CEO Tobi Lütke now requires teams to prove that a job cannot be performed by AI before requesting new hires, making AI competence a baseline expectation included in performance evaluations.[8] This directive signals a fundamental shift in how work is both done and evaluated.

The imperative is clear: connect training to transformation. Encouraging safe experimentation must also mean sharing successful use cases across teams and embedding AI into daily workflows, turning isolated innovation into enterprise-wide capability. Leading organizations are already moving in this direction. In China, government incentives are helping businesses upskill their workforce in robotics and AI, not just for operational support, but also for strategic roles. Workers are being redeployed from routine tasks into areas like predictive maintenance, product innovation, and workflow digitization, directly fueling project portfolios and business growth.

PDOs create a skilled workforce ready to lead the future by investing in targeted, forward-looking development programs. These teams don't just operate systems—they advance strategy. They don't just adapt to change—they accelerate it. And in the fast-moving transformation age, that's not a luxury—it's a necessity.

Shifting the Center of Value Creation from Operations to Projects

As product life cycles shorten, advantage is more ephemeral, and innovation accelerates, organizations increasingly find more value created through projects that launch new products, develop customer solutions, or enhance digital capabilities, not just through ongoing operations. In PDOs, operations provide the foundation, while projects drive growth.

The Erosion of Value Created by Operations

In many industries, the traditional reliance on optimizing operations as a primary value lever no longer delivers the returns it once did. Efficiency gains alone are insufficient in rapidly shifting market dynamics and rising customer expectations. (See the sidebar, "The Role of the Chief Operating Officer.")

Take the electronics sector, where product life cycles are increasingly compressed. Consumers demand constant updates and innovation, forcing manufacturers to accelerate development timelines and launch new models relentlessly. This puts immense pressure on production planning, inventory management, and after-sales support, leaving little time to recoup investments before products are outpaced or commoditized.

Rising production and material costs and intense competition have led companies to adopt practices like "shrinkflation," where product sizes are reduced without lowering prices to maintain margins. This approach can erode customer trust and brand value over time.

The Role of the Chief Operating Officer

Leadership roles are changing rapidly to support the new project-driven organization. According to McKinsey, the unsung role of the COO is undergoing a major transformation. The reason is clear:

> The COO role is evolving from its roots in the back office into a catalyst for technology-driven growth, strategic expansion, and employee empowerment. As chief executives increasingly become the public face of organizations and deal with external constituencies and stakeholders, it often falls to COOs to provide internal leadership and direction. And as operations face extraordinary disruptions, COOs are now key players in boosting organizational resilience and value creation.[a]

This evolution is especially pronounced in PDOs, where COOs are pivotal in dynamic resource allocation, operational agility, and strategic execution. Their responsibilities have expanded to include enabling technology adoption, fostering cross-functional collaboration, and aligning operations with project priorities—all while maintaining stability and efficiency in a world of constant change.

The shift toward project-based operations is central to this transformation. In a PDO, operations increasingly integrate with strategic projects, creating adaptable systems and processes that align operational activities with project priorities. By embracing project-based operations, COOs enable their organizations to balance short-term flexibility with long-term resilience. Here are several ways COOs can lead this shift effectively:

- **From back office to strategic partner.** Traditionally viewed as a behind-the-scenes executor, the COO is now a key strategic partner, driving initiatives that enable the organization to adapt and thrive. In a PDO, this means moving beyond routine operational oversight to actively shaping resource allocation and ensuring alignment between projects and long-term goals.

- **Enabling operational agility.** To support dynamic resource allocation, COOs streamline processes, removing inefficiencies that hinder resource flexibility. By fostering a culture of continuous improvement, they free up capacity for high-priority projects.

COOs must also leverage advanced technologies like AI and automation to optimize workflows, enabling operations to function as a responsive and efficient support system for strategic initiatives.

- **Bridging projects and operations.** The COO serves as the bridge between day-to-day operations and strategic project execution. This involves creating systems allowing operational insights—such as emerging bottlenecks or shifting market demands—to inform real-time project decisions. It also means ensuring that operational teams are aligned with project teams, promoting seamless collaboration and knowledge sharing across functions.

- **Balancing stability and innovation.** One of the most significant challenges for COOs is balancing operational stability with the agility needed to support continuous transformation. They must ensure the organization's core remains resilient and efficient while enabling resources to be deployed dynamically to strategic projects. This dual focus helps the organization maintain continuity while driving innovation and adapting to disruption.

NOTE
a. Darryl Piasecki, "Stepping Up: What COOs Will Need to Succeed in 2023 and Beyond," McKinsey & Company, October 31, 2022, https://www.mckinsey.com/capabilities/operations/our-insights/stepping-up-what-coos-will-need-to-succeed-in-2023-and-beyond.

As markets become saturated, operational efficiency alone no longer creates competitive advantage. When products feel interchangeable, competition shifts to price and eroding margins. To stay competitive, organizations must turn to project-based initiatives that spark innovation and deliver differentiated value to customers.

The New Core of Competitive Advantage

Companies are now reorienting their strategies to prioritize project-based value creation while maintaining operational foundations. (For more information, see the sidebar, "Assessment: Is Your Operating Model Ready for Project-Driven Value Creation?")

Assessment: Is Your Operating Model Ready for Project-Driven Value Creation?

As more organizations pivot from traditional operations to project-led innovation, evaluating whether your current operational setup supports—or stalls—this shift is crucial. This assessment is designed to help leaders identify whether their operations are still geared toward past efficiencies or ready to enable future growth.

Ask yourself the following:

- **Are operations still optimized for scale and repeatability, even as market demand requires speed and customization?** Legacy processes and systems may still deliver stable outputs but often lack the flexibility to support rapid project deployment and adaptation.

- **Do operational processes support frequent product launches or customer-specific solutions?** If operational bottlenecks delay go-to-market timelines or make delivering tailored outcomes difficult, value is left on the table.

- **Is most capital and staffing still spent maintaining operations rather than delivering projects?** Operational excellence alone rarely drives differentiation anymore. Projects often carry the responsibility for innovation, yet they may lack adequate support or resourcing.

- **Are project teams dependent on traditional operational workflows that weren't built for speed or flexibility?** Rigid systems and approval processes slow down transformation. Agile projects require operational backing that can move just as fast.

- **Do operations generate insights that actively inform and accelerate project work?** Data trapped in operational silos can't be leveraged effectively by innovation teams. Project-driven value creation depends on real-time feedback loops across both worlds.

If the answer to three or more of these questions is no, operations may need to be reconfigured for efficiency and to enable insights that directly inform and accelarate project work. In a PDO, operations are not the past but the platform that powers the future.

Mastercard exemplifies this dual approach. While continuing to operate its core payments infrastructure reliably and at scale, it is increasingly creating value through new service offerings delivered via project-driven innovation and transformation initiatives.

In October 2023, Mastercard announced the expansion of its Advisors consulting business with new practices in artificial intelligence and economics—part of a broader pivot toward business transformation services.[9] Similarly, its Digital Labs initiative supports internal teams and enterprise clients by providing immersive environments that apply digital technologies, design thinking, and user experience expertise to rapidly prototype and refine new products and services. These new capabilities, built and scaled through internal transformation projects, enable Mastercard to cocreate solutions with clients, deepen strategic relationships, and unlock new revenue streams beyond traditional transaction services.

Traditionally known for its oil and gas operations, BP is building a new growth engine through project-based ventures that prioritize agility, innovation, and long-term value over traditional volume-driven operations. In June 2020, it sold its petrochemicals unit to INEOS for $5 billion, signaling a move away from traditional operations and freeing up resources to invest in new strategic initiatives.[10] One key example is its $4.1 billion acquisition of Archaea Energy in October 2022.[11] Rather than simply expanding operational capacity, this move added a dynamic portfolio of renewable natural gas projects that generate value through continuous development and delivery. Each biogas facility operates as a stand-alone project with specific milestones, outcomes, and alignment to BP's low-carbon strategy, moving it further from steady-state operations toward agile, innovation-led growth.

In November 2024, BP and its partners committed $7 billion to developing the Ubadari gas field in Indonesia and deploying carbon capture, utilization, and storage technologies.[12] Set to begin production in 2028, this large-scale initiative is structured as a multiphase transformation project, combining infrastructure development, environmental technology, and long-term sustainability targets.

Selling Projects Instead of Products

Companies are transitioning from offering stand-alone products to delivering comprehensive projects that achieve specific outcomes. This evolution addresses the limitations of traditional product sales, such as commoditization and high customer attrition.

Traditional product sales are typically one-off transactions, where the customer relationship ends after delivery. In contrast, selling projects involves providing integrated, long-term solutions that combine products, services, and ongoing support. This approach not only delivers continuous value but also fosters deeper, more strategic partnerships with clients.

Philips, responding to rapid technological change and increasing market competition, shifted its focus from selling stand-alone medical devices to delivering comprehensive health-care solutions. A prime example is its partnership with Westchester Medical Center Health Network, a 1,700-bed health-care system in New York. Through this long-term collaboration, Philips offers advanced medical technologies, clinical consulting, and IT integration services aimed at transforming patient care.[13]

This shift from product to project has produced measurable results: a 20 percent reduction in patient wait times, earlier first-case starts, improved lab utilization, and higher satisfaction among both patients and staff. By embedding itself as a transformation partner rather than a product vendor, Philips demonstrates how project-based execution can drive sustained competitive advantage.

This project-centric approach deepens customer engagement, unlocks recurring revenue opportunities, and positions companies as long-term partners rather than onetime suppliers. By aligning delivery with measurable outcomes, businesses can stand out in crowded markets and build loyalty through ongoing value creation.

Selling projects demands an agile delivery model that integrates software, hardware, consulting, and support into seamless solutions tailored to client needs. Operations must evolve from rigid, standardized systems into dynamic service platforms that support customization, scalability, and sustained impact across the full customer journey.

This transition underscores the core principle of project-driven operations: value is no longer embedded solely in what is produced, but in how that output supports broader transformation goals. Leaders must build operational infrastructures that support product flow and accelerate solution delivery, integrate cross-functional expertise, and scale innovation. The organizations that master this shift will be best positioned to lead in the transformation age.

Orchestrating Operations through Project-Aligned Service Models

As value creation shifts toward project-based work, traditional operational models must be reimagined. To support rapid transformation, operations must evolve into dynamic platforms, capable of flexibly deploying expertise, data, and services in response to the changing demands of projects.

The Pitfalls in a Project-Driven Organization

In a project-driven organization, operations must evolve from efficiency engines into platforms for strategic value creation, supporting adaptability, innovation, and transformation at scale. Yet many companies adopt enabling tools like automation, AI, and shared services without changing how they structure, staff, or measure success. The result? Temporary gains in cost or speed, but missed opportunities for deeper, sustained impact. Here are three pitfalls that often undermine this shift:

Failing to Lead the Reinvestment of AI Automation Gains into Value-Driven Projects

Many operations-driven organizations still treat AI and robot process automation as a blunt instrument for reducing costs, cutting headcount, and banking immediate savings. This approach may yield short-term

(continued)

gains but often undermines long-term competitiveness. Too frequently, leaders fail to look beyond costs and efficiency, treating automation solely as a way to trim budgets rather than a catalyst for growth. Instead of redeploying freed-up capacity to fuel high-impact projects or investing in workforce reskilling, they allow those gains to evaporate. Without a deliberate reinvestment strategy, the potential of automation is not just missed—it becomes a missed opportunity that stalls transformation and weakens the organization's future readiness.

At one logistics firm, robotics streamlined operations and slashed costs. Yet leadership focused solely on margin gains, freezing even strategic hires and delaying project investments. The result was a leaner operation with no added agility or growth—automation gains were absorbed into the bottom line rather than fueling innovation or transformation. Projects stalled, momentum for broader change faded, and within a year, leadership was again under pressure to find new sources of savings.

Overcommitting to the Core, Undervaluing the Future

In many organizations, core operations still command the most resources, attention, and leadership focus—even as the market shifts and opportunities for value creation increasingly emerge through innovation and transformation initiatives. Projects, by contrast, are often treated as peripheral experiments: underfunded, loosely governed, and disconnected from the organization's main engine of growth.

Intel's recent trajectory illustrates this pitfall. While maintaining heavy investment in its legacy chip manufacturing operations, Intel underresourced its innovation efforts—such as Intel Labs—which remained isolated from core strategy and execution. This imbalance contributed to a 60 percent drop in share value and the largest financial loss in the company's fifty-six-year history in 2024, as faster-moving competitors outpaced Intel in AI, advanced chip design, and next-gen computing. The company has now started to rebalance its focus, spinning off noncore units and channeling investment toward transformative initiatives.[a]

Limiting Shared Services to Noncore Functions

Shared services often remain narrowly focused on noncore support functions like finance, HR, and procurement—driven primarily by cost-cutting objectives. While this model improves consistency and reduces overhead, it reinforces a siloed mindset and overlooks the strategic potential of shared services. By limiting these platforms to back-office roles, organizations miss the opportunity to bring flexibility and scale to core operations. This constraint hampers the ability of project teams to access the expertise, tools, and data they need.

A global pharmaceutical company had centralized support for basic tasks like admin and finance but left critical areas like regulatory and clinical operations stuck in traditional, siloed units. When new innovation projects launched, teams had to fight through slow approvals and disconnected processes. Without flexible, project-aligned support for these core functions, the company lost valuable time and couldn't maintain momentum—missing a key opportunity to lead in a fast-moving market.

These pitfalls reflect a familiar pattern: adopting transformation tools without aligning operating models to support continuous, project-based value creation. Overcoming them requires not just automation or reorganization, but a fundamental rethinking of how operations contribute to growth in the project economy.

NOTE

a. Laura Bratton and Yasmin Khorram, "How Innovation Died at Intel: America's Leading-Edge Chip Manufacturer Faces an Uncertain Future and Lawsuits," Yahoo! Finance, December 20, 2024, https://finance.yahoo.com/news/how-innovation-died-at-intel-americas -only-leading-edge-chip-manufacturer-faces-an-uncertain-future-and-lawsuits-130018997 .html

Historically, shared-services centers (SSCs) were designed for efficiency, scale, and standardization, focusing on cost reduction and uniform processes. For instance, Procter & Gamble (P&G) established a Global Business Services (GBS) unit that centralized functions such as finance, accounting, HR, and IT across its global operations. This consolidation aimed to streamline operations, reduce redundancy, and leverage economies of scale. GBS supported over 170 services for P&G's 127,000 employees and 300 brands in 180 countries, delivering nearly $800 million in cost savings.

This model thrived in a business environment where stability, control, and standardization were the cornerstones of value creation. However, in a PDO, operational functions must do more than deliver efficiencies—they must become enablers of speed, agility, and innovation.

Evolving Shared Services into Project-Enabling Platforms

The evolution to project-enabling platforms involves integrating advanced technologies such as AI and robotic process automation to enhance responsiveness and scalability. By doing so, shared services can provide on-demand expertise and resources, aligning operational capabilities with strategic project goals.

For instance, some automobile manufacturers have evolved their internal technology units into shared service platforms that support multiple brands and vehicle lines across the enterprise. Rather than treating technology firms as external service providers, these manufacturers have integrated them into a shared services model—centralized hubs that provide real-time data analytics, predictive maintenance systems, and in-vehicle connectivity as a reusable capability across projects. This internal service structure allows cross-functional project teams from engineering to customer experience to access the same high-performance tools and insights, ensuring consistency, scalability, and strategic alignment across connected vehicle initiatives.

The shift from standardized operations to strategic enablement requires fundamentally changing how organizations design, manage, and measure their shared services. Success is now defined by efficiency metrics and the ability to contribute to project outcomes and drive innovation. Crucially, this transformation is not limited to traditional support functions. Increasingly, core operational processes are also being migrated into shared service environments, functions that were once considered too critical or complex to outsource or centralize. These include:

- *Customer operations and experience,* where service centers are equipped with AI-driven CRM tools to support personalized, multichannel engagement at scale.

- *Manufacturing oversight,* particularly in industries with distributed production, which involves centralized units monitoring quality, maintenance, and performance using IoT and digital twin technologies.

- *Product life-cycle management,* which involves integrated platforms that coordinate design, testing, and iteration across cross-functional project teams and external partners.

With this broadening of scope, SSCs are evolving from internal cost centers to strategic execution hubs. They no longer support the business—they cocreate value with it. And SSCs can take multiple forms. Internally, companies are creating cross-functional service platforms like internal consultancies, offering plug-and-play capabilities to project teams, including data science, rapid prototyping, or regulatory expertise. Externally, organizations are partnering with specialist providers or forming joint ventures, not merely as outsourced vendors, but as extensions of their shared service ecosystems, to tap into niche capabilities and innovation pipelines, extending their ecosystem without increasing internal headcount.

A powerful example of this transformation is Ping An's health-care ecosystem, Good Doctor, built on its Smart Healthcare shared-services platform.[14] Originally designed as cost-effective support, it has evolved into a project-enabling foundation powering China's largest health-tech collaboration:

- *Scale and reach.* As of 2021, Smart Healthcare was live in 90 cities, supporting 20,000 medical institutions and 450,000 doctors with AI-driven diagnostics, which helped cut average diagnosis time from fifteen minutes to fifteen seconds.

- *Modular services for projects.* Teams across Ping An now deploy shared capabilities like its AskBob AI assistant—used 33 million times in its first fourteen months—and one-hour prescription delivery in 249 cities, integrating these plug-and-play services into localized projects.

- *Business and social impact.* By mid-2023, the ecosystem had generated 400 million registered users and 20 million family doctor subscribers, and connected 4,000 hospitals and 226,000 pharmacies—transforming operations into a health-tech backbone and major customer acquisition channel.

This evolution reflects a deeper structural shift: from standardized, function-based delivery to modular, project-aligned enablement. In practice, it requires rethinking how SSCs are staffed, governed, and measured. Traditional KPIs focused on efficiency and cost reduction are giving way to value contribution metrics: how well a shared service supports strategic goals, accelerates project timelines, or enables innovation.

For PDOs, the strategic benefits of this model are clear:

- *Faster time-to-value.* Agile SSCs can mobilize capabilities for new projects quickly, reducing startup friction and eliminating delays in execution.

- *Scalable innovation.* Centralizing advanced services (e.g., AI modeling, R&D analytics, or regulatory interpretation) allows for faster experimentation and reuse across multiple initiatives.

- *Talent optimization.* Moving standardized work into SSCs liberates internal teams to focus on transformative efforts, while service hubs attract and retain niche specialists in high-demand fields.

- *Ecosystem integration.* Modular platforms enable smoother collaboration with external partners, making it easier to launch joint ventures, codevelop products, or integrate third-party innovation.

- *Alignment and transparency.* Shared visibility into SSC performance and contribution to project outcomes improves decision-making and organizational alignment.

From isolated administrative engines, SSCs are becoming orchestrators of transformation—nodes in a broader operational network designed to power project execution and continuous value creation.

Operational Reinvention at BNP Paribas Fortis

Over the past decade, the banking industry has undergone a quiet revolution. What once required face-to-face meetings, paper-based processes, and physical branches now happens entirely online, instantly and independently. Customers open accounts, apply for credit, and manage investments without speaking to a banker or setting foot in a branch. Banks increasingly resemble technology firms in this new landscape: they employ more data engineers than branch managers, and their competitive edge depends on innovation, not just compliance or efficiency.

BNP Paribas Fortis, Belgium's largest bank and a subsidiary of the French multinational BNP Paribas, which serves over 4.7 million customers and employs approximately eighteen thousand people, is leaning into this shift. In early 2025, the bank announced a bold restructuring: transferring five hundred employees from its client service center to a newly created entity within Accenture. These employees will now work under Accenture management, marking a shift from internal operations to an outsourced services model. These roles span critical operational areas such as credit processing and investment administration— functions that, while vital, are no longer sources of differentiation in a digital-first economy.

In the short term, outsourcing these functions allows BNP Paribas Fortis to preserve service continuity while focusing internal talent on more strategic priorities. However, the deeper impact lies in the longer-term opportunity to redesign the operating model. Freed from the burden of maintaining high-touch administrative processes, the bank can redirect energy and expertise toward initiatives that drive customer value and business growth. This could mean accelerating the rollout of AI-powered service platforms, fast-tracking sustainability-linked financing initiatives, or scaling new digital banking experiences in response to shifting market demands.

Importantly, this isn't just about being more efficient—it's about being more responsive. In a market shaped by heavy regulation, fast-moving fintech competitors, and rising customer expectations, BNP Paribas Fortis is betting that the future of operational excellence is the ability to support transformation at speed.

This is the essence of project-driven operations: turning stability into speed and routine into opportunity. This might not be happening in your industry just yet, but it will most likely happen sooner rather than later. And when it does, it will happen very fast.

Conclusion

As value creation shifts toward shorter product life cycles, heightened customer expectations, and continuous innovation, traditional operations—designed for stability and standardization—can no longer remain static support structures. They must evolve into dynamic enablers of transformation.

When viewed not merely as cost-saving tools but as enablers of strategic reinvestment, automation and AI offer organizations the opportunity to release capacity and channel it into high-impact initiatives. Realizing this potential requires clear leadership, a strong project agenda, and a deliberate focus on reskilling, reallocation, and human-digital collaboration.

The transition from siloed operations to modular, project-aligned service models further reinforces this shift. Shared services—whether centralized, federated, or platform-based—must be designed to flex with the demands of project portfolios. The BNP Paribas Fortis case illustrates both the opportunities and challenges of this evolution, emphasizing the importance of internal alignment, ecosystem collaboration, and thoughtful change management.

The next chapter will shift the focus to speed—exploring how organizations transform work. It will examine the adoption of agile, hybrid, and AI-enabled delivery models that enable teams to execute with greater velocity, adaptability, and strategic impact.

CHAPTER 8

Project-Driven Execution

None of Haier's accomplishments described throughout this book would have been possible without the crowning characteristic of a project-driven organization: disciplined and sustained project-driven execution. The company's success lies in its ability to *drive alignment and focus among stakeholders* with a shared purpose and clear, measurable benefits. Its Ren-DanHeYi model provides a unified framework that addresses foundation (core philosophy and purpose), people (employees, partners, and users), and creation (projects and initiatives). By focusing on these domains, Haier ensures that every project contributes directly to its strategic objectives.

This clarity allows teams across Haier's global operations to engage deeply with the company's purpose: creating user value. For instance, in its smart IoT refrigerators, Haier brought together engineers, data scientists, and UX designers to cocreate systems that detect expiring food and send real-time alerts to users. These connected fridges—deployed after rapid prototyping—reduced household food waste by around 30 percent in early pilots, aligning stakeholder efforts around a shared, measurable benefit.[1] This shared focus ensured alignment across diverse stakeholders and accelerated project execution.

Haier has also embraced a *hybrid approach to execution*, tailoring methods to the unique requirements of each project rather than rigidly adhering to a single methodology. While traditional waterfall methods are still used for linear, predictable tasks (e.g., infrastructure upgrades or manufacturing process automation), Haier has adopted agile principles for more dynamic and iterative initiatives, such as developing user-centric IoT platforms.

This hybrid approach is evident in the development of the COSMO-Plat platform, which required long-term planning and rapid iteration. Teams integrated waterfall planning for the platform's underlying infrastructure while using agile cycles to add user-facing features based on real-time feedback. This model allowed Haier to break free from the limitations of one-size-fits-all approaches, enabling it to deliver robust and adaptable solutions.

By encouraging teams to apply the proper methods and tools to the right project, Haier has demonstrated the effectiveness of hybrid approaches in balancing structure and adaptability. This pragmatism ensures that IT projects align with broader organizational goals without sacrificing agility.

Finally, Haier's *integration of AI and other emerging technologies* into its projects has revolutionized how it executes transformations. AI is used extensively to enhance decision-making through real-time insights and predictive analytics. For example, Haier leverages AI-powered tools to monitor production lines, predict maintenance needs, and optimize workflows in its smart factories. These tools provide actionable data that helps teams anticipate challenges and make informed decisions quickly. AI also plays a critical role in forecasting and resource allocation. By analyzing historical data and current trends, Haier's AI systems provide teams with accurate projections of project timelines, costs, and resource needs. This capability has been instrumental in the company's ability to deliver projects on time and within budget.

Haier's IT strategy extends beyond AI, exploring other emerging technologies to maintain its competitive edge. For instance, its IoT platforms enable real-time interaction between users and manufacturing systems, allowing for mass customization at scale. This innovative use of technology positions Haier as a leader in digital transformation, ensuring that its projects remain user-focused and future-ready.

---

n my work with leadership teams across industries, one discussion keeps surfacing—and it always stops the room. We will review their portfolio: hundreds of projects, millions of dollars at stake, all critical to their company's future. Then I ask a simple question: "How do you manage all this?" And often, the answer is: with a decades-old system and a single delivery method applied to everything. Agile or waterfall. One or the other. No nuance, no adaptability.

I pause and ask the group to imagine trying to drive across Europe today using only a paper map. That's what their teams are doing—navigating the most critical transformation efforts without real-time guidance, feedback, or adaptive tools. We've moved from paper maps to GPS, and now to self-driving cars. But when executing transformations, most organizations are still stuck in the paper map era.

Compounding this issue is the insistence on a one-size-fits-all approach to project delivery. Declaring an organization "agile only" or "waterfall only" may sound decisive, but it fails to reflect the complexity of real work. Some projects need speed and iteration; others require structure and compliance. No wonder so many initiatives stall or fall short—they're forced into frameworks that don't fit.

We're still far from fully self-driving project systems—but we're getting closer to something just as powerful: GPS-like AI tools that guide execution in real time. These tools don't automate the entire journey, but they help teams make better decisions, faster, with fewer blind spots. That's why I encourage every transformation team I work with to explore how AI and data-driven tools can automate some elements of project execution. It's time to leave the paper map behind.

This chapter explores how project-driven organizations are transforming the way work is executed—moving beyond rigid delivery models and outdated tools to embrace flexible, tech-enabled, and value-focused ways of working. We focus on three essential capabilities reshaping how execution happens in high-performing PDOs (see figure 8-1): driving alignment and focus with the project canvas, embracing hybrid execution methods, and integrating AI and emerging technologies to elevate execution.

These shifts reflect a fundamental truth: in the transformation age, *how* you execute is as important as what you accomplish. Organizations that invest in advancing their ways of working—anchored in simplicity, flexibility, and technology—create a decisive advantage. Execution, when done right, becomes a strategic capability. (See the sidebar, "A New Critical Role in the C-Suite: The Chief Project Officer.")

FIGURE 8-1

Project-driven execution

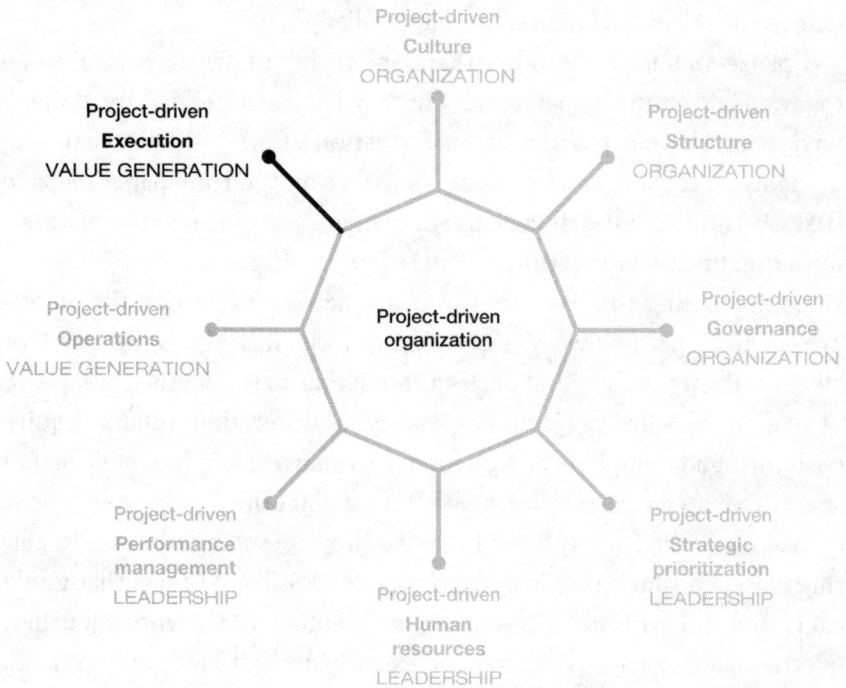

Project-driven
Culture
ORGANIZATION

Project-driven
Execution
VALUE GENERATION

Project-driven
Structure
ORGANIZATION

Project-driven
Operations
VALUE GENERATION

Project-driven
organization

Project-driven
Governance
ORGANIZATION

Project-driven
Performance
management
LEADERSHIP

Project-driven
Human
resources
LEADERSHIP

Project-driven
Strategic
prioritization
LEADERSHIP

Driving Alignment and Focus
with the Project Canvas

One of the most significant gaps in transformations and projects has been the lack of a simple, universally accessible tool for managing and communicating about projects. Historically, project management has been viewed as overly technical, bureaucratic, and process-driven—a perception that has created a disconnect between project leaders and the broader organization. This complexity has hindered stakeholder engagement and obscured the strategic value that projects are meant to deliver.

To address this gap, I have worked to introduce and amplify modern project management concepts such as the *project canvas*, the central framework of my *HBR Project Management Handbook*.[2] Since its introduction in 2021, the project canvas has become one of the most widely

A New Critical Role in the C-Suite: The Chief Project Officer

As organizations increasingly operate through projects rather than permanent structures, a new leadership role has emerged in the C-suite: the chief project officer (CPO) sometimes known as the chief transformation officer.[a] This leader is responsible for turning bold strategies into tangible outcomes, ensuring that vision translates into execution at scale and speed.

The CPO's role is not simply about project oversight; it is about leading the strategic orchestration of initiatives across the organization, maintaining focus, momentum, and measurable results. Unlike operational, financial, or HR leaders, the CPO sits at the intersection of strategy execution, resource allocation, and transformation leadership, ensuring that high-value projects accelerate the organization's growth agenda. The CPO's key areas of responsibility include:

- **Aligning project portfolios with strategic goals.** The CPO ensures that every project directly supports the organization's highest priorities. For example, Katie Mullen, as chief digital and transformation officer at JCPenney, spearheaded digital transformation initiatives tightly aligned with strategic goals for growth and customer engagement, showing how targeted execution drives measurable business results.

- **Establishing project governance and standards.** The CPO builds fit-for-purpose governance frameworks to maintain consistency without stifling flexibility. This includes setting decision rights at the correct level, escalation paths, and execution standards, enabling faster delivery without compromising oversight.

- **Fostering a culture of accountability and outcome ownership.** The CPO drives a results-driven mindset, ensuring project leaders and teams are empowered and accountable for delivering outcomes, not just completing activities. This includes setting clear expectations, aligning incentives with impact, and enabling project leaders to make decisions, driving stronger commitment and measurable results.

(continued)

- **Optimizing resource capacity.** In partnership with CHROs and CFOs, the CPO ensures that project resources—funding, talent, and technology—are allocated dynamically based on evolving priorities. Unlike traditional staffing models, this dynamic deployment approach ensures that top talent fuels the highest-value initiatives at the right time.

- **Breaking down silos and enabling cross-functional execution.** Transformation often cuts across multiple functions and business units. The CPO champions cross-department collaboration, ensuring that knowledge flows freely, obstacles are removed quickly, and complex initiatives remain cohesive from end to end.

Why Organizations Need a Chief Project Officer

The CPO plays a pivotal role in embedding a project-first mindset into the organization's heart, ensuring that projects are not isolated activities but the primary engine for executing strategy, driving innovation, and delivering measurable results. Rather than treating projects as one-off efforts, the CPO builds an integrated, value-creating project ecosystem—one where initiatives are tightly aligned to long-term goals and collective impact matters more than individual wins.

This leadership role demands relentless focus across the entire project portfolio: concentrating resources, talent, and leadership attention on the highest-impact initiatives. By curating a disciplined, strategic portfolio, the CPO prevents resource dilution, eliminates low-value distractions, and channels energy into projects that truly move the organization forward.

At the same time, the CPO champions a culture of agility and ownership. Through streamlined governance frameworks, dynamic resource reallocation, and cross-functional collaboration models, CPOs break down traditional silos and build flexible pathways for teams to adapt quickly to evolving priorities. Crucially, by setting a tone of accountability and shared purpose, they empower teams to take full ownership of outcomes, reinforcing resilience, speeding up execution, and helping the entire organization become faster, sharper, and more strategically aligned.

NOTE

a. Antonio Nieto-Rodriguez, "The Rise of the Chief Project Officer," hbr.org, April 26, 2022, https://hbr.org/2022/04/the-rise-of-the-chief-project-officer.

used tools in project execution, helping organizations—like L'Oréal, Euronext, KLM, DHL, and many others—navigate the project economy, where initiatives and transformations are the primary drivers of value. Many organizations have adopted the framework to simplify how they manage their projects and enhance collaboration across teams, achieving remarkable results.

After a speech I gave at a conference, a professional approached me to share how he used the project canvas to present his organization's transformation project to their CEO. The CEO exclaimed, "This is the first time in years that I've understood what this project is about!" This underscores the power of the project canvas: its ability to deliver clarity and accessibility, aligning all stakeholders around the purpose, goals, and value of a project.

The project canvas simplifies modern project management into a single-page framework with three domains: foundation, people, and creation, each broken into three essential building blocks (see figure 8-2). It provides transformation leaders, project managers, and team members with a shared language, increasing strategic alignment and stakeholder engagement throughout the project.

The Three Domains of the Project Canvas

Three core domains at the heart of the project canvas—foundation, people, and creation—bring clarity and coherence to even the most complex initiatives. Each captures a vital dimension of project success, from strategic intent to team dynamics to value delivery. Together, they provide a comprehensive yet intuitive structure for planning, executing, and communicating project work. See the sidebar, "Key Advantages of the Project Canvas" for more information.

Foundation: The Strategic Base of Every Project. The foundation domain emphasizes the "why" behind the project and connects it to organizational goals. It comprises three essential building blocks:

- *Purpose.* As detailed in chapter 4, purpose answers the question, Why are we doing this project? It identifies the problem to be

FIGURE 8-2

The project canvas

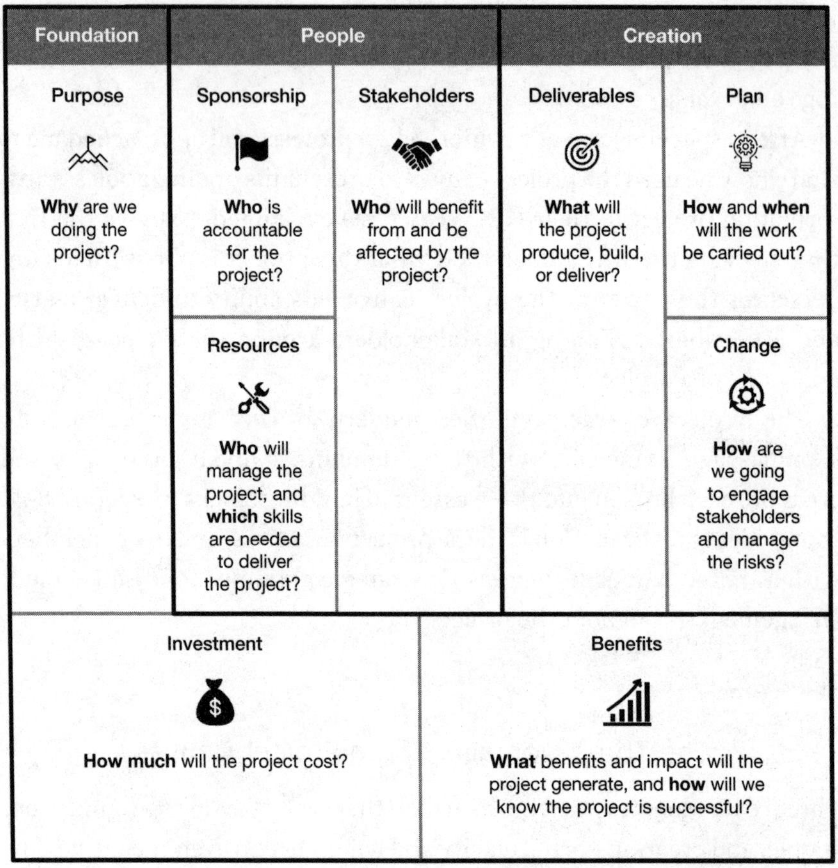

Foundation	People		Creation	
Purpose	**Sponsorship**	**Stakeholders**	**Deliverables**	**Plan**
Why are we doing the project?	**Who** is accountable for the project?	**Who** will benefit from and be affected by the project?	**What** will the project produce, build, or deliver?	**How** and **when** will the work be carried out?
	Resources			**Change**
	Who will manage the project, and **which** skills are needed to deliver the project?			**How** are we going to engage stakeholders and manage the risks?
Investment		**Benefits**		
How much will the project cost?		**What** benefits and impact will the project generate, and **how** will we know the project is successful?		

Source: Antonio Nieto-Rodriguez, *Harvard Business Review Project Management Handbook: How to Launch, Lead, and Sponsor Successful Projects* (Boston: Harvard Business Review Press, 2021).

solved or the opportunity to be captured. A strong purpose must be SMART (specific, measurable, achievable, relevant, and time-bound). It should not only inspire but also provide a clear, measurable outcome with a deadline. For example, a purpose like "improving customer satisfaction" is vague, whereas "reducing customer complaints by 30 percent within twelve months" provides clarity, direction, and focus.

Key Advantages of the Project Canvas

The project canvas stands apart from other frameworks due to its focus on simplicity, adaptability, and strategic alignment. Here are nine ways it delivers value:

- **Is simple and designed for all.** The canvas eliminates complex jargon, making it accessible to executives, board members, managers, and newcomers to project management. It empowers everyone involved in a project to contribute meaningfully.

- **Applies to all project types.** Whether you're managing a traditional, agile, or hybrid project—or even a large program or strategic initiative—the framework provides a universal structure that adapts to the methodology being used.

- **Focuses on value and benefits.** Unlike frameworks that prioritize processes and controls, the project canvas centers on delivering measurable benefits and maximizing value for stakeholders.

- **Enables rapid delivery of value.** By focusing on the elements of the project that deliver the most value first, the canvas encourages iterative progress, allowing teams to adjust as needed while delivering results quickly.

- **Aligns projects with organizational strategy.** Every project starts by clarifying its purpose and ensuring alignment with the organization's strategic goals, preventing wasted resources on low-priority initiatives.

- **Prioritizes implementation over bureaucracy.** Focus shifts from overly detailed plans to execution and results, ensuring that projects remain dynamic and responsive.

- **Covers the entire project life cycle.** The framework expands beyond the traditional project life cycle to consider pre-project justification and post-project evaluation, enabling continuous improvement.

(continued)

- **Is fast and flexible.** The canvas is a living framework, designed to accommodate changes in scope, resources, or objectives throughout the project life cycle.

- **Encourages collaboration and shared understanding.** By providing a shared language, the project canvas breaks down silos between teams, stakeholders, and leadership, ensuring alignment and clarity.

- *Investment.* This includes all resources—financial, human, and material—required to achieve the project's goals. Leaders must ensure the organization is willing to commit the necessary resources up front. Failing to secure adequate investment often leads to delays, compromises, or failure.

- *Benefits.* Also emphasized in chapter 4, each project needs a well-defined benefit plan, yet it is often missing. Benefits are both the financial and nonfinancial outcomes that the project is expected to deliver. A benefit must have both a clear metric and a date to be achieved. For example, rather than "improve operational efficiency," a measurable benefit would be "Reduce processing times by 25 percent by the end of Q3." This ensures alignment, accountability, and focus on delivering tangible value.

People: Empowering Teams and Stakeholders. The people domain ensures that the right individuals are engaged, aligned, and empowered to deliver the project successfully. It focuses on accountability, collaboration, and resources. Its three building blocks include:

- *Sponsorship.* The executive sponsor serves as the bridge between the organization and the project team, providing guidance and decision-making authority, and ensuring accountability for the project's success. Strong sponsorship is essential for driving any transformation, resolving conflicts, and securing buy-in at all levels.

- *Stakeholders.* A stakeholder is anyone affected by or benefiting from the project. Engaging stakeholders early helps identify potential risks, build trust, and maintain alignment. For example, in a digital transformation initiative, stakeholders may include IT teams, department heads, and customers. Mapping their needs and expectations reduces resistance and increases support.

- *Resources.* These are the individuals and skills required to deliver the project. Beyond technical capabilities, leaders must ensure team members are motivated, fully dedicated, well supported, and equipped to adapt to challenges. In today's remote work environments, fostering strong virtual collaboration is more critical than ever.

Creation: Delivering Tangible Results. The creation domain covers the visible outputs of the project, ensuring that outputs are met efficiently while managing risks and stakeholder engagement. Creation can be broken down into three parts:

- *Deliverables.* Clearly define what the project will produce, such as products, services, technology, new capabilities, or a new business model. Deliverables must align with stakeholder expectations and project benefits. For example, a hospital upgrading its IT infrastructure may have a deliverable of implementing a fully operational patient management system.

- *Plan.* The plan outlines how and when work will be carried out, detailing tasks, timelines, and responsibilities. Breaking down long and complex projects into smaller manageable ninety-day phases is essential in modern plans. While flexibility is important, a strong plan provides structure and minimizes ambiguity.

- *Change.* Projects often are met with resistance. Effective change management ensures that stakeholders buy in, risks are mitigated, and resistance is minimized. For example, a large retail chain deploying a new logistics system must manage staff training and operational adjustments as part of the project's change strategy.

How to Use the Project Canvas

Leaders should start every initiative by mapping it on the project canvas, assessing whether it is well-defined, whether there is enough buy-in, and whether it is ready to launch. During execution, the canvas serves as a road map, helping teams track progress, address risks, and evaluate success. At the end of the project, it becomes a tool for postmortem analysis, enabling organizations to capture lessons learned and refine future projects.

Over the past five years, the project canvas has evolved from a planning tool into a dynamic execution framework. In mature execution environments, it is embedded across the project life cycle—from ideation and prioritization to delivery and benefits realization. Teams use it to initiate projects, then revisit and update it during key milestones, ensuring alignment and adaptability in fast-changing environments. This continuous engagement with the canvas fosters a culture of shared ownership and strategic focus.

The most advanced organizations are now institutionalizing the project canvas across enterprise systems, using it as the common architecture for funding decisions, resource planning, and strategic portfolio reviews. When project sponsors present updates to executives or request additional investment, it provides the single source of truth. It brings cohesion to cross-functional transformation initiatives, ensures clear accountability, and accelerates decisions. In this way, it becomes not just a planning or delivery tool, but the backbone of execution and value creation across the entire organization.

The project canvas isn't just a framework—it's a mindset that fosters clarity and accountability and results in execution. By focusing on the essential elements of success, it empowers PDOs to deliver better outcomes and thrive in the transformation age.

Embracing Hybrid Execution Methods

In earlier chapters, we explored how transformation success requires strong leadership, cultural change, and prioritization. As we now turn our attention to value creation and project-driven execution, it becomes clear that new delivery models are also critical.

Organizations today operate in volatile, complex environments—especially those involving technologies like AI, big data, and platform ecosystems. Yet when it comes to navigating these environments, most are still caught in an outdated debate between waterfall and agile methodologies. And that misses the bigger point: transformation execution demands flexibility and precision at the same time.

To meet the demands of the transformation age, leaders must move beyond this dichotomy and embrace hybrid execution methods that blend the structure and predictability of waterfall with the adaptability and customer-centricity of agile. Hybrid approaches provide a pragmatic pathway to deliver complex, high-value projects at speed—anchoring execution in both discipline and agility.

The Useless Battle between Waterfall and Agile

For the past two decades, project execution has been defined by an unproductive debate: waterfall versus agile.[3] Each method has brought valuable approaches but also significant limitations. Worse, this debate has created a cultural divide between traditional project managers, who prioritize structure and governance, and agile practitioners, who champion flexibility and iteration.

While each approach has strengths, neither is sufficient for today's transformative initiatives. Waterfall, with its linear, phase-driven approach, excels in projects with stable requirements and predictable outcomes, such as infrastructure or compliance-driven initiatives. However, its rigidity makes it unsuitable for fast-moving or uncertain projects, where adaptability is critical. Agile, on the other hand, focuses on iterative delivery, continuous feedback, and collaboration, making it ideal for dynamic projects like software development. Yet agile often neglects long-term planning, stakeholder alignment, and governance, which can create challenges in complex, multiphase projects.

The problem lies not in the methods themselves but in the binary thinking that forces organizations to choose between them. Applying a single execution method to every project is like using the same tool for every repair—it inevitably leads to inefficiencies, delays, and unnecessary risks. Each project brings its own mix of complexity, uncertainty, and strategic importance, requiring leaders to tailor their approach.

The Emergence of Hybrid

Hybrid methodologies represent a new era of execution that blends the structure of predictive techniques with the flexibility of adaptive methods, while incorporating disciplines like program management, lean startup, and design thinking. This integrated approach allows organizations to apply the right level of control and adaptability based on the nature of each initiative.

However, while the benefits of hybrid methods are clear, our research shows that adoption is still in its early stages. Only 8 percent of organizations have fully embedded hybrid execution models across their portfolios. The majority still lean toward either traditional or agile approaches, often inconsistently. And 16 percent of organizations report having no standardized methods at all—a critical gap that undermines execution consistency and transformation impact.

For transformation leaders, this represents both a challenge and an opportunity. Adopting hybrid is a complex process and will almost certainly encounter resistance. However, by engaging more directly with hybrid delivery methods—such as participating in sprint reviews or reviewing cross-functional road maps—leaders can make smarter decisions, accelerate delivery, and build greater resilience into their transformation efforts.

Key characteristics of hybrid execution methods include:

- *Flexibility and structure.* Hybrid approaches balance agile's adaptability with waterfall's predictability. For example, when Philips adopted a hybrid method for its HealthSuite digital platform, agile allowed for iterative software development, while waterfall ensured compliance with strict safety standards. This combination improved quality, reduced time to market, and delivered cost predictability while reinforcing a project-driven innovation culture.

- *Phased and iterative execution.* Hybrid methods allow projects to combine structured phases for predictable components with iterative cycles for dynamic elements. DBS Bank used this model during its digital transformation, employing waterfall for IT infrastructure upgrades and agile for customer-facing services.

This strategic balance enabled DBS to modernize operations while maintaining agility in a project-driven business environment.

- *Customer involvement and predictability.* By blending agile's customer-centric feedback loops with waterfall's reliable delivery schedules, hybrid approaches strike an effective balance. British Telecom used agile for its 5G rollout, gathering early feedback, while leveraging waterfall to deliver on-time, on-budget data center projects.

Hybrid execution methods deliver the following benefits:

- *Balanced approach.* By integrating the best of waterfall and agile, hybrid execution methods offer a tailored solution for diverse project needs within a PDO. For instance, Ubisoft used waterfall to design core game elements for *Assassin's Creed Valhalla* while employing agile to refine gameplay mechanics iteratively.

- *Risk mitigation.* Combining structured planning with iterative adaptability helps organizations manage risks effectively while maintaining strategic alignment across project portfolios. Tesla, for example, followed a waterfall approach for constructing its gigafactory while using agile to deliver over-the-air updates for its Model 3.

- *Efficient resource allocation.* Hybrid approaches optimize re-source usage by blending long-term planning with the ability to adapt to real-time changes—a critical capability for PDOs. Zara employs waterfall to plan its supply chain while using agile cycles to respond to fashion trends, ensuring minimal waste and high responsiveness.

Flexibility with Focus

As we have seen, project success is not about the method itself but about aligning the approach to the nature of the project. The implementation matrix shown in figure 8-3 maps three types of projects—efficiency,

FIGURE 8-3

Implementation methods matrix

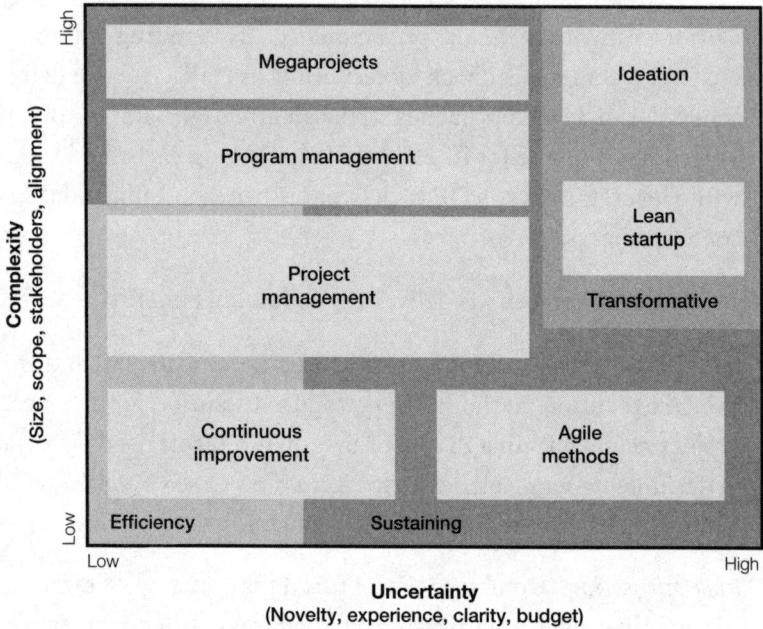

Source: Antonio Nieto-Rodriguez, *Harvard Business Review Project Management Handbook: How to Launch, Lead, and Sponsor Successful Projects* (Boston: Harvard Business Review Press, 2021).

sustaining, and transformative—against their levels of complexity (size, scope, stakeholders, alignment) and uncertainty (novelty, experience, clarity, budget).

Transformation leaders must recognize that successful execution is about choosing the right approach for the right project at the right time. Selecting the wrong execution model isn't just a technical error; it's a leadership failure that results in wasted energy, disillusioned teams, and stalled transformation when momentum is critical. Smart, transformation-focused leaders guide execution choices by matching method to context—complexity, uncertainty, and strategic value. This discipline sharpens focus and protects the organization's capacity to transform at speed and scale. Here's how:

- *Continuous improvement: Simplifying efficiency projects.* Efficiency initiatives—those aimed at incremental gains—operate under low complexity and uncertainty. These projects benefit from light-touch, decentralized execution that empowers teams to drive change continuously at the source. For example, Toyota's frontline teams continuously optimize assembly lines through local problem-solving, demonstrating how transformation at the operational level can be sustained without heavy project overhead.

- *Traditional project management (predictive/waterfall).* Medium-complexity projects, such as process upgrades or regional capability builds, benefit from stability and structure. Leaders must resist the temptation to over-adapt methods when predictability and disciplined delivery are critical to strategic success. Airbus used structured project management principles to consolidate European manufacturing operations, turning complex coordination into a strategic operational advantage.

- *Program management (hybrid).* Large-scale transformation requires connecting multiple interdependent initiatives under a unified strategy. Program management demands both high-level governance discipline and the flexibility to adapt components to changing conditions without losing momentum. The HS2 rail program in the UK, for instance, blends classic project controls with adaptive approaches to community engagement—balancing infrastructure delivery with social license to operate.

- *Megaproject management (hybrid).* Transformations at national or global scale—new airports, digital nations—demand both rigor and responsiveness. Leaders must hold a dual focus: protecting critical-path stability while flexibly managing political, social, and technological uncertainties. Saudi Arabia's planned city, NEOM, integrates megaproject management frameworks with adaptive innovation hubs, ensuring vision execution while embracing the unknowns inherent to building future cities.

- *Agile and adaptive approaches.* Rapidly evolving transformations such as launching new digital ecosystems or next-generation customer platforms require agility, speed, and constant customer feedback. Leaders must prioritize iteration over perfection, accepting that transformation journeys unfold through learning, not rigid planning. Adobe's Creative Cloud team releases features continuously using agile sprints, aligning product innovation closely with fast-changing user needs and expectations.

- *Lean startup: Driving radical innovation.* Where organizations seek breakthrough transformation—not incremental change—lean startup methods accelerate learning cycles and minimize the cost of failure. Leaders should champion experiments over assumptions, creating safe spaces for small bets that lead to outsized impact. For example, Amazon uses MVP pilots and rapid customer testing to validate transformation bets before scaling—preserving resources and intensifying focus.

- *Design thinking: Managing uncertainty in ideation.* The front-end of transformation—where the "right problem" still needs to be found—demands empathy-driven, iterative exploration. Leaders must guide teams to suspend assumptions, immerse in user realities, and cocreate new possibilities with those they serve. Kaiser Permanente redesigned its patient intake experience through design thinking, ensuring that early innovation efforts were grounded in real user needs rather than internal assumptions.

Modern project management isn't about choosing sides—it's about equipping PDOs with the right tools and strategies to adapt and thrive. Hybrid methods create the foundation to unlock the full potential of efficiency, sustaining, and transformative projects in this new era. (See the sidebar, "Leveraging Waterfall and Agile for Better Project Outcomes.")

Revolutionizing Projects and Transformations with AI

Now, let's examine a game-changing force for PDOs: the massive application of AI in project management. Just as AI has reengineered project-driven operations (see chapter 7), it is poised to revolutionize projects and transformations, radically changing how organizations plan, execute, and deliver value through their initiatives.[4] With its ability to

Leveraging Waterfall and Agile for Better Project Outcomes

In 2015, the Danish Industry Foundation, Implement Consulting Group, Aarhus University, and Denmark Technical University came together to launch a radical new project delivery framework called "half double," which was an attempt to reconcile the disconnect that only 30 percent of projects create the intended impact but still are considered successful. In conjunction with twenty-five partners, Implement Consulting Group examined the research and best practice examples to identify what elements differentiate successful projects from unsuccessful ones.

At the heart of the movement are three specific measures: impact, which is based on stakeholder satisfaction (and which correlates with the ideas around value described in this book); flow, which favors progress and resource optimization; and leadership, which embraces uncertainty and aims to make things happen by "shifting from control to facilitation, involvement, and ownership."[a]

The methodology aligns well with the concepts of the PDO by placing benefits at the center of projects, emphasizing cocreation with stakeholders, delivering value rapidly through shorter phases, and empowering teams that drive ownership and impact.

NOTE

a. Half Double Institute home page, https://halfdoubleinstitute.org/.

---

enhance decision-making, automate repetitive tasks, and provide predictive insights, AI offers unprecedented opportunities to address the complexities of modern projects and boost their success rates.

Traditional tools and methodologies fall short in meeting the demands of today's dynamic and complex transformation landscape. Many organizations still rely on spreadsheets and static project management software, which are limited in adapting to real-time changes or providing actionable insights. Even newer tools focused on collaboration and task management lack the automation and intelligence needed to fundamentally shift how projects are executed.

The Pitfalls in Project-Driven Execution

Delivering projects in the transformation age requires more than resources and ambition—it demands execution systems that are clear, adaptive, and outcome-focused. Yet even the most visionary organizations can falter when the way projects are executed fails to evolve. While many companies talk about becoming more agile, tech-enabled, and aligned, they fall into execution traps that slow delivery, dilute impact, and frustrate teams.

Here are three common pitfalls that undermine project execution in modern organizations:

Misalignment and Inconsistency Creep In from the Start

In many organizations, teams struggle to align because there's no consistent understanding of what qualifies as a project. Departments use different definitions, templates, and processes, leading to confusion, duplication, and misaligned priorities. Without a shared understanding of what constitutes a project and the best way to deliver it, focus fractures early and execution becomes scattered.

One global consumer goods company initiated multiple innovation initiatives across regional teams. Each unit had its own approach to defining and managing projects. With no common execution language or structure, collaboration broke down, reporting became chaotic, and leadership struggled to assess progress. Momentum stalled not because of strategy, but due to fragmentation in how execution was framed.

Locking into a One-Size-Fits-All Delivery Method

Too often, organizations adopt a rigid methodology—declaring themselves "agile" or "waterfall" shops—and force all projects into that mold. However, transformation initiatives require different levels of iteration, speed, and structure. The failure to tailor methods to project needs leads to wasted effort, misaligned resources, and disengaged teams.

A classic example is the 2013 launch of HealthCare.gov.[a] The project employed a traditional waterfall approach, emphasizing sequential development and late-stage testing. This methodology proved ill-suited for the site's complexity, leading to significant issues: only six users managed to enroll on the first day, and the site's capacity was far below expectations. The lack of iterative testing and flexibility contributed to a launch that was both delayed and over budget, with costs escalating to over $2 billion. This case underscores the importance of selecting a delivery method aligned with a project's specific needs and challenges.

Underutilizing Intelligent Execution Technologies

Many organizations use software tools to execute their projects but only scratch the surface—using it to monitor deadlines rather than drive more intelligent decisions. AI-powered tools can forecast risks, allocate resources, enhance decision-making, and streamline collaboration, yet too often, these functionalities go unused. Execution remains manual, reactive, and dependent on individual effort.

A major telecom provider rolled out a next-generation project platform with predictive analytics and automated resource planning. However, the teams continued to operate as before—managing capacity through Excel files, holding weekly status meetings to chase updates, and reacting to delays only after they happened. Despite the platform's potential, poor adoption and outdated habits neutralized its impact. The technology existed—but intelligent execution did not.

NOTE

a. Michael C. Daconta, "Media Got It Wrong: HealthCare.gov Failed Despite Agile Practices," Route Fifty, November 1, 2013, https://www.route-fifty.com/digital-government/2013/11/media-got-it-wrong-healthcaregov-failed-despite-agile-practices/316537/.

AI is closing this gap by enabling real-time decision-making, automating labor-intensive tasks, and generating precise forecasts for resources, timelines, and risks. These advancements are empowering project leaders and teams to work smarter, reduce inefficiencies, and deliver projects with far greater agility and impact. The technology is transforming project management in three critical areas: decision-making and predictive analytics, automation of routine tasks, and AI-driven forecasting for better resource allocation and outcomes.

Bridges to Prosperity, a nonprofit connecting remote communities in the Global South, is using AI to dramatically accelerate infrastructure planning. Its WaterNet model analyzed over 3 million satellite images to identify 124 million kilometers of previously unmapped waterways—crucial for locating isolated populations.[5] Meanwhile, their Fika Map platform uses AI to recommend bridge locations and forecast costs, shrinking planning timelines from years to months.

This creates a powerful feedback loop: smarter tools drive faster insights, which in turn enable better decisions and more impactful outcomes. Bridges to Prosperity's work shows how thoughtful AI integration can turn logistical challenges into scalable, sustainable solutions—even in the world's most remote areas.

AI in Decision-Making and Predictive Analytics

One of AI's most transformative contributions to projects lies in its ability to enhance decision-making through predictive analytics. By harnessing advanced machine learning capabilities, AI tools empower organizations to make data-driven decisions with greater precision and confidence.

Smarter Project Selection and Prioritization. Selecting the right projects has always been a critical challenge for organizations. AI-powered tools like AI Predictor tackle this issue by providing data-backed insights to assess project viability.

AI Predictor uses a detailed data set derived from over ninety yes/no questions, based on the project canvas framework, to analyze key project characteristics such as clarity of purpose, stakeholder alignment, resource availability, and anticipated benefits. It calculates a project's likelihood of success, ranking initiatives to guide decision-making and resource allocation. This approach ensures alignment with organizational priorities while reducing the influence of biases or incomplete information.

AI Predictor has already demonstrated its effectiveness. A US-based food production company used this tool to evaluate and prioritize its portfolio of initiatives, improving both focus and resource efficiency. Similarly, an international business school applied it to its transformation projects, identifying critical gaps and redirecting efforts toward higher-impact activities. The more AI Predictor is used, the smarter it becomes, thanks to machine learning algorithms that continuously re-fine its analysis as the database grows.

Proactive Risk Management. AI tools are also redefining how risks are identified and addressed. Machine learning models can process vast amounts of historical and real-time project data to detect patterns and predict potential risks before they materialize. These applications analyze variables such as resource constraints, interdependencies, and shifting market conditions, flagging areas of concern early in the project life cycle.

For example, machine learning algorithms might identify that certain tasks are more likely to delay timelines due to previous bottlenecks or resource shortages. Future iterations will take this a step further by offering automated risk-mitigation strategies, dynamically adjusting project plans, and reallocating resources to minimize disruptions.

Improved Reporting and Insights. AI is transforming the traditionally static and manual process of project reporting. AI-driven dash-boards provide real-time visualizations of project metrics, enabling transformation leaders and stakeholders to track progress, identify bottlenecks, and respond swiftly to emerging challenges.

Automation of Repetitive Tasks

AI agents are also reshaping projects by significantly reducing the time and effort spent on repetitive and labor-intensive tasks. These advancements free project managers and teams to concentrate on high-value activities, enabling faster execution and greater focus on strategic goals.

Streamlining Scope Definition and Planning. Defining a project's scope and building detailed plans have traditionally required extensive manual effort, stakeholder involvement, and iterative revisions. AI-powered tools simplify these processes by analyzing project requirements to detect ambiguities, inconsistencies, or missing details. This early analysis ensures that potential issues are resolved before execution begins, saving both time and resources.

In addition to requirement analysis, AI agents automate resource planning and cost estimation, tasks that previously consumed significant amounts of time. By leveraging historical data and real-time project insights, these tools can generate actionable plans in minutes. For example, they might recommend optimal staffing levels, budget allocations, and timelines tailored to the project's complexity and objectives, eliminating guesswork and reducing planning overhead.

Dynamic Monitoring and Adjustments. In transformation projects, maintaining alignment with timelines, budgets, and deliverables requires constant updates and adjustments. AI tools excel at real-time monitoring, flagging deviations, and recommending changes based on project performance.

Digital assistants use machine learning to analyze evolving project data and provide real-time insights. This dynamic interaction helps prioritize key actions and maintain momentum, ensuring projects stay on track. Moreover, AI tools continuously scan project updates to detect potential misalignments or resource constraints. By identifying such challenges early, these systems can recommend timely corrective measures, such as reallocating resources or modifying schedules, ensuring that progress continues smoothly.

Automating Routine PMO and Transformation Office Functions. Within the PMO and transformation offices, routine tasks such as compliance monitoring, reporting, and stakeholder analysis often occupy a disproportionate amount of time and resources. AI is streamlining these functions, enabling the PMO to transition from administrative oversight to strategic project enablement. For example, AI-powered compliance tools can automatically assess transformation activities against regulatory standards, eliminating the need for manual reviews. Similarly, reporting tools generate real-time, visually engaging dashboards that highlight key metrics, such as progress, risks, and resource utilization, ensuring stakeholders have instant access to critical insights.

Stakeholder analysis, another essential but time-intensive task, benefits from AI's ability to process large volumes of data. Machine learning models can identify influential stakeholders, assess their engagement levels, and recommend strategies for fostering alignment, all while reducing manual effort.

AI-Driven Forecasting for Improved Resource Allocation

AI is revolutionizing how organizations predict, allocate, and adjust resources throughout the project life cycle. By leveraging advanced data analytics, AI-driven forecasting tools provide actionable insights that help teams plan effectively, mitigate risks, and optimize performance in real time.

Enhanced Forecasting Accuracy. Traditional forecasting methods often rely on static models and human estimates, leaving room for inaccuracies that can derail projects. AI-powered tools bring a new level of precision by analyzing vast amounts of historical and real-time data. These tools identify patterns, correlations, and anomalies that human analysis might overlook, generating highly accurate predictions for timelines, costs, and resource requirements.

For instance, Octant AI tracks project data dynamically, enabling organizations to update forecasts as conditions evolve. Rather than relying on fixed assumptions, the system continuously refines predictions based on real-time input, flagging potential budget overruns or timeline delays before they occur. This proactive approach allows transformation teams to adapt their strategies, ensuring that resources are deployed efficiently and costs are kept under control.

Beyond budgets and schedules, AI-enhanced forecasting models also improve planning for material resources, personnel, and dependencies. These insights are particularly valuable for complex initiatives with multiple moving parts, where accurate forecasting can mean the difference between success and failure.

Real-Time Adaptability. As transformations and projects progress, unexpected challenges can arise, such as delays in critical tasks, shifting stakeholder priorities, or changes in scope. AI-driven tools are designed to respond to these disruptions with real-time adaptability, ensuring that projects remain on course. For example, AI algorithms can monitor task progress and resource utilization, identifying where bottlenecks are likely to occur. If a specific task begins to fall behind schedule, the tool can recommend reallocating resources, adding personnel, or adjusting timelines to prevent delays from cascading through the project.

AI tools also optimize resource allocation across multiple projects in a portfolio, identifying underused assets that can be redeployed to high-priority initiatives. This dynamic approach ensures that every resource—whether time, budget, or personnel—is used to its full potential.

Scenario Planning and Predictive Simulations. AI's predictive capabilities extend beyond real-time forecasting to scenario planning, where multiple what-if simulations help transformation leaders and project managers evaluate potential strategies. For example, an AI tool can model the impact of different resource allocation decisions, such as adding an extra team member to a high-priority task or delaying a non-essential deliverable. These simulations provide data-backed insights into the most effective course of action, reducing guesswork and enhancing confidence in decision-making.

Predictive simulations also help teams plan for contingencies, such as disruptions in the supply chain or fluctuating resource availability. By testing various scenarios before challenges arise, project leaders can develop preemptive strategies that minimize risks and keep projects on track.

The Challenges of AI Adoption

While AI holds transformative potential for projects, effective implementation hinges on overcoming significant challenges—chief among them, issues surrounding data. AI systems rely on vast amounts of high-quality data to generate insights, make predictions, and automate processes. However, most organizations face considerable hurdles in managing their project-related data, which is often scattered, unstructured, and incomplete. This may help explain why, according to our research, only 4 percent of organizations currently use AI extensively across all projects and just 9 percent have integrated it significantly but not universally. A full 50 percent are still in the exploratory phase, using AI minimally as they begin to understand its potential, while 28 percent have yet to adopt AI in project management at all. Addressing these challenges and bridging the knowledge gap around AI is essential to unlocking its full value in project management.

The Importance of High-Quality Data. Data is the lifeblood of AI. For project management AI systems to function effectively, they require accurate, consistent, and comprehensive data sets that reflect project realities. Poor-quality data—whether due to missing information, discrepancies, or inconsistencies—can lead to flawed predictions, misleading insights, and suboptimal decisions. For example, an AI tool analyzing project timelines might struggle to deliver reliable forecasts if the historical data contains gaps in task completion dates or misaligned milestones. Similarly, unstructured data sets, such as fragmented stakeholder feedback stored in disparate systems, can hinder AI's ability to identify patterns or provide actionable recommendations.

Centralizing and Organizing Data. One of the foundational steps for AI adoption is creating a centralized inventory of project data. Many organizations store data across multiple platforms, teams, or departments, leading to silos that make it difficult to gain a holistic view of projects. Consolidating this information into a single, unified database ensures that AI systems can access the full scope of relevant data.

In addition to centralization, organizations must focus on standardizing taxonomies—the terminology, classifications, and formats used to capture project-related information. For example, project timelines must use consistent date formats, risk assessments should follow uniform scoring systems, and resource categories must align across teams. Standardization ensures that data from different sources is comparable and can be seamlessly integrated for analysis.

Investing in Data Cleaning and Structuring. Even after centralizing and standardizing data, organizations must identify and correct errors, fill gaps, and convert unstructured data—such as free-text descriptions of project risks—into structured formats that AI systems can interpret. For instance, tools like natural language processing can help convert stakeholder feedback or meeting notes into structured data sets that AI can analyze for trends or insights. Similarly, data validation protocols can identify inconsistencies, such as duplicate entries or mismatched categories, ensuring the database remains accurate and reliable over time.

Scaling Data Collection Efforts. To fully leverage AI's capabilities, organizations must also scale their data collection efforts to capture a broader range of project-related variables. This includes tracking new types of data, such as real-time team sentiment, resource utilization patterns, or external factors like market conditions. By incorporating richer data sets, AI systems can generate deeper insights and support more nuanced decision-making.

E nsuring data quality is a strategic imperative for organizations aiming to adopt AI in their transformations and projects. By centralizing data, standardizing taxonomies, and investing in cleaning and structuring processes, organizations can build a robust foundation that allows AI systems to deliver accurate, actionable insights.

Beyond Artificial Intelligence: Exploring Other New Technologies

While AI has taken center stage in transforming how projects and transformations are executed, it is only one of a much larger array of tech tools. According to the Project Management Institute, the field is on the brink of a technological renaissance, with innovations such as digital twins, the metaverse, avatars, and neural interface implants redefining the very fabric of how initiatives are planned, managed, and delivered.[6] These technologies promise not only to enhance efficiency but also to fundamentally reshape the roles of transformation leaders and the processes they oversee.

The Rise of Digital Twins in Projects and Transformations. Digital twins—virtual replicas of physical systems or processes—are offering transformation leaders an unparalleled ability to simulate, analyze, and optimize their initiatives. By mirroring real-world environments, digital twins enable proactive decision-making and risk mitigation, ensuring higher success rates and smoother execution.

- *Applications across industries.* Transformation leaders in construction can use digital twins to simulate entire building designs or infrastructure projects before breaking ground. This preemptive modeling helps identify potential issues, reduces costly errors, and ensures that timelines and budgets remain intact. Similarly, in manufacturing, digital twins can model production lines to optimize workflows and predict maintenance needs, minimizing downtime and maximizing efficiency.

- *Real-time scenario planning.* By integrating data from IoT sensors, digital twins provide real-time insights that enable transformation leaders to adapt swiftly. For instance, in a large-scale transportation initiative, a digital twin could simulate traffic flow changes caused by new road designs, allowing leaders to make evidence-based decisions that optimize outcomes.

The Metaverse: A New Dimension for Collaboration and Training. The metaverse—a shared virtual space that merges physical and digital realities—creates powerful new opportunities for managing transformations, building stronger teams, and engaging stakeholders across global initiatives:

- *Immersive collaboration for distributed teams.* In the metaverse, transformation leaders and their teams can interact with life-size, three-dimensional models of their initiatives, enabling more intuitive and effective collaboration regardless of physical location. For instance, a global team working on a renewable energy transformation can virtually examine wind turbine designs, troubleshoot issues, or explore site layouts, reducing miscommunication and accelerating progress.

- *Hands-on training and skill development.* The metaverse provides an ideal immersive training and development platform. Transformation teams can engage in lifelike simulations to practice scenarios such as disaster recovery or emergency responses without the risks or costs associated with real-world drills. This approach is particularly beneficial for complex transformations requiring high levels of coordination and specialized skills.

- *Stronger stakeholder engagement through avatars.* Digital avatars allow leaders and team members to represent themselves in real-time virtual sessions, guiding stakeholders through complex project updates and strategic reviews. This visual, interactive approach enhances understanding, accelerates decision-making, and sustains leadership visibility even across multiple initiatives.

Neural Interface Technologies and the Future of Thought-Based Collaboration. Neural interface technologies create a direct interface between the brain and digital systems. Tools such as those being developed by Neuralink are pushing the boundaries of collaboration and innovation in transformations. These technologies could radically redefine how teams communicate, solve problems, and execute complex initiatives. Potential uses include:

- *Seamless communication and idea sharing.* With neural interfaces, team members could transmit complex ideas instantaneously without the need for lengthy discussions or documentation. For example, transformation leaders brainstorming solutions for a new health-care initiative could visualize and refine concepts collectively, using thought-based inputs to adjust 3D models or simulations in real time.

- *Enhanced decision-making agility.* Neural interfaces could enable faster, more informed decision-making by allowing transformation leaders to interact directly with dashboards, simulations, or digital twins through neural commands. This capability would eliminate the friction of manual inputs, enabling leaders to focus on refining strategies and driving outcomes.

In the transformation age, where the pace of change is unprecedented, technologies like AI, digital twins, the metaverse, and neural interfaces go beyond incremental improvements. Additional leading-edge technologies offer the tools and frameworks necessary for PDOs to collaborate globally, anticipate disruptions, and align stakeholders around shared goals. They empower transformation leaders to break free from traditional constraints, enabling bold initiatives that drive competitive advantage and prepare organizations to meet the demands of an increasingly dynamic world.

Conclusion

Organizations are redefining execution for the transformation age—aligning stakeholders through the project canvas, applying hybrid methodologies tailored to project complexity, and harnessing AI and emerging technologies to drive smarter, faster outcomes. Together, these shifts move execution from a technical discipline to a core enabler of value creation and strategic agility.

As we transition to the final chapter of this book, we look ahead to shaping the future through project-driven organizations. We will examine the competencies, structures, and cultures required to lead the next wave of innovation and ensure that the project economy delivers its full potential for individuals, organizations, and society.

Shaping the Future through Project-Driven Organizations

What lies ahead for project-driven organizations and the lasting impact they can create? These organizations are not simply responding to the demands of a rapidly changing world—they are leading the charge, leveraging projects as engines of transformation, innovation, and societal progress.

In this chapter, we look into three critical dimensions that define the future of project-driven organizations: their lasting legacy, the critical role of leadership in navigating uncertainty and complexity with purpose, and the ongoing journey of reinvention. Finally, we review all that we've learned about PDOs and how to take your next steps forward.

The Future of the Project-Driven Organization

We can safely predict some aspects of the future because the forces driving them are already visible today. AI is part of a stream of technology-enabled change that in time will include quantum computing and new generations of human/AI interfaces. At the time of writing this book, the second term of US President Donald Trump has had extraordinary political and economic repercussions on global systems. We are seeing radical social changes, from the growing centenarian demographic to the revolution in how we influence those around us on both the local and international scale. Climate change and resource scarcity will have a profound human and economic toll, while green technologies to mitigate them may generate entirely new industries in the coming decade.

The PDO needs to adapt to these and many other fast-emerging challenges but also requires a proactive approach so that they are actively shaping the future—not simply responding to the external environment.

The Future of Resilience through Value Creation

In this context, the successful organization will need a level of *antifragility* (a term popularized by Nassim Taleb), which moves beyond resilience to an ability not simply to adapt to challenges and obstacles but to leverage them, to generate an innovation bounce—almost a living system. Here's what will move organizations forward to this state:

- *Predictive AI and data systems.* Organizations will use predictive analytics and machine learning to foresee disruptions before they occur. AI will provide decision-makers with clear scenarios and recommendations, ensuring rapid activation of mitigation projects.

- *Proactive crisis playbooks.* Organizations will invest in project-based playbooks with which they can simulate a wide variety of different delivery options and outline predesigned responses to various types of disruptions for those options they adopt. These playbooks will allow for rapid mobilization of resources and teams.

- *Resilience-focused talent ecosystems.* Leading organizations will cultivate a flexible, project-ready workforce that includes internal talent, contingent workers, and strategic partners. By building ecosystems that can be reshaped as needed, companies can ensure that the right capabilities are available to meet emerging challenges and seize new opportunities.

For PDOs, value creation isn't just a metric to be measured in financial terms—it's a reputation that sets enduring organizations apart. It shapes how investors view long-term potential, how employees decide where to work, and how communities perceive the organization's relevance and contribution. Sustained value ensures continued investment, attracts ambitious talent, and builds deeper connections to the societies the organization serves. It must be reframed to reflect a broader, more resilient approach—one that may not be fully future-proof, but that actively shapes the emerging agenda.

The future of value creation in PDOs will be defined by four core shifts. First, organizations will manage holistic portfolios of projects that go beyond profit maximization. Portfolios will intentionally balance financial returns with societal and environmental outcomes—tracking success through metrics like enhanced biodiversity, increased access to education, improved health outcomes, or reduced inequality. Value will be understood as multidimensional—economic, human, and ecological.

Second, value creation will be rooted in localized solutions delivered at scale. Rather than imposing uniform solutions, organizations will cocreate projects with local communities, tailoring them to specific social, cultural, and environmental needs. These models will then scale globally through networks, partnerships, and open platforms—amplifying impact without sacrificing context.

Third, we will see a shift toward long-term ecosystem commitments. Projects will no longer be isolated interventions—they will be designed with generational time horizons, embedding regenerative practices that not only restore ecosystems but also deliver compounding value to all stakeholders over time. This means thinking not just about a project's ROI but also its legacy.

Fourth, and perhaps most critically, the entire value-creation model will move away from static structures and transactional relationships. There can be no fixed commercial or organizational blueprint, no reliance on a limited internal workforce, and no dominance of hierarchical relationships. Instead, value will emerge from fluid ecosystems—cross-sector collaborations, open innovation models, and dynamic networks of people and partners who contribute as needed from wherever they are, often without formal employment.

For the PDO, this new value approach is not optional but existential. In an era where impact matters as much as efficiency, where ecosystems move faster than hierarchies, and where trust is earned through action, the ability to continuously redefine and deliver value will determine who leads, who follows, and who fades.

The Future Is Adaptive

The project-driven organization will continue to evolve into an adaptive, responsive system—one designed to thrive in constant transformation. At the heart of this evolution is the shift toward ecosystem-based structures. Organizations will no longer function as self-contained units, but as nodes in a broader network of collaborators—working dynamically with external partners, independent contractors, startups, academic institutions, and even competitors. These ecosystems will form and reform around specific challenges and opportunities, with trust, data-sharing, and aligned purpose. Projects will become the currency of collaboration, and value will be cocreated across boundaries.

Internally, the talent model will become radically more fluid. The era of static roles and fixed departments is ending. In its place, we will see the rise of fluid talent systems, where individuals bid on projects based on their skills, interests, and growth aspirations. Employees will move in and out of initiatives as needed—often across functions and geographies or within ecosystems. This shift will unlock deeper engagement, faster learning, and a more entrepreneurial workforce continuously aligned with where the organization needs to go.

Driving this adaptive model will be the emergence of self-optimizing organizations. Powered by AI and intelligent platforms, they will constantly monitor execution, collaboration, and outcomes—identifying friction points and recommending adjustments in real time. Whether it's reconfiguring a project team, reallocating resources, or suggesting a workflow design shift, the system will become a copilot in organizational agility. Leaders will no longer have to wait for quarterly reviews to spot what's not working—the organization will adapt continuously.

Together, these shifts point to a future where adaptability is a condition of survival. The PDO will become less about what it owns and more about how it connects, less about stability and more about responsiveness. (See the sidebar, "Project-Driven Organizations in Possible Futures.") Those that embrace this model will be better equipped to lead not only through change—but remain ahead of it.

Project-Driven Organizations in Possible Futures

The following four scenarios are fictional, but they reflect real trends that are reshaping how organizations create value through projects. Set in 2030, 2035, 2040, and 2050, each explores a possible future shaped by shifts in strategy, technology and society at large.

2030: Organization-Community Partnerships

A clean energy company redefines how organizations create long-term value. Partnering with emerging economies, it launches interconnected projects to install modular, off-grid solar power systems in underserved rural areas. These projects don't just aim to sell a product; they aim to create lasting value for the communities involved.

Laura Becks, a senior program leader at the company, oversees one of the flagship initiatives in the United Arab Emirates. Her team coordinates 120 local installations across three countries, reaching more than 15,000 households. However, the real impact stems from the model's integration with the community: each solar installation is paired with localized training programs, which teach over 900 residents how to maintain and repair the systems, thereby ensuring sustainability.

The projects are designed to generate economic opportunities. Within eight months, the region recorded a 19 percent increase in small business activity, particularly in food refrigeration, sewing, and mobile charging services. Impact metrics tracked a 26 percent reduction in carbon emissions, improved education outcomes from extended evening study hours, and a 35 percent rise in local entrepreneurship registrations.

2035: Predictive AI Powers Crisis Teams

Facing a critical challenge posed by simultaneous climate-related disruptions—severe floods in North America and droughts in South America—a global logistics company activates its AI-powered crisis management center. This system monitors global weather patterns and supply chain data, triggering autonomous project teams across San Francisco, Montreal, São Paulo, and Lima.

(continued)

At the center of this mobilization was Alex Nelson, a regional transformation leader based in Singapore. With over twenty years in the field, he had never faced such a dual-continent emergency. Within thirty-six hours, Alex's team rerouted over 1,200 shipping containers, shifted inventory to resilient hubs, and introduced low-emission rail options to maintain service levels, achieving a 92 percent on-time delivery rate despite the turmoil.

Each project team is decentralized and empowered to make decisions without waiting for top-down approvals. Leveraging real-time insights, they adjusted logistics flows, collaborated with local governments, and minimized customer disruption. The financial impact, originally projected to be $270 million in potential losses, was reduced to less than $12 million. This fast response not only protected customer relationships but also reinforced the company's brand promise in a volatile world.

2040: Responsive Reconfiguration at Speed

NovaHealth, a multinational health-care consortium, addresses challenges by constantly reconfiguring itself. When a new viral outbreak emerges in a remote region, the consortium launches projects within hours, pulling experts from a global network of biotech firms, universities, and government agencies.

At the helm of this initiative is a young leader, Selma Singh, a standout graduate of NovaHealth's Leadership Futures Program—a unique training initiative designed to prepare leaders for high-stakes, high-complexity transformation projects. Selma's task is monumental: she must manage fourteen cross-functional teams spanning three continents, oversee partnerships with seven regulatory agencies and three major global nonprofits, and ensure the project remains financially viable while prioritizing equitable access to a lifesaving treatment.

But Selma is ready. Drawing on her training in purpose-driven leadership, she aligns more than 180 project contributors around a mission that transcends profit: saving lives and curbing the outbreak. She uses systems thinking to navigate the complexity of regulatory approvals and supply chain logistics. Leveraging AI-powered analytics, her team models multiple scenarios, identifying potential supply risks three months in advance and reducing approval timelines by 48 percent. Through this project, NovaHealth not only develops a breakthrough treatment but also inspires a new model of leadership for the transformation age.

2050: Autonomous Adaptive Organizations

By 2050, the very idea of an organization has been redefined. There are no job titles and no departments—only fluid, intelligent networks that self-organize around purpose. Work no longer follows fixed processes. It flows through dynamic, temporary structures—each one forming, operating, and dissolving around a project.

At Cultura, a global experience platform, contributors are selected based on verified impact, not tenure. When the company identifies a need to reimagine public space across thirty global cities, Lucas Okoye is chosen to lead the initiative—nominated and voted in by his peers based on his track record of high-trust, high-impact transformation projects.

Lucas's project isn't managed—it's orchestrated, and humans and robots collaborate seamlessly. In London, service robots cofacilitate multilingual workshops with residents. In Madrid, autonomous construction drones fabricate modular seating and shade structures based on live community feedback. In just eight weeks, the project delivers adaptive, community-owned spaces in all thirty cities—spaces that evolve in real time, based on usage patterns and emotional data. Public satisfaction jumps by 67 percent. Local economic activity increases. Most importantly, trust in shared spaces is visibly restored.

In this world, transformation isn't something organizations strive for. It's how they exist—through people like Lucas Okoye, who don't manage tasks but catalyze lasting impact through agile, autonomous, and deeply human projects.

Challenges and Opportunities for Leaders of PDOs

For CEOs and senior leaders, the journey ahead offers immense opportunities to lead with purpose, inspire innovation, and build ecosystems that thrive in a dynamic world. It also comes with challenges that demand vision, adaptability, and the courage to disrupt traditional norms.

An Appetite for Decentralization and Innovation

Although the need to delegate authority to empowered teams presents a challenge for CEOs who are accustomed to centralized decision-making, it creates an opportunity to build a culture of trust and accountability. Leaders who embrace decentralized models can unlock innovation and entrepreneurship at all levels, with teams acting as autonomous units capable of responding quickly to change. Integrating AI systems will allow them to improve communication, risk management, and opportunity sharing across the whole portfolio, which will help align and accelerate projects and strategy. At the same time, predictive AI will offer leaders unparalleled foresight, enabling them to act decisively in high-stakes situations.

The Long-Term Vision

Balancing short-term pressures with long-term commitments will remain a significant challenge. CEOs will face increasing scrutiny from stakeholders who demand quarterly performance results while advancing strategic initiatives that may take time to deliver their full impact. Yet, this tension also provides an opportunity to redefine organizational success. By championing value-driven projects, leaders can attract new types of investors, deepen customer loyalty, and boost employee engagement.

The Continuously Shifting Landscape

The continuous evolution of organizational structures will challenge leaders to navigate ambiguity and manage resistance to change. However, this evolution also creates immense opportunities for innovation and talent retention. By fostering a dynamic and adaptive culture, CEOs can attract top global talent eager to work on meaningful projects. Additionally, embracing ecosystem-based collaboration allows organizations to extend their influence, share risks, and drive larger-scale impact.

Developing a New Generation of Project Leaders

Leadership development will focus on those who can provide meaning to their teams, help employees work effectively with emerging technologies like AI, and guide collaboration through constant change. Tomorrow's project leaders will grow by delivering outcomes, building trust, and adapting in real time—regardless of what comes next.

Purpose-Driven Leadership. The leaders of the future will operate with a deep sense of mission. Leadership development will prioritize embedding purpose into business strategy, teaching leaders how to evaluate the societal and environmental impact of every project. Community-centric leadership models will emerge, requiring leaders to work closely with diverse stakeholder groups—including employees, customers, and local communities—to provide meaning to everyone's work in their organizations.

Leaders who embrace purpose will drive competitive advantage, using projects to address global challenges while building stronger connections with consumers and employees. For CEOs, the challenge will be creating a culture that values purpose as much as profit, while the opportunity lies in enhancing organizational reputation, talent attraction, and market differentiation.

Leading in Constant Disruption. Future leadership will focus on building systems thinking—equipping leaders to see patterns, understand interdependencies, and anticipate the ripple effects of decisions across projects and ecosystems. Comfort with uncertainty will be essential, as leaders increasingly rely on AI-powered tools to simulate scenarios, guide decisions, and respond in real time. Developing these capabilities will be core to preparing leaders who can thrive in environments defined by speed, ambiguity, and continuous change.

Experiential Leadership Development. Advanced simulations will complement a shift toward immersive, experiential learning. Future organizations will design leadership pathways that move beyond traditional classroom-based training, prioritizing experiential and hands-on learning. Companies will immerse rising leaders in live projects, allowing them to develop skills in real-world, high-pressure environments. Project-based development programs will give leaders direct experience managing resources, risks, and teams in dynamic environments. Innovation hubs and internal incubators will play a complementary role, offering safe spaces where emerging leaders can test ideas, engage in rapid learning cycles, and build resilience through experimentation. And rotational leadership tracks will expose leaders to different industries, functions, and regions, equipping them with the versatility needed to lead in the transformation age.

The Journey Ahead: A Continuous Evolution

The road to becoming a project-driven organization is not a onetime destination but a continuous journey. In the transformation age, the pace of change will only accelerate, making perpetual adaptation a requirement for survival and success. Below, we explore four pillars that will define the journey ahead, guiding PDOs toward lasting relevance and leadership in a dynamic world.

Learning Every Day: Turning Adaptation into a Habit

Continuous learning will no longer be a separate activity but will be seamlessly integrated into everyday workflows. This means transforming each project, meeting, or challenge into an opportunity to gain insights, refine skills, and share knowledge across teams.

Organizations will establish "learning loops," where teams pause at regular intervals to assess what's working, what's not, and how to improve. These insights will be immediately applied, creating a culture of real-time adaptability. Leaders will also leverage advanced tools like AI-driven platforms to identify emerging skill gaps and provide employees with personalized training recommendations.

To amplify this culture of everyday learning, organizations will formalize partnerships with external think tanks, universities, and innovation hubs, ensuring that fresh knowledge flows constantly into the organization. This approach will create a virtuous cycle of adaptation, where teams become better equipped to tackle new challenges with every project they complete.

Future organizations will also use every project as a chance to innovate and evolve, treating setbacks not as failures but as opportunities to improve processes and outcomes. By doing so, they will create a sustainable competitive advantage that allows them to adapt faster than the competition.

Building a Transformation-Ready Workforce: Making Change Everyone's Job

Organizations will embed transformation capabilities into onboarding programs and professional development initiatives, ensuring that every employee understands how to lead and adapt to change. Real-world simulations, such as virtual scenarios replicating organizational crises or high-stakes pivots, will give employees hands-on experience in problem-solving and cross-functional collaboration.

Transparency will be key to this effort. Organizations will adopt real-time transformation dashboards that allow employees to track the progress of ongoing initiatives. This visibility will help individuals see how their contributions fit into the bigger picture, fostering a sense of ownership and accountability. Mentorship and reverse mentorship networks will further support this cultural shift, pairing seasoned transformation leaders with emerging talent to exchange insights, accelerate learning, and bridge generational perspectives.

Accelerating Innovation: Integrating Technology as a Strategic Capability

Technology will become deeply embedded in the organization's fabric, evolving alongside strategy, structure, and culture. Employees will need to learn to live and work with technology as partners, much as we already do with tools like GPS navigation or mobile phones. This shift demands a new mindset that treats technology not as a onetime investment or fixed asset but as an adaptive capability.

To accelerate innovation, organizations will create tech sandbox environments where teams can test and refine technologies on smaller, less critical projects before scaling them enterprise-wide. This approach minimizes risk while enabling fast learning cycles. Additionally, companies will codevelop solutions with tech providers, ensuring that tools are customized to fit their specific needs and can be implemented without lengthy adaptation periods.

Technology integration will also require cultural shifts. Organizations must train employees to use new systems effectively while fostering an attitude of curiosity and experimentation. AI-driven project analytics tools will help track the impact of technology in real time, allowing leaders to optimize deployment strategies dynamically. Digital twins will further enhance agility by enabling leaders to simulate project outcomes and mitigate risks before implementing changes on the ground.

Leading with Impact: Redefining How Change Is Seen and Felt

In the transformation age, leadership impact will no longer be judged solely by business outcomes, but rather by how visibly and meaningfully leaders guide their organizations through ongoing change. Leading with impact means creating clarity in ambiguity, progress in motion, and purpose in every decision.

Future-fit leaders won't just track KPIs—they'll narrate transformation as it happens. They'll utilize real-time data and AI-powered storytelling to demonstrate how their initiatives drive tangible value, from accelerating net-zero transitions to expanding equitable access to technology and health care.

Impact will be made visible, both internally through transparent feedback loops and externally through living dashboards that demonstrate how each action aligns with broader societal goals. Quick wins will serve not as endpoints but as proof points that long-term change is underway.

Ultimately, leading with impact means making transformation both measurable and meaningful—so teams feel it, stakeholders trust it, and the world can see it.

The Path Ahead

One truth is clear: the future of business and society will be shaped by organizations that adopt a project-driven approach. These organizations leave a legacy of resilience, adaptability, meaning, and long-term relevance, transcending short-term objectives to create meaningful and lasting value. They are powered by a new generation of leaders—individuals who balance profit with purpose, inspire teams to tackle complex challenges, and prioritize societal and environmental progress alongside organizational goals. By fostering cultures of empowerment, these leaders ensure their organizations remain relevant in an ever-changing world.

But this journey has no end; it is a continuous process of learning, reinvention, and innovation. The transformation age demands constant evolution: integrating emerging technologies, embedding transformation capabilities at every level, and making visible progress that inspires trust and engagement. The path forward will be challenging, but for those who embrace these principles, the rewards are immense. PDOs have the unique potential to solve global challenges, lead with impact, and create a future defined by purpose, progress, and resilience. It is this sustained commitment to leading through projects that will define their long-term success.

Becoming a project-driven organization is not linear, it is not a checklist, it is a continuous act of leadership—a commitment to clarity, focus, adaptability, and purpose.

This book has offered the tools, principles, and practices to guide that journey. From the project canvas to the CPO role, from governance shifts to talent reinvention, from project-first cultures to intelligent execution. The PDO blueprint is now in your hands.

To the leaders reading this, your organization's future will be defined not by how well you execute routine tasks but by how boldly you lead through transformation. By how well you mobilize people around purpose. By how you prioritize. By how fast—and how well—you deliver. Remember, you're already a project-driven leader—and hopefully while reading this book, you've taking a few steps forward on your journey.

The project economy is not a trend. It is a structural shift. This is a once-in-a-generation opportunity to redesign how we work, lead, and create value.

The opportunity is here. The future is waiting. The question is: *Will you lead as you always have—or will you lead the shift to a project-driven organization built for the future?*

NOTES

Introduction

1. "The Five Key Forces of Change," Accenture, April 25, 2023, https://www
.accenture.com/us-en/insights/five-key-forces-of-change.

2. Antonio Nieto-Rodriguez, *The Project Management Handbook: How to
Launch, Lead, and Sponsor Successful Projects* (Boston: Harvard Business Review
Press, 2021).

3. Stephen Foley and Simon Foy, "EY Took on $700 Million in Debt for Doomed
'Project Everest' Spin-Off Plan," *Irish Times*, February 12, 2024, https://www
.irishtimes.com/business/2024/02/12/ey-took-on-700m-in-debt-for-doomed
-project-everest-spin-off-plan/.

4. Amy Francombe, "Nike's New CEO Has One Hell of a Challenge Ahead,"
Wired, September 24, 2024, https://www.wired.com/story/nikes-next-ceo-has
-one-hell-of-a-challenge-ahead/.

5. Jacques Bughin, Laura LaBerge, and Anette Mellbye, "The Case for Digital
Reinvention," *McKinsey Digital*, February 9, 2017, https://www.mckinsey.com
/capabilities/mckinsey-digital/our-insights/the-case-for-digital-reinvention.

6. Saurabh Mathur, "The Impact of a Company's Organizational Structure on
Project Management," Project Management Path, September 11, 2023, https://
projectmanagementpath.com/the-impact-of-a-companys-organizational
-structure-on-project-management/.

7. Michael Mankins, "In Uncertain Times, the Best Strategy Is Adaptability,"
Harvard Business Review, August 24, 2022, https://hbr.org/2022/08/in-uncertain
-times-the-best-strategy-is-adaptability.

8. Martin Reeves and Mike Deimler, "Adaptability: The New Competitive
Advantage," *Harvard Business Review*, July–August 2011, https://hbr.org/2011/07
/adaptability-the-new-competitive-advantage.

9. Chip Cutter, "One CEO's Radical Fix for Corporate Troubles: Purge the
Bosses," *Wall Street Journal*, March 22, 2024, https://www.wsj.com/business
/bayer-cuts-bosses-recovery-plan-f3c94865; Bruce Crumley, "Bayer's American
CEO Plots Management Revolution from Above," *Inc.*, March 22, 2024, https://
www.inc.com/bruce-crumley/bayers-american-ceo-plots-management-revolution
-from-above.html.

10. "Humble Beginnings," gore.com, https://www.gore.com/system/files/2022
-10/Gore-Culture-Press-Kit-English-September2022.pdf?.

11. European Commission, "The Digital Economy and Society Index (DESI),"
https://digital-strategy.ec.europa.eu/en/policies/desi, accessed April 3, 2025.

12. "Digital Transformation Drives Development in Africa," World Bank
Group, January 18, 2024, https://www.worldbank.org/en/results/2024/01/18
/digital-transformation-drives-development-in-afe-afw-africa.

13. "Asian Development Policy Report: Harnessing Digital Transformation for
Good," Asian Development Bank, May 2025, https://www.adb.org/adpr/editions
/digital-transformation.

14. "Shattering the Status Quo: A Conversation with Haier's Zhang Ruimin," *McKinsey Quarterly*, July 27, 2021, https://www.mckinsey.com/capabilities/people-and-organizational-performance/our-insights/shattering-the-status-quo-a-conversation-with-haiers-zhang-ruimin.

Part 1

1. Darius Adamczyk, "The Chair of Honeywell on Bringing an Industrial Business into the Digital Age," *Harvard Business Review*, March–April 2024, https://hbr.org/2024/03/the-chair-of-honeywell-on-bringing-an-industrial-business-into-the-digital-age.

2. Honeywell, "Honeywell Announces Fourth Quarter and Full Year 2023 Results; Issues 2024 Guidance," press release, February 1, 2024, https://investor.honeywell.com/news-releases/news-release-details/honeywell-announces-fourth-quarter-and-full-year-2023-results?.

Chapter 1

1. Albert Bandura, "Self-Efficacy Mechanism in Human Agency," *American Psychologist* 37, no. 2 (1982): 122–147.

2. Franklin Covey, "The 7 Habits of Highly Effective People," learning course, https://www.franklincovey.com/the-7-habits/.

3. Daniel Gayne, "'World-Leading' Net Zero Policy Sees Wales Cancel Road Building Projects," February 15, 2023, https://www.building.co.uk/news/world-leading-net-zero-policy-sees-wales-cancel-road-building-projects/5121784.article.

4. Simon Harvey, "Nestlé Misses on Key Growth Metric as CEO Mark Schneider Leaves Curtain Down on Future Pricing," JustFood, February 16, 2023, https://www.just-food.com/features/nestle-misses-on-key-growth-metric-as-ceo-mark-schneider-leaves-curtain-down-on-future-pricing/.

5. Ingka Group, "Sustainability Is the New Business Model: Jesper Brodin, CEO, Ingka Group," news release, June 8, 2020, https://www.ingka.com/newsroom/sustainability-is-the-new-business-model-jesper-brodin-ceo-ingka-group/.

6. "Boyan Slat," The Ocean Cleanup, https://theoceancleanup.com/boyan-slat/.

7. Ilias Krystallis and Dr. Michel-Alexandre Cardin, "Managing Uncertainty in Megaprojects," *Bartlett Review*, https://bartlett-review.ucl.ac.uk/managing-uncertainty-in-megaprojects/index.html.

8. "Sony CEO History," History Oasis, https://www.historyoasis.com/post/sony-ceo-history.

9. Lords University, "A Commitment to CSR: Tata Group Sets the Standard for CSR in Indian Business," https://www.lordsuni.edu.in/blog/commitment-to-corporate-social-responsibility.

10. John Lynch, "Why Netflix CEO Reed Hastings Calls His Company 'the Anti-Apple,'" *Business Insider*, April 16, 2018, https://www.businessinsider.com/netflix-ceo-reed-hastings-calls-company-the-anti-apple-2018-4.

11. GlaxoSmithKline, "GSK Gives Update on Plans to Share Detailed Clinical Trial Data as Part of Its Commitment to Transparency," press release, May 7, 2013, https://www.gsk.com/en-gb/media/press-releases/gsk-gives-update-on-plans-to-share-detailed-clinical-trial-data-as-part-of-its-commitment-to-transparency/.

12. Marion Terrill, Owen Emslie, and Greg Moran, *The Rise of Megaprojects*, The Grattan Institute, November 2020, https://grattan.edu.au/wp-content /uploads/2020/11/The-Rise-of-Megaprojects-Grattan-Report.pdf.

13. Marc Benioff, "2023 Letter to Stakeholders," Salesforce, April 19, 2023, https://www.salesforce.com/news/stories/2023-letter-to-stakeholders/.

14. Collin Smith and Naomi Mathers, *Data Analytics for Informed Decision-Making in Complex Projects: Exploring the Human-Data Relationship*, Australian Department of Defence, https://iccpm.com/report-data-analytics-for-informed -decision-making-in-complex-projects/.

Chapter 2

1. Mohi U. Ahmed, interview by author, May 16, 2024.

2. "Laboratory Medicine/Pathology," Sonic Healthcare, https://www .sonichealthcare.com/our-services/laboratory-medicine-pathology/.

3. "The Buurtzorg Model," Buurtzorg, https://www.buurtzorg.com/about-us /buurtzorgmodel/.

4. "In First Person: Jos de Blok," SHRM, February 22, 2024, https://www.shrm .org/executive-network/insights/people-strategy/first-person-jos-de-blok.

5. Jeff Galvin and Laura LaBerge, with Evan Williams, *The New Digital Edge: Rethinking Strategy for the Postpandemic Era*, McKinsey, May 26, 2021, https:// www.mckinsey.com/capabilities/mckinsey-digital/our-insights/the-new-digital -edge-rethinking-strategy-for-the-postpandemic-era.

6. General Motors, "GM Will Boost EV and AV Investments to $35 Billion through 2025," news release, June 16, 2021, https://investor.gm.com/news-releases /news-release-details/gm-will-boost-ev-and-av-investments-35-billion-through -2025.

7. Anders Olesen, *Creating Value with Performance Management: Coloplast*, Beyond Budgeting, https://bbrt.org/wp-content/uploads/bb-case-study_a.pdf.

8. Laura London, Stephanie Madner, and Dominic Skerritt, "How Many People Are Really Needed in a Transformation?" McKinsey, September 23, 2021, https:// www.mckinsey.com/capabilities/transformation/our-insights/how-many-people -are-really-needed-in-a-transformation.

9. "Multitasking: Switching Costs," American Psychological Association, March 20, 2006, https://www.apa.org/research/action/multitask.

Chapter 3

1. Axel Welinder, *Legitimizing Sustainability Talk in Retail: The Case of IKEA's Sustainability Journey* (PhD dissertation, Lund University, 2023), https://lup.lub.lu .se/search/files/135263883/Axel_Welinder_Dissertation_Legitimizing _sustainability_talk_in_retail_talk.pdf

2. "Exploring Morning Star's Mission Focused Self-Management Model," Morning Star, https://www.morningstarco.com/exploring-morning-stars-mission -focused-self-management-model/.

3. Gary Hamel and Michele Zanini, "The End of Bureaucracy: How a Chinese Appliance Maker Is Reinventing Management for the Digital Age," *Harvard Business Review*, November–December 2018, https://hbr.org/2018/11/the-end-of -bureaucracy.

4. "A Data-Driven Journey: How TechCorp United Transformed Their Business," *Processology* (blog), https://blog.processology.net/data-driven-journey.

5. Laura Heller, "Walmart Launches Tech Incubator Dubbed Store No. 8," *Forbes*, March 20, 2017, https://www.forbes.com/sites/lauraheller/2017/03/20/walmart-launches-tech-incubator-store-no-8/.

6. Mary Meisenzhal, "Walmart Closes Startup Incubator Store No. 8," Digital Commerce 360, January 23, 2024, https://www.digitalcommerce360.com/2024/01/23/walmart-closes-startup-incubator-store-no-8/.

7. *NASA Systems Engineering Handbook*, SP-610S, June 1995, https://spacecraft.ssl.umd.edu/design_lib/Systems_Eng_Handbook.pdf.

8. "Our Ambition 2025 Strategy," *Integrated Report for the Year Ended 31 December 2023*, MTN Group, https://mtn-investor.com/mtn-ir2023/our-ambition-2025-strategy.php.

9. *Advancing Corporate Governance in the Middle East and North Africa: Stories and Solutions*, Center for International Private Enterprise, February 2011, https://www.ifc.org/content/dam/ifc/doc/mgrt/mena-casestudies-web.pdf.

10. MTN Group, "In a Challenging Macro, MTN Group Reports Strong Underlying 2024 Performance," press release, March 17, 2025, https://www.mtn.com/in-a-challenging-macro-mtn-group-reports-strong-underlying-2024-performance/.

Chapter 4

1. Phil Driver and Ian Seath, "There Are No Shortcuts from Projects to Benefits!" *Simply, Improvement . . .* (blog), January 2014, https://ianjseath.wordpress.com/wp-content/uploads/2014/04/prub-thinking_for_pm_journal_final.pdf.

2. Matthew de Klerk, "The Real-World Positive Outcomes and Examples of Benefits Realisation," OpenSky, October 14, 2022, https://www.openskydata.com/blog/real-world-examples-of-benefits-realisation-and-its-positive-outcomes.

3. Antonio Nieto-Rodriguez and Whitney Johnson, "6 Questions to Ask Before Starting a Big Project," hbr.org, February 12, 2020, https://hbr.org/2020/02/6-questions-to-ask-before-starting-a-big-project.

4. Antonio Nieto-Rodriguez, "How to Prioritize Your Company's Projects," hbr.org, December 13, 2016, https://hbr.org/2016/12/how-to-prioritize-your-companys-projects.

5. Nils O. Fonstad, Martin Mocker, and Jukka Salonen, "Scaling at Scale: Realizing Big Value from Digital Innovations," Research Briefing XXII-12, MIT CISR Research, December 15, 2022, https://cisr.mit.edu/publication/2022_1201_ScalingatScaleRepsol_FonstadMockerSalonen.

6. Fonstad, Mocker, and Salonen, "Scaling at Scale."

7. Antonio Nieto-Rodriguez, *Harvard Business Review Project Management Handbook: How to Launch, Lead, and Sponsor Successful Projects* (Boston: Harvard Business Review Press, 2021).

8. Personal interview with Kate Duchene, June 10, 2024.

9. Roger L. Martin, "Rethinking the Decision Factory," *Harvard Business Review*, October 2013, https://hbr.org/2013/10/rethinking-the-decision-factory.

10. Project Management Institute, *Success in Disruptive Times: Expanding the Value Delivery Landscape to Address the High Cost of Low Performance*, 2018, https://www.pmi.org/learning/thought-leadership/pulse/pulse-of-the-profession-2018.

11. Tata Steel, *Transforming for Tomorrow: Integrated Report and Annual Accounts 2023–24, 117th Year* (Mumbai, Tata Steel, 2024), https://www.tatasteel.com/investors/integrated-report-2023-24/pdf/tata-steel-limited-ir-2024.pdf.

12. "How to Beat the Transformation Odds," McKinsey & Company, 2015, https://www.mckinsey.com/~/media/mckinsey/business%20functions/people%20and%20organizational%20performance/our%20insights/how%20to%20beat%20the%20transformation%20odds/how_to_beat_the_transformation_odds.pdf.

Chapter 5

1. Jurriaan Kamer, "How Haier, Bayer, and Roche Unblock Value at Scale with Mission-Based Teams," Medium, November 28, 2024, https://jurriaankamer.medium.com/how-haier-bayer-and-roche-unblock-value-at-scale-with-mission-based-teams-61efbaf3b794.

2. Stephen Hall, Dan Lovallo, and Reinier Musters, "How to Put Your Money Where Your Strategy Is," McKinsey, March 1, 2012, https://www.mckinsey.com/capabilities/strategy-and-corporate-finance/our-insights/how-to-put-your-money-where-your-strategy-is.

3. "Insights: Jonathan Smart," Barclays, January 4, 2018, https://home.barclays/news/2018/02/insights-jonathan-smart/.

4. "Insights: Jonathan Smart."

5. *Mik + One* (podcast), "Episode 9: Jon Smart on Why Agile Is No Longer the Answer," Flow Framework, November 12, 2019, https://flowframework.org/ffc-podcast/jon-smart/.

6. "Neri Karra Sillaman," 50 Thinkers, https://thinkers50.com/biographies/neri-karra-sillaman/.

7. David Burkus, "What Makes Some Teams High Performing?" hbr.org, August 29, 2023, https://hbr.org/2023/08/what-makes-some-teams-high-performing.

8. Jim Harter, "World's Largest Ongoing Study of the Employee Experience," Gallup, September 4, 2024, https://www.gallup.com/workplace/649487/world-largest-ongoing-study-employee-experience.aspx.

9. Bryan Hancock and Bill Schaninger, "Workplace Rituals: Recapturing the Power of What We've Lost," *Talks Talent* (podcast), McKinsey, January 25, 2023, https://www.mckinsey.com/capabilities/people-and-organizational-performance/our-insights/workplace-rituals-recapturing-the-power-of-what-weve-lost.

10. Amy C. Edmondson, *The Fearless Organization: Creating Psychological Safety in the Workplace for Learning, Innovation, and Growth* (Hoboken, NJ: John Wiley & Sons, 2019), https://amycedmondson.com/psychological-safety/.

11. "Google's Project Aristotle," Psych Safety by Iterum, March 28, 2024, https://psychsafety.co.uk/googles-project-aristotle/.

12. World Economic Forum, *The Future of Jobs Report 2023*, April 30, 2023, https://www.weforum.org/publications/the-future-of-jobs-report-2023/.

Chapter 6

1. Mark Greeven, "Haier's AI Evolution: Charting the Course for GE Appliances," *Forbes*, September 13, 2024, https://www.forbes.com/sites/markgreeven/2024/09/13/haiers-ai-evolution-charting-the-course-for-ge-appliances/

2. dFackto, "Steering All the Transverse Transformation Programs of a Large European Bank," blog, n.d., https://www.dfakto.com/steering-all-the-transverse -transformation-programs-of-a-large-european-bank/.

3. Antonio Nieto-Rodriguez, *Harvard Business Review Project Management Handbook: How to Launch, Lead, and Sponsor Successful Projects* (Boston: Harvard Business Review Press, 2021).

4. Gary Hamel and Michele Zanini, *Humanocracy: Creating Organizations as Amazing as the People Inside Them* (Boston: Harvard Business Review Press, 2020), 36.

5. Heidi K. Gardner, "When Senior Managers Won't Collaborate," *Harvard Business Review*, March 2015, https://hbr.org/2015/03/when-senior-managers -wont-collaborate.

Part 3

1. Chrissy Kapralos, "AI Must Consider Human Dignity, Well-Being, and Jobs, Says Stanford AI Expert Dr. Fei-Fei Li," Digital Journal, December 26, 2023, https://www.digitaljournal.com/tech-science/ai-must-consider-human-dignity -well-being-and-jobs-says-stanford-ai-expert-dr-fei-fei-li/article.

2. Antonio Nieto-Rodriguez, *Harvard Business Review Project Management Handbook: How to Launch, Lead, and Sponsor Successful Projects* (Boston: Harvard Business Review Press, 2021).

Chapter 7

1. Valerio Dilda, Lapo Mori, Olivier Noterdaeme, and Christoph Schmitz, "Manufacturing: Analytics Unleashes Productivity and Profitability," McKinsey, August 14, 2017, https://www.mckinsey.com/capabilities/operations/our-insights /manufacturing-analytics-unleashes-productivity-and-profitability.

2. Ford, "Ford Choreographs Robots to Help People—and Each Other—on the Fiesta Assembly Line," news release, September 26, 2019, https://media.ford.com /content/fordmedia/feu/en/news/2019/09/26/ford-choreographs-robots-to-help -people--and-each-other--on-the-.html.

3. OIA Team, "Warehouse AI: How OIA Uses Artificial Intelligence," Ocado, December 6, 2024, https://ocadointelligentautomation.com/insights /warehouse-ai.

4. "Priestley's Gourmet Delights Opens New $53m AI-Powered Food Facility," *Food Technology and Manufacturing*, May 28, 2024, https://www.foodprocessing .com.au/content/the-food-plant/article/priestley-s-gourmet-delights-opens-new -53m-ai-powered-food-facilty-305074954.

5. "Doing 90% Mundane HR Tasks Like Promotion, Assessment of People with AI: IBM CEO Arvind Krishna," *Economic Times*, August 25, 2023, https:// economictimes.indiatimes.com/tech/technology/doing-90-mundane-hr-tasks-like -promotion-assessment-of-people-with-ai-ibm-ceo-arvind-krishna/articleshow /103055354.cms.

6. Ka-Ho Li, George Georgiou, and ICE Publishing, *Systems Architecture Models in Crossrail Design and Delivery—Client's Perspective*, Crossrail Learning Legacy, September 30, 2017, https://learninglegacy.crossrail.co.uk /documents/systems-architecture-models-crossrail-design-delivery-clients -perspective/.

7. Nicole Gillespie, Steven Lockey, Tabi Ward, et al., *Trust, Attitudes and Use of Artificial Intelligence: A Global Study 2025* (University of Melbourne and KPMG, 2025), DOI 10.26188/28822919.

8. Jay Peters, "Shopify CEO Says No New Hires without Proofs That AI Can't Do the Job," The Verge, April 7, 2025, https://www.theverge.com/news/644943 /shopify-ceo-memo-ai-hires-job.

9. Mastercard, "Mastercard Further Expands Consulting Services with AI and Economics Practices and Digital Labs for Fast-Tracked Solutions," press release, October 23, 2023, https://www.mastercard.com/news/press/2023/october /mastercard-further-expands-consulting-services-with-ai-and-economics -practices-and-digital-labs-for-fast-tracked-solutions/.

10. BP, "BP Agrees to Sell Its Petrochemicals Business to INEOS," press release, June 29, 2020, https://www.bp.com/en/global/corporate/news-and-insights/press -releases/bp-agrees-to-sell-its-petrochemicals-business-to-ineos.html.

11. BP, "BP Completes Acquisition of Archaea Energy," December 28, 2022, https://www.bp.com/en/global/corporate/news-and-insights/press-releases/bp -completes-acquisition-of-archaea-energy.html.

12. "BP and Partners to Invest $7 Billion in Carbon Capture Project in Indonesia's Papua," Reuters, November 21, 2024, https://www.reuters.com/business/energy /bp-partners-invest-7-billion-carbon-capture-project-indonesias-papua-2024-11-22/.

13. "Improving Clinical Process Performance," Philips, 2017, https://www .philips.com/c-dam/b2bhc/master/services/success-stories/managed_services _case_study_wmc.pdf.

14. "Ping An Insurance Group's Future Strategy: AI, Health Tech, and the Challenge of 2030," Abita LLC and Marketing Japan, February 10, 2025, https:// 1xmarketing.com/news/en/world-marketing-diary-250210083903/.

Chapter 8

1. Xiaojie Shi, Yufeng Zhang, and Zhuquan Wang, "Sustainable Value-Sharing Mechanisms of the Industrial Internet of Things Platforms: A Case Study of Haier's Service Oriented Transformation," *Sustainability* 16, no. 11 (2024): 4814; https://doi.org/10.3390/su16114814.

2. Antonio Nieto-Rodriguez, *Harvard Business Review Project Management Handbook: How to Launch, Lead, and Sponsor Successful Projects* (Boston: Harvard Business Press, 2021).

3. Antonio Nieto-Rodriguez, "It's Time to End the Battle between Waterfall and Agile," hbr.org, October 10, 2023, https://hbr.org/2023/10/its-time-to-end-the -battle-between-waterfall-and-agile.

4. Antonio Nieto-Rodriguez and Ricardo Viana Vargas, "How AI Will Transform Project Management," hbr.org, February 2, 2023, https://hbr.org/2023/02 /how-ai-will-transform-project-management.

5. Freya Graham, "A Nonprofit Used AI to Document 77 Million Miles of Unmapped Waterways. Here's Why That Matters," *Business Insider*, May 22, 2025, https://www.businessinsider.com/bridges-to-prosperity-nonprofit-ai-mapping -waterways-rural-communities-2025-5.

6. Project Management Institute, "The Future of Project Work: Moving Past Office-Centric Models," *Pulse of the Profession Report* 2024, 15th edition, https:// www.pmi.org/-/media/pmi/documents/public/pdf/learning/thought-leadership /pmi-pulse-of-the-profession-2024-report.pdf.

INDEX

ACKNOWLEDGMENTS

This book—my seventh, and my second with Harvard Business Review Press—marks a very personal milestone and perhaps the one closest to my heart. Twenty years ago I set out with a simple yet ambitious goal: to bring projects and the discipline of modern project management into the C-suite conversation, where they've always belonged. With *Powered by Projects*, that vision is finally becoming a reality.

To my children—Laura, Alexander, Selma, and Lucas—and my wife, Clarisse, thank you for your love, patience, and constant support. You are my greatest source of strength. To my parents, María José and Juan Antonio, and to my brothers, Javi, Iñaki, and José Miguel—thank you for always believing in me.

I'm deeply grateful to Dave Lievens and the exceptional team at the Press for their trust, collaboration, editorial thoroughness, and tireless support, not only in shaping the manuscript but also for placing the book into the hands of leaders who need it most. To Jonathan Norman, who has been by my side since my very first book, thank you for your thoughtful guidance. And to everyone who reviewed, endorsed, or provided feedback during the writing process: your insights, encouragement, and generosity helped shape not just this book but a broader movement toward a more project-driven world.

Finally, I dedicate this book to every leader with the courage to embrace radical change and take the leap toward building a truly project-driven organization—and to every project manager whose work behind the scenes fuels this transformation. May this book serve as a blueprint for a future in which project thinking drives progress, innovation, and meaningful impact at every level.

ABOUT THE AUTHOR

ANTONIO NIETO-RODRIGUEZ is recognized as the world's leading champion of modern project management. He is the author of the *Harvard Business Review Project Management Handbook*, the HBR magazine Spotlight feature "The Project Economy Has Arrived," and four other books. He is the most published project management author in *Harvard Business Review* and the creator of breakthrough concepts such as the project economy and the project canvas.

Nieto-Rodriguez is a fellow and former Global Chairman of the Project Management Institute and is currently Vice President of the Association for Project Management (APM). He is the creator of the Brightline initiative, founder of Projects & Company, and cofounder of the Strategy Implementation Institute. Thinkers50 recognized his global impact by naming him one of the world's Top 50 most influential management thinkers, and he also won the Thinkers50 Ideas into Practice Award. In addition, he is a member of Marshall Goldsmith's 100 Coaches program.

As the founder and CEO of Projects & Company, Nieto-Rodriguez leads a global team of transformation experts that helps organizations build world-class transformation capabilities and accelerate strategic impact. He works with executive teams to focus on what matters most: cutting low-value initiatives, executing critical projects with precision, and driving enterprise-wide change. He also supports organizations in embedding a project-driven culture and upskilling their entire workforce to thrive in the transformation age. This includes adopting AI-powered tools to enhance decision-making, execution, and value creation.

Through this work, Nieto-Rodriguez has trained and advised thousands of professionals and senior leaders from global organizations such as L'Oréal, Euronext, ING Group, Nestlé, AB InBev, Saudia Airlines, Lonza, Qatar Petroleum, Cleary Gottlieb, and Moët Hennessy.

Prior to his advisory work at Projects & Company, Nieto-Rodriguez held senior executive roles across leading global organizations. He served as Sustainability Transformation Program Director and Head of the Global Program Management Office at GlaxoSmithKline, where he led critical transformation initiatives. Before that, he was Head of Project Portfolio Management at BNP Paribas Fortis, and before that, Head of Post-Merger Integration at Fortis Bank, where he led the integration of ABN AMRO—at the time the largest acquisition in financial services history. Earlier in his career, he spent a decade at Pricewater-houseCoopers, ultimately becoming the firm's global lead practitioner for project and change management.

Nieto-Rodriguez's thought leadership focuses on the future of work, the rise of the project economy, strategy execution, and modern project management. In addition to his Harvard Business Review Press books, he is the author of *Lead Successful Projects*, *The Project Revolution*, *The Focused Organization*, and coauthor of *The Strategy Implementation Playbook*.

A recognized authority in project-based ways of working, Nieto-Rodriguez teaches MBA students, and also develops and delivers customized transformation programs for leading organizations worldwide. He serves as a visiting professor at institutions including Hult International Business School, Instituto de Empresa, and Solvay Brussels School of Economics.

He is also a globally sought-after speaker and has delivered keynote speeches at more than five hundred conferences worldwide—including the European Business Summit, Presidents Summit, Gartner conferences, TEDx, and the EU Cohesion Conference.

Born in Madrid and educated in Germany, Mexico, Italy, and the United States, Nieto-Rodriguez is fluent in five languages. He is an economist and holds an MBA from the London Business School and INSEAD's International Board Director Program.

He can be reached via email at antonio@projectsnco.com or LinkedIn at be.linkedin.com/in/antonionietorodriguez or you can visit his website at www.antonionietorodriguez.com.